Cultivating Victorians

Cultivating Victorians

Liberal Culture and the Aesthetic

DAVID WAYNE THOMAS

PENN

University of Pennsylvania Press

Philadelphia

10   9   8   7   6   5   4   3   2   1

Published by
University of Pennsylvania Press
Philadelphia, Pennsylvania 19104-4011

Library of Congress Cataloging-in-Publication Data

Thomas, David Wayne.
    Cultivating Victorians : liberal culture and the aesthetic / David Wayne Thomas.
      p. cm.
    Includes bibliographical references and index.
    ISBN 0-8122-3754-4 (cloth : alk. paper)
    1. English literature—19th century—History and criticism. 2. Liberalism in literature. 3.
Culture—Political aspects—Great Britain—History—19th century. 4. Culture—Social
aspects—Great Britain—History—19th century. 5. Liberalism—Great Britain—History—19th
century. 6. Great Britain—History—Victoria, 1837–1901. 7. Great Britain—Civilization—
19th century. 8. Aesthetics, British—19th century. I Title.

PR468.L52T48 2004
820.9'358—dc22   2003061627

Contents

Illustrations

Preface

In recent years, numerous literary scholars have tried to reassert aesthetic values without resorting to a neoconservative nostalgia for a dubiously conceived golden era of appreciation. Elaine Scarry has called for a return to beauty; George Levine has invited us to rethink the widespread reduction of aesthetics to ideology; and a renewed "reading for form" is being debated in conferences, books, essays, and special issues of journals.[1] The challenge confronting such recuperative efforts is how to get past the reduction of aesthetics to ideology while still giving ideological critique its due. The impetus to take up this challenge comes, in turn, from at least two specifiable anxieties reflecting current disciplinary conditions. Some of these critics propose that a prevailing hermeneutics of suspicion has so foreclosed on projects of appreciation that readings in literature and the arts have gradually become flattened or routine. Others argue on wider cultural grounds that the disciplinary rationale of literary and artistic scholarship is dangerously obscured when literary scholars—to say nothing of onlookers in the larger culture—are hard pressed to explain current work as anything but an unaccountably oblique form of history, ethics, or politics.

While sympathetic to these and perhaps other motives driving this recent movement, I argue in this study that aesthetics cannot be reclaimed along such lines until we reassess the character of modern liberal culture as well. Thus I offer here not so much an account of aesthetic value as a preliminary reconsideration of liberal agency, understood as a crucial feature of modern aesthetic culture. My linkage of aesthetic culture and liberal culture is premised on a point of methodological critique: to affirm the integrity and the importance of aesthetic experience, we must invoke, at least implicitly, the idea of self-reflecting individuality that informs liberalism's conceptions of agency and autonomy. Such affirmation poses special challenges today, however, when liberalism's distinctive commitment to rational autonomy is widely understood to encode a baleful atomistic individualism and to perpetuate dominant interests of gender, class, race, and nation. I write, then, with a broadly modern set of problems in mind, and with a keen interest in current theoretical debates about aesthetics and liberalism.

By way of concretizing these quite general issues, my focus goes to a historically specific terrain: the latter half of the nineteenth century in Britain. This focus lights up a time and place that saw both liberal culture and aesthetic culture taking on crucially new forms, with lasting consequences. I order this twofold engagement through a flexibly conceived rubric of *cultivation*. Various ideas about cultivation—understood here as self-improvement and as social amelioration—drove many famously "Victorian" contexts, from self-help manuals to educational reforms and philanthropic interventions. The two scenes of cultivation treated here—liberalism and aestheticism—remain especially problematic and contested. In the mid-Victorian years, figures such as Matthew Arnold, J. S. Mill, Charles Dickens, and George Eliot brought new prominence to a liberal vision of "many-sidedness," a temperamental and intellectual attainment involving practices of self-criticism, open-mindedness, and earnest conduct. And from the 1870s onward, we find the establishment of a high-cultural aesthetic ethos, set against practices deemed uncultivated, common, and vulgarly materialistic. Concerning both liberal culture and aestheticism, scholarly debates in recent decades have turned on the balance we should strike in understanding persons and classes as cultivating or as cultivated, as subjects or as objects of cultivation.

Regarding this question—who or what is doing the cultivating of Victorians?—the present study yields a twofold answer. I confirm recent understandings of the socially charged character of aesthetic culture. Artists, writers, and critics came in these years to claim for high art the rhetoric of self-determining power that had been at the core of liberal agency, with all its social and political investments. But I also urge—drawing on a theoretical argument for a roughly neo-Kantian view of agency—that we need to critique our tendency today to construe both liberalism and aestheticism simply as hegemonic ideological effects. For theorists, the result is a measured but generally redemptive account of modern liberal agency, one that recognizes the ideological work of the concept and emphasizes, at the same time, its salience as a regulative ideal in aesthetic and critical work to this day. For historians, the result is a strengthened sense of the Victorian period's share in ongoing controversies about aesthetic culture and the social work of criticism.

The study's introductory chapter surveys historical and conceptual dimensions of liberal and aesthetic agency. The historical narrative begins with the mid-Victorian discourse of many-sidedness, which I show to have gained special prominence in political and cultural debates of the 1860s. My historical claim is that artists, writers, and critics subsequently claimed for art the very idea of self-determining agency that had been at the core of this liberal many-sidedness. I also argue, at a conceptual level, that numerous literary-critical approaches of our own time repeat this gesture by simultaneously enacting and disavowing liberal ideals. I canvas some contemporary lines of opposition to liberal culture, including communitarian and pragmatist objections, and I assert the resilience of a regulative conception of liberal agency, with "regulative" set over against a more problematic "substantive" conception of liberalism. The opening chapter concludes by outlining an overlap between the liberal and the aestheticist rhetoric of agency beginning in the 1870s, looking W. J. Courthope's conservative objections to the vision of agency that he perceived—rightly, I allow—as a literary liberalism. For Courthope, that vision of human agency paradigmatically challenged his preferred traditionalism by grounding itself merely in the contingencies of individual experience, not only the sort of flux that Walter Pater is noted for esteeming, but also a less obvious style of subjectivism such as Arnold enacts.

In several respects, the vantage point on liberal culture offered in my opening chapter recalls Stefan Collini's *Public Moralists*, which looks to periodical debates and other topical contexts to show how an overarching "moral aesthetic of Individualism" constituted a practically dominant discourse of agency from the mid-Victorian years into the twentieth century.[2] And like Collini, I have found that the vantage point I seek has seemed to necessitate (or at least to invite) a rather idiosyncratic array of cases in this study's body chapters, which embrace high-cultural, political, and popular contexts. My hope is that such a variety of cases will help us to pose sharper questions about how liberal culture and its aesthetic offshoots took shape alongside quite various dimensions of Victorian public life. This particular variety of cases also lets me look squarely at some respects in which Millite and other liberalisms were sometimes constituted by concrete acts of cultural and political exclusion, undertaken by the progressive-minded high-cultural intelligentsia on which Collini focuses more or less exclusively.

Chapter 2 looks to John Ruskin's lifelong relation to the city of Venice, seeing in his combined vexation and fascination a projection of his own concerns about creative and critical individuality. With this most particular of cities, that is, Ruskin played out his own anxieties about what it means to be particular— a question key in modern individualism. The project of reading Venice turns out in Ruskin's case to be charged with an antagonism of religious and post-religious authorizations of agency. In that sense Ruskin's issues fit well within a familiar conception of the Christian sensibility threatened by modern secularism. What also emerges here, I argue, is a tendentially liberal individualism built into Ruskin's practices as an interpreter or seer. Famously, Ruskin's treats aesthetic creation and reception as matters to be engaged for their objective truth or falsity, their healthfulness or their degeneracy, but his procedures as a reader also document his stake in a perspectivalist conception of interpretive agency with debts to the emerging liberal conception of many-sidedness.

Ruskin is but one individual, of course, and quite an unusual one at that. In Chapter 3, therefore, I turn to a broad-based cultural episode: the public contestation surrounding the Tichborne Claimant. This case concerns a low-born impostor who came forth in the late 1860s to lay claim to a noble inheritance, and the public reckoning with his gambit provides us today with as large-scale a social conversation as one could imagine. The case has long been understood as much ado about class contestation, with the poor understood to favor the Claimant while the well-to-do deplored him. My reading shows how debates about the Claimant's subjective agency and about his objective authenticity—is he or is he not the real Sir Roger Tichborne?—also reflect mid-Victorian contention over emerging tendencies in liberal culture. The best explanation for public divisiveness concerning the Claimant's authenticity, I argue, is the increasingly interventionist nature of liberal culture during Gladstone's first ministry (1868–74), years in which working-class voters in fact shifted in large numbers to the conservative Tory Party.

The study turns in its second half to ideas of agency developed in and around Victorian aesthetic culture. Chapter 4 sets Dante Gabriel Rossetti's high-cultural case alongside a case in popular culture via the figure of replication. Rossetti's practice as a painter fashioning replicas of his own works allows us a unique vantage point on the relation of creativity and the art market in the late Victorian period. At the same time, reportage on life-scale historical city replicas fashioned for the 1887 Manchester Exhibition shows how the uncertain character of these replicas as historical recovery mirrors the uncertain relations of history and reflective agency to an emerging consumerist sensibility. Regarding each of the chapter's contexts—painter and city—I argue that replicas gain their specific interest in part because their fusion of authenticity and inauthenticity mirrors a feature of the evolving liberal conception of selfhood, insofar as that selfhood embraces an interpretive mobility implied in the value of many-sidedness. I conclude the chapter with a larger methodological point concerning the interpretive stakes of my linkage between two admittedly disparate contexts of "replication." In part, the issue is what it takes to treat this relation as more than a merely verbal play on the word *replica*. My special concern, however, is to show that latter-day literary critics must finally betray commitments to an aggrandized conception of aesthetic agency, precisely in the suggestion that these two contexts should "obviously" be treated as profoundly different from one another. Thus the next chapter foregrounds postmodern-era critical debates concerning aesthetic agency even as it also fleshes out the study's account of late Victorian aestheticism as such.

Concluding the study, Chapter 5 shows how Oscar Wilde's concerns for individual self-realization were staged through a vertiginous authorial discourse of antioriginality. I support our latter-day views of Wilde as a writer of surpassing critical suggestiveness, virtually a literary philosopher of modern subjectivity. In this light, his refusals of originality as a value come to look like one more sign of his prescience concerning the critique of liberal humanism and romantic creative agency that current literary scholars know well. But I also insist that Wilde enacts a value of strategic critical mobility with sources precisely in the modern liberal ideal of self-reflecting agency. Thus I complicate the commonplace view of him as an apostle for antiessentialist subjectivity, and I also call into question the cogency of postmodern-era routines of thought concerning authorial agency more generally. A brief conclusion to this chapter extrapolates on points made in respect to Wilde to argue for a conception of aesthetic agency along neo-Kantian lines. In staking a claim for the functional force of human reflective capacities, this conclusion serves as a kind of bookend in the study, partnered with, while drawing on, the opening chapter's recuperation of certain features of modern liberal culture through a similar neo-Kantian defense.

I point out here the overarching Kantianism informing the present study, precisely because that Kantianism is more often implicit than explicit. Two very general effects are notable. First, all the study's chapters touch upon themes of originality and authenticity. Second, and more abstractly, the chapters develop and largely affirm a vision of interpretive agency in which reflection enables and orients individual and even collective action.

I treat originality in both conceptual and historical aspects. The conceptual level embraces general questions about the kind of *doing* that originality is supposed to indicate or memorialize. Such questions of agency arise directly, first in chapter one, on J. S. Mill's thinking, and then throughout the final chapter, where I take the elusive Wilde to embody a view of original genius foretold in Kant: "Genius is a *talent* for producing something for which no determinate rule can be given."[3] For the most part, however, I engage the theme of originality in more indirect ways—in particular, my opening treatment in chapter 1 of George Eliot's *Middlemarch*. To a degree that surprised even me in final revisions of this study, Eliot's equivocal celebration of one character's "imitation of heroism"—precisely in its recourse to the term *imitation*—condenses key tensions within many ideas of cultivated agency treated in this study. For on the one hand, the contexts that we read today as liberal and aesthetic reflect an aggrandizement of purposive action, a liberal heroics. On the other hand, those same visions are haunted by specters of inauthenticity or artificiality. Thus do accounts of cultivated selfhood or agency along liberal lines contend endlessly with the threat of hypocrisy.

My distinctive historical point concerning originality is that mid-Victorian liberal views of cultivated agency essentially took over the cultural work that had earlier been performed by high-romantic conceptions of original agency. Where romantic originality was, there would Victorian liberal heroics be. While there is good reason to view such generalization with some wariness, this account does go some way, at least, toward explaining why postmodern-era critical treatments of originality ritually leapfrog the mid-Victorian period, apparently regarding it as an interregnum reflecting neither romantic affirmations of originality (genius, organic imagination) nor modernist and postmodernist uncertainties about it (technological reproduction, simulacrum).[4] To take up this account, we may begin by recalling that romantic visions of original agency typically had a properly middle-class work to do after the French Revolution of 1789, in that the authorities to be superseded by revolutionary agency were still chiefly clerical, aristocratic, and monarchical. By the 1840s, however, revolutionary momentum had come to signify lower-class contention with middle-class hegemony. The year 1848 saw popular revolutions across Europe, of course, but a correlative English context at that time is more telling: the collapse of Chartism on the Kennington Common, when the radical mass platform had its final gasp. Commonly adduced factors in the failure of English radicalism include widespread public alarm at Continental revolution and at the supposed complicity of Chartists with Irish conspiracy.[5] But the sheerly romantic aspect of these agitations was also losing its uptake. By 1848, the specifically romantic elements of Chartist speechifying—as in Feargus O'Connor's opposition of natural and artificial (industrial) society—had come to seem rather stale.[6] The economic boom of the 1850s left only a dogged few holdouts in the Chartist line, and the same period is generally seen as the seedbed of properly Victorian Liberal politics. At this point ideas of liberalism and ideas of originality become linked in a newly powerful fashion through their bearing on questions of cultivated agency.[7] In effect, the revolutionary dimensions of romantic agency became incendiary in a way that was not congenial to much of the middle class, although there remained room for middle-class women to welcome scenes of identification in more or less romantic terms.[8] In the mid-Victorian context, then, the most pressing concern for the dominant middle-class culture was no longer how to valorize industrialistic agency but how to cultivate its forms along specific lines among plebeians.

Cast in those terms, of course, the rubric of cultivation looks plainly like middle-class condescension or hegemony. But implicit in my Kantian account of agency, noted above, is a more affirmatively or generously readable aspect of cultivated agency. I spotlight a metapositional potential of human thought, variously performed or thematized in the cases that follow. Where human agency is understood as self-interpretation and as a protocol of decision-making respecting the forms of life that one is ready to credit, we have at hand another vision of cultivation than that of hegemony. The account offered here entails a fairly strong view of reflection, and that view itself is consciously promoted by most Victorian liberal figures—consider George Eliot and her appeals to tolerant judgment, or Matthew Arnold with his concern for a many-sided "Hellenic" temperament. At other times, this vision of reflective agency is more implicitly and surprisingly in force, as when John Ruskin cheerfully offers his self-contradictions as preferable to any intrinsically inadequate devotion to a single-minded vantage point, or when the historical city replica of "Old Manchester and Salford" comes to look like an occasion for exhibition-goers to occupy a provocatively mobile and tangled sense of their own placement in history. In what follows, I often read these themes of positional mobility and self-reflection as bound together with *identification*, by which I mean an emotional-critical dynamic, whereby an individual or collective consciousness seizes on an image of itself in some thing or idea. Ruskin's interest in Venice seems a species of identification, for instance, insofar as his personal concern with the nature of self-reflecting moral agency seems fundamentally to define his interest in that city's historical rise and fall. Likewise with D. G. Rossetti's replicas: in monumentalizing for him both his creative agency and his subscription to economic exigencies, they function as foils for self-reflection on his life as an artist. Generally at issue in such moments is what interest agents or collectives can be said to take in an imagined rationalization of their own agency—or, likewise, what interest they take in imagined threats to such rationalization. In my view, this interest echoes features of Kantian moral agency (in which agents are presumed to have a stake in "making sense" of themselves) and of Kantian aesthetic judgment (in that aesthetic pleasure reflects, in the end, not objects but the *subject* in a position to take pleasure in perceiving form). For the most part, I read the Victorian cases with this rather transhistorical or broadly modern logic of interest very much in the background. With my closing chapter, however, I carry the claim forward to our current viewpoints on the Victorians. Thus I suggest that contemporary critical interest in Oscar Wilde is sustained, in large part, by an interested identification, in which modern readers sense a common likeness between his critical canniness and their own self-valorizing sense of critical mobility and insight.

Throughout this study, I proceed from a sense that current scholarship needs to devote less dismissive and routinized attentions to the historical expressions of reflective agency. I also remain watchful throughout for the claims that this very vision of agency maintains on contemporary critical practices, however loathe we sometimes have been to recognize those claims.

Part I
Victorian Liberal Culture

Chapter 1
Cultivating Victorians

In 1859 Samuel Smiles declared, "National progress is the sum of individual industry, energy and uprightness, as national decay is of individual idleness, selfishness and vice."[1] With *Self-Help* and subsequent improving manuals—all filled out with instructive examples of perseverance rewarded—Smiles had his popular role to play alongside the philanthropic interventions and educational reforms that made up mid-Victorian Britain's burgeoning discourse of cultivation. The urgency of that discourse is little mystery, provided one accepts Smiles's notion that the fate of a nation is directly to be read from the quality of its individuals. And while Victorian projects of individual and social improvement had various wellsprings, including Evangelicalism and paternalistic Toryism, liberal culture was the privileged determinant. Not only does the quotation from Smiles celebrate liberal keywords like *progress* and *individuality*; his point also implies a methodological individualism that has been understood as distinctively liberal. For in arguing that society must finally be seen as "the sum" of its individuals, Smiles implies that society is, in effect, strictly reducible to its parts, with those parts construed as autonomously responsible individuals. Thus Smiles's version of J. S. Mill's assertion that same year: "The worth of a State, in the long run, is the worth of the individuals composing it."[2]

Numerous critics since the nineteenth century—from some Comtean positivists to most Marxists and latter-day sociologists—have blanched at the short shrift that such methodological reduction gives to collectivity in social life.[3] With no ambition here to settle hoary debates about the priority of individuality or sociality, I spell out the presence of this liberal reduction only to rationalize this study's treatment of Victorian cultivation both as self-improvement and social amelioration. For in mid-Victorian liberal discourse, liberals routinely and necessarily fused sociopolitical concerns and individualism in their rhetoric of cultivation. The priority of individuality for Victorian liberals themselves is nonetheless clear, and in this initial chapter I focus primarily on the liberal project of cultivated agency at the individual level.

Several decades of academic discourse have established largely skeptical attitudes toward liberal culture, whether Victorian or broadly modern. When viewed in the light of its classical individualism, liberal culture correlates with present-day conservatism's opposition to the welfare state. Thus can modern

1. "A Party of Working Men at the National Gallery," *The Graphic* (6 August 1870), 136.

cultural and political conservatives—from Gertrude Himmelfarb and William Bennett to Newt Gingrich and Margaret Thatcher—line up in praise of Victorian liberal nostrums on character, diligence, and the like.[4] When viewed in the light of its democratizing and egalitarian energies, in turn, liberal culture has seemed constitutionally incapable of taking conclusive steps toward genuine collectivism and the abolishment or serious redistribution of property. The true colors of modern liberalism are understood to come out in a Lockean commitment to the self as property-maker and property-bearer.[5] Liberalism has also received a well established line of critique from feminists who have shown how routinely liberal individualism has been aligned with masculinist and exclusionary energies.[6]

While accepting the substantive character of these views and esteeming their cultural work in recent decades, I intend with this study to carve out some space for a relatively affirmative reading of liberal agency, and on terms other than those of a conventionally neoconservative nostalgia for the humanist subject. Through a measured affirmation of broadly modern liberal culture, I mean to confront an ambiguity courted by the rubric *cultivating Victorians*. The ambiguity arises because we can so easily privilege either agency or passivity in imagining this figure of cultivation. Will we envision Victorians as cultivating or cultivated? That is, are they to be seen as heroic self-fashioning subjects, or as unwitting objects, of cultivation?

These alternatives of agency and passivity might seem oversimple, so let me reassert my concerns in a more concrete fashion. In an 1870 depiction of a guided visit to the National Gallery, a neatly dressed and trimmed docent points out features of a painting to two men whose social status is suggested not only by their rougher clothing and appearance but even more subtly by their body positions (Figure 1). Leaning forward candidly to take in their instruction, they contrast with nothing so much as the erect authority of their instructor. What are the working men lapping up here, and at whose hands? An article accompanying the engraved image tells of a Working Men's Club and Institute Union, newly created as an umbrella organization to oversee the proliferating groups aimed at the education of working men. Unlike the earlier Mechanics' Institutes, notes the writer, these new groups are controlled by working men and dedicated to the proposition that plebeian horizons can be valuably broadened without in the least impairing the "independence and self respect" of those taking such instruction. In addition to guided tours of such public institutions as the National Gallery, the new clubs maintain well-lit gathering spaces, collections of enlivening reading, and affordable, high-quality refreshments. The writer concludes that such efforts seem more likely than most other current charitable designs to "wean a man away from the public house," while adding as well that much of the chatter among "charitable gentlefolk" about working-class drunkenness is, at the same time, so much "cant."[7] It seems fair to say that the article accompanying the engraving reflects careful efforts on the writer's part to respect the uncultivated citizens depicted in the image. Equally plain, however, is the writer's view that specific pleasures and pastimes, such as gallery visits, are more estimable than others, such as beer drinking. How should we read the rhetoric of cultivation in such a case, a rhetoric that seems to stand with one foot on each side of a line dividing solicitude and sanctimony? Rather than argue any detailed claim about this particular scene's placement in Victorian liberal culture—chapter 3 below, on the Tichborne case, will be much better placed to take on the intricacies of such a social characterization—I want now to lay down my governing claims concerning how critics today tend to read occasions such as this one.

In recent literary and cultural histories, Victorian and other scenes of cultivation have most often been read as scenes of hegemony, much as liberal culture itself has been read. And a wary view of liberal cultivation is plainly warranted regarding contexts such as British imperialism and middle-class hostility to democracy, both cases in which dominant cultural interests argued that subordinated social groups were as yet insufficiently cultivated to demand treatment as equals. Likewise, many aspects of aesthetic culture have clearly helped to consolidate and perpetuate the economic and social relations of capitalism.[8] But a generalized sense that cultivation is reducible to hegemony has come to permeate current scholarly readings. Thus Victorian philanthropy, for example, amounts to bourgeois surveillance, and David Copperfield's self-disciplined heart reflects the internalization of middle-class society's disciplinary requirements.[9] The concern from which such readings proceed—a concern to expose social power relations to critique—must be regarded as an ongoing project, but I also contend that we need at this moment to think again about the ease with which such readings can take shape and claim authority. The stakes bear equally on the character of our readings in the period and on the wider public profile of current academic criticism.

Regarding debate within the academic humanities, recent work on the Victorian period by Amanda Anderson has voiced the viewpoint that I take up. She argues that an overly generalized hermeneutics of suspicion forecloses on ideas of critical distance by reading them as false objectivity; and ideas of self-reflective agency, she continues, come to look simply like artifacts of a properly exploded Enlightenment rationalism. What goes lost, according to Anderson, is any coherent idea about how Victorians themselves actually conceptualized critique.[10] Arguing in terms more generally of modern aesthetic culture, Charles Altieri insists that "postmodern idealizations of heterogeneity and resistances to categorical thinking have left us with a very thin set of psychological concepts for exploring the internal dynamics of subjective agency."[11] Altieri aims to remedy this problem through an elaborate theory of expressivist agency that I will return to in this chapter's conclusion. Here I will simply embrace his problem statement, as I do Anderson's. Common to all our standpoints is a perception that prevailing critical paradigms enjoin such vigorous bracketing of ideas like agency, judgment, and critique, that those very ideas have become embattled, and, when wagered, they are prone to distorting preoccupations with sheer apologetics.

These academic stakes stand alongside a larger consideration. To the extent that current work in the humanities forecloses on nuanced but still affirmative standpoints regarding human agency—either by reducing such agency to a transmission of objective social structures or by locating its truth in radical decenteredness or lack—our ways of rationalizing the humanities within the larger public culture would seem to be inevitably and detrimentally affected. At issue, very generally, is whether academics in the humanities can coherently explain their image of the human to themselves and to their surrounding culture. Of course, critics are offering fascinating and compelling claims about the constructedness of humanity and the advent of posthumanity, and my viewpoint is in no way an a priori contention against such lines of thought. But so long as our critical readings continue to give us forth as critical practitioners—therefore as images of critical agency—we expose ourselves to suspicions regarding the cogency and the ultimate honesty of our critical practices, once we radically foreshorten questions of critical agency. Such readings will tend to account obscurely, if indeed at all, for the possibility of agency or even of "reading."

With those general points in the background, this chapter's closer work will be to specify some key themes in mid-Victorian and largely middle-class discourses of agency and self-culture. It falls to later chapters to detail the complexities of mid-Victorian thinking about agency in individual and collective contexts, including questions of religious and class difference (Chapters 2 and 3); likewise, I defer detailed treatment of mid-Victorian liberal culture's relations to late Victorian aesthetic culture (Chapters 4 and 5). Because liberalism is such a multiform and highly cathected term, my concern at this point is to make a usefully concrete and deliberate beginning.

I start off with a literary reading, concentrated on a minor plotline in George Eliot's *Middlemarch* (1871–72). The literary case dramatizes what I call *liberal heroics*, meaning a reflectively endorsed, self-regulating agency with both promising and problematic features. Through an account of the readerly identifications solicited by Eliot's text, I can tender some crucial points about the appeal of liberal aspiration and, at the same time, about the disturbing artificiality of liberal subjectivity in its overly concretized forms. This reading will light up the difference between a regulative conception of liberal agency, which I endorse, and a more problematic, substantive conception of such agency. Very generally, I contend that current critiques of liberal agency bear powerfully only on a naively substantialist view of liberal subjectivity. I also suggest that those critiques are prone to underread their own implication in the regulative view of liberal subjectivity. To make good on these latter claims, the chapter's next section briefly canvases current critiques of liberalism and then looks more closely to an exemplary recent argument, Uday Singh Mehta's *Liberalism and Empire*, which exposes liberal complicity with imperialism in the nineteenth century. My general concern is to wager a detailed rejoinder to those critiques that assimilate liberalism to an arid or supercilious moral rationalism. My special concern with Mehta's argument is to critique its assumption that communitarianism and antifoundationalist pragmatism sustain coherent objections to liberalism. Next, returning to primary sources in the Victorian context, I examine a liberal rhetoric of many-sidedness in J. S. Mill and Matthew Arnold; and, in a final section, I explore overlapping ideas of agency in broadly liberal and specifically aestheticist argumentation in the 1870s.

Liberal Heroics in George Eliot's *Middlemarch*

Midway in Eliot's *Middlemarch*, the young Fred Vincy and the reverend Camden Farebrother both look like prospective husbands for Mary Garth, who seems to love Fred and admire Farebrother. Farebrother is a minor character in the scheme of Eliot's grand novel, but I take him to stand just short of Dorothea Brooke as the figure most positively affirmed within that novel's moral vision.[12] Indeed, Farebrother spends the entire novel occupying a generous, flexible, tolerant position of judgment that Dorothea has to attain to in the course of her experiences, which have her shedding the residual sternness and myopia of her ardent religiosity in favor of an implicitly secularized but still ardent devotion to earthly works. Farebrother's nature has already been signaled by his generous bearing toward the doctor Tertius Lydgate, who was unhappily compelled, on social and financial grounds, to prefer another candidate to Farebrother for the chaplaincy of Lydgate's new hospital. At that juncture, the narrator observed that Farebrother was unlike most others in this regard: "he could excuse others for thinking slightly of him, and could judge impartially of their conduct even when it told against him."[13] The congenial but immature Fred, meanwhile, has been racking up debts in pathetic anticipation of an inheritance. Because Mary is a practical young woman, she warns Fred that no marriage between them will be possible until he becomes responsible. Fred enters a spell of diligence and self-command, but soon he is frequenting the billiards room and seems unlikely to refrain much longer from betting.

Through Farebrother's intervention into this situation, Eliot gives us a telling instance in the mid-Victorian vision of cultivated agency that I mean in this study to examine, to generalize upon, and to redeem in some ways. Despite his own genuine affection for Mary, Farebrother understands the deep mutual attachment of Mary and Fred and he finally decides to act on Fred's behalf by taking him aside and making bluntly clear how things stand among them all. Says Farebrother, "I am sure you know that the satisfaction of your affections stands in the way of mine" (674)—which is to say, if Fred wins Mary, Farebrother's desire to have her must be foiled. Fred initially misinterprets Farebrother's message as a threat, observing, "I thought you were friendly to me" (675). Eliot brings Fred to the light with Farebrother's reply:

"So I am; that is why we are here. But I have had a strong disposition to be otherwise. I have said to myself, 'If there is a likelihood of that youngster doing himself harm, why should you interfere? . . . If there is a chance of him going to the dogs, let him—perhaps you could nohow hinder it—and do you take the benefit.' . . . But I had once meant better than that, and I am come back to my old intention. I thought that I could hardly *secure myself* in it better, Fred, than by telling you just what had been going on in me. And now, do you understand me? I want you to make the happiness of her life and your own, and if there is any chance that a word of warning from me may turn aside any risk to the contrary—well, I have uttered it." (675–76)

Farebrother epitomizes a specific vision of moral reflection: we see his inward voice, implying a self-addressable self; his bracketing of "a strong disposition" to follow an emotionally pressing desire; and his determination to act according to what seems morally correct. In these respects, Farebrother's conduct exemplifies an enlightened moral rationalism—an alignment of the will with a universalizable maxim to act only as one would have any person act in the given circumstance.[14]

His conduct exemplifies the most general features of what I am calling liberal heroics, which look here something like an ambition to fulfill oneself by denying oneself. The idea entails not paradox, necessarily, but a hierarchically divided portrait of subjective agency. In this view, a valorized reflective individuality is cultivated precisely through the considered bracketing of other, less creditable aspects of one's individuality. This idea of reflective agency has had rather poor press in literary and cultural studies for some decades, mostly out of a sense that it naively brackets the urgency of human desires and too casually grants to human agency a character at once essentialist and transcendentalist. The liberal cast of Farebrother's enlightened conduct emerges especially in his determination to utter these words to Fred, aware that he can better "secure" himself in this vision of normative morality by tendering an informal promissory note regarding the vision of conduct he subscribes to—and might be held accountable to, in the future. Like Ulysses securing himself to the ship-mast as an expedience against the Sirens, Farebrother contrives to hear his desires while placing them in suspension, thereby confirming a specific ideal of identity.[15] This vision of personal conduct is also a vision of social contract in which agents consent to the occasional frustration of their own immediate satisfactions. In interpersonal relations, of course, those who esteem altruism—if this act be counted such—can fear that right action will not find further echoes in the thinking of its beneficiaries, but the possible futility of altruism is not Eliot's concern: "Fred was moved quite newly. Some one highly susceptible to the contemplation of a fine act has said, that it produces a sort of regenerating shudder through the frame, and makes one feel ready to begin a new life. A good degree of that effect was just then present in Fred Vincy" (676).

Victorian novels are famously prone to such scenes: figures wavering on the moral borderline finally step toward their best self when inspired by example. If Eliot's scene is in that respect generic, its suggestiveness for my argument comes out clearly in the phrasing offered by the narrator after Fred and Farebrother part. In indirect narration of Farebrother's thinking, Eliot writes: "To think of the part one little woman can play in the life of a man, so that to renounce her may be a very good imitation of heroism, and to win her may be a discipline!" (676).

By amalgamating ideas of imitation, heroism, and discipline into a single sentence, Eliot touches with remarkable conciseness on much of what this entire study will have to say about liberal culture and, later, about aesthetic culture from the 1870s onward. I propose that Victorian liberal culture reads self-discipline as heroism, as an overcoming of self that counts as another and better kind of self accomplished. Further, the figure of imitation turns out to be but one of many possible figures that capture anxieties concerning whether and how the self-disciplining liberal subject can lay claim to authenticity. This question of authenticity reflects an important dimension of precariousness and uncertainty in the self-reflection upon which liberal agency is founded. Thus I share with liberalism's critics a sense that something is being overstated when critical self-reflection is viewed as a means to triumphal self-conviction or self-righteousness. Permutations on Eliot's terms here—heroism, discipline, and imitation—will arise throughout this study, then, but most distinctively in respect to problems surrounding imitation: the architectural casts of John Ruskin, the imposture of the Tichborne Claimant, the painted replicas of Dante Gabriel Rossetti, and the discourse of antioriginality in Oscar Wilde. To see how richly the Victorian context takes up these points is to see how fully that context anticipated what we commonly understand as modernist and postmodernist conceptions of simulacrum and decentered subjectivity.

At this juncture, my chief concern is to bring immediate substance to these large claims, so I will return to the *Middlemarch* narration quoted above. There, Farebrother's perspective on Mary tells that "to renounce her may be a very good imitation of heroism, and to win her may be a discipline!" In this phrase, the discipline appears to indicate Fred's challenge to regulate his gambling appetites in pursuit of a finer end, namely, a life with Mary. The heroism, in turn, would seem to be Farebrother's. But what does it mean to style Farebrother's renunciation as an *imitation* of heroism?

The word *imitation* suggests a qualification of some sort, or at least a difference between an authentic or primary heroism and Farebrother's act of heroism. At the same time, it does not seem that the secondariness of Farebrother's heroism is given to us as cause to regret that his act takes this form rather than some other, more genuinely heroic, form. What could account for this apparent demotion of authentic heroism? But then again, what room would there be in the moral universe of Eliot's story for any more authentic heroism than this one? None at all, I suggest. For no such authentic heroism seems in any position to retain credibility. Among the traits of the hero in a Western mythological context is a mixed ancestry, a divine and a mortal parent—with Hercules, for example, a son of Zeus and Alcmene. In that scheme, the hero possesses by divine contribution a greater range of powers than do mere mortals, and the hero also draws on the special regard of an overseeing deity more often than not on his side. But the modern environment cannot take heroism seriously in those terms, nor even—if you are George Eliot or a similarly postreligious sensibility—in any theological or spiritual terms. The imitation of heroism, in this light, is modernity's "authentic" heroism. This heroism amounts to a secularized appropriation of transcendence as an element of the self. In stepping back from himself, in transcending his immediate desires, Farebrother imitates a defunct kind of heroism but he performs the truth of another kind.

Thus Farebrother's heroism comes strikingly to resemble the *discipline* that seemed at first like Fred's charge: valorized in each case is a kind of self-overcoming. But neither are the two cases identical. Fred's discipline is modeled on an image of right conduct that seems more or less external to him, given in the visions of himself that Mary, Farebrother, and others have urged upon him. Farebrother's discipline seems to have primarily an inward origin, and his image of himself is externalized through his own volition, as he decides to secure himself by telling his feelings to Fred. Fred and Farebrother, respectively, embody the distinction that Elaine Hadley proposes between respectability—a matter of struggling to live up to a set of roughly middle-class virtues—and character, valorized by Victorians as a kind of self-possession and wrapped up, according to Hadley, with the liberal linkage of autonomous agency and alienable property.[16] Given the privileges of Fred Vincy's upbringing, we cannot strictly assimilate him to the distinctively lower-middle-class character of Victorian respectability. But it is in fact that inner-directed nature of Farebrother's agency that privileges his moral conduct over Fred's.

In her account of John Stuart Mill's liberalism, Maria H. Morales almost seems to be reading this *Middlemarch* encounter: "Mill learned from his crisis that exclusively relying on external sanctions can erode the moral part of human nature. In his view, utility requires much more than acting in certain ways. More importantly, it requires being *a certain kind of person*: the kind who can develop concerns with the good of others and can learn to take an active interest in sympathetic associations."[17] What Morales means to isolate can be called a *substantive* liberal agency in the sense that a claim is made here not merely about acts but indeed about the "being" of the liberal agent.[18] In Farebrother, then, we have what can seem a paradigm of individual moral reflection by a substantive agent, bringing itself into relation with a domain of interpersonal relations. The general shape of his heroism is a pretension to, as it were, fulfill oneself by denying oneself.

In the credibility of that pretension lies the credibility of liberal heroics more generally. A crucial feature in my measured defense of this idea is a distinction between a regulative conception of liberal agency, affirmed in my account, and a more problematic conception of such agency as something that one might embody in any definitive or pure sense. We can allow the sort of criticism that would see in Farebrother's character a "view from nowhere"—in

Thomas Nagel's memorable phrase—even as we also refuse to take that diagnosis as a conclusive argument against the viewpoint's historical functionality or ongoing utility. Indeed, Nagel himself supports the tenability of the view from nowhere, although his practical-minded critics sometimes think that his provocative phrase makes much of their case for them.[19] At issue, finally, is whether this liberal agency—even when understood as a view from nowhere—amounts to a coherent and historically powerful regulative ambition, sustained through what is perhaps modernity's most fundamental element in cultivation: self-reflective agency.

Accepting the fragility of this liberal standpoint, I suggest that most good readers are bound to find something difficult about the figure of Farebrother. Once we grant Eliot's concerns to portray him in a generally warm light and to align him, in particular, with the high-minded moral conduct adumbrated by Victorian liberal culture in its intellectual and political forms, we might well ask what to make of his marginality in the novel. Farebrother is not the Jesus of Eliot's testament, much less its St. Theresa. Dorothea is clearly the most "interesting" figure in this novel. She is more interesting than Farebrother, however, for this specific reason: Dorothea strives, struggles, and advances, feeling her way toward a viewpoint carrying with it what Eliot calls "that distinctness which is no longer reflection but feeling"—a sort of feeling, in other words, not prior to, but consequent on, reflection (211). By comparison, Farebrother is characterized in terms largely of moral reflection, and as a result he is something like liberal culture's version of a flat character.

The extent to which liberal heroics can take shape as a regulative force might be gauged by this study's readers from their own assessments of Dorothea's appeal as a character. What her plotline conjures is a promise of reflective agency, much more than its realization and static maintenance. And I contend that readerly identification and interest accrue to her largely for this reason. Farebrother is not a dynamic character but instead one fixed in the relatively bloodless and dispassionate space that critics often see as proper to liberalism—as, for example, in its privileging of abstract rights over positive conceptions of the good. If it is clear that readers of all sorts are invited to identify not with Farebrother but with Dorothea, that is because Farebrother's substantive liberal agency is less persuasive finally than the regulative ideal of liberal conduct apparent in Dorothea.

Of course, from a vantage point in which each character is understood as mere fiction, it can seem nonsensical to suppose that the difference between substantive and regulative liberalism in these characterizations should matter. Farebrother, as a fiction, is in no position to render his ethos literally substantial. It seems unduly arch, however, to suppose that fiction makes such compartmentalized claims on readerly perceptions and interests: making sense of fictional characters calls on energies that overlap very much with everyday living, from ostensibly benign efforts of caring to potentially importunate projections of rationality onto others construed as intentional systems.[20] Thus the plausibility of fictional characters is deeply relevant to their abilities to effect the kind of ethical and moral solicitation that has recently been seen as the special work of Victorian novelistic realism.[21] Just as Mary loves Fred and (only) admires Farebrother, we might suppose that Eliot would have us love Dorothea and, at best, admire Farebrother, with a sense of his impossibility or flatness keeping us from going any further.

The impossibility of Farebrother is, however, none too clear-cut. Indeed, the threat of becoming that impossibility animated a good deal of mid-Victorian social debate. As I will soon argue, our tendency today is to read this particular liberal threat in terms of the aridness of abstract moral rationalism and its attendant difficulties in recognizing human difference and particularity. Victorians generally perceived the threat in terms of diminished power or agency, however, with the liberal agent understood as lacking in vigor and conviction.

A *Saturday Review* commentary on "Intellectual Vigour" illustrates the point. The author opens with a general observation that, "among intellectual as among moral virtues, there is a constant tendency to allow the cultivation of one good quality to edge out another," issuing in, among other problems, "the repugnance entertained by the men of detail to generalizing their facts, and by the men of generalization to accurate and wide verification of their principles." The writer continues, "But there is a special complaint in our own time, that the culture of the admirable group of intellectual virtues which may be comprehended in the name of tolerance, or impartiality, or sympathy, is being allowed to drain off the sources of the no less admirable virtue of conviction or earnestness. What men gain in manysidedness, it is said, they are losing in vigor."[22] Whether to see a boon or an ill in "many-sidedness" is very much at issue in the rationalization of liberal agency in the 1860s. Newly post-Darwinian and on their way to the Second Reform Bill, the readers of this article would see much currency in the predicament that the writer spells out: even "highly trained minds"—especially such minds, indeed—are paralyzed by uncertainties concerning "democratic government" and "the province of reason in religious inquiry."[23] Eliot's characterization of Farebrother touches on many of the same points. The strain between the Higher Criticism and religious dogma is at hand, for example, as the Evangelical hypocrite Bulstrode distrusts Farebrother for reading in the new sciences and philology. And Farebrother's vigor is in doubt from at least some vantage points: even as Lydgate is thankful for the reverend's warm constancy after the chaplaincy election, he cannot help but see in Farebrother "a pitiable infirmity of will" (187). Lydgate, that is, enjoys the fruits of Farebrother's indulgence while also concluding that a real man would probably have given him a rougher time. Elsewhere Eliot's narrative shows that Farebrother's life will feature perpetual economic marginality and bachelorhood in common housekeeping with his mother, an aunt, and an elder sister. In this light, Farebrother's conduct embodies paralysis and emasculated agency.

For my argument's purposes, this overall situation spotlights a challenging contradiction. On the one hand, liberal heroics must be styled as a sort of self-overcoming, an idea that most critical argumentation of our time aligns with a masculinist and individualistic set of values, and many critics would also see an identifiably liberal set of precepts at stake here, as when an embodied subjectivity is thought to fly in the face of liberal humanism's ambition to deny the body by recourse to rationalism. (Farebrother seems to signify, among other things, the priority of rational decision over carnal or worldly considerations.) But as we have also seen, Farebrother is a strangely diffident superman. James Eli Adams has cogently argued that such Victorian male heroics might best be viewed in the light of a crisis of masculinity, with sources in the increasing uncertainties of Victorians concerning the manliness of intellectual labor.[24] Regarding the Victorian context, I must defer these issues of self-inspection and agency until my upcoming discussions of J. S. Mill and Matthew Arnold. For the Farebrother plotline, as read here, presses issues that had best be handled now. Liberal agency, whether as a regulative or substantive matter, has numerous lines of argument arrayed against it today, and I will turn now to a fuller, conceptual consideration of those points. Although this study is concerned primarily with mid-Victorian liberal culture and some of its consequences in late Victorian aesthetic culture, the historical cases in the following chapters can be treated more clearly if I compartmentalize my outlines of the conceptual commitments that lie in the argument's background. Most pressing at this early stage of the study is what I mean by liberalism.

Critique of Liberalism

At a general level, liberalism indicates a doctrine whereby individuals bear equivalent rights of free thought and action within a sociality to which they adhere through their own volition. So understood, liberalism has been widely criticized as a naive voluntarism, a perniciously atomistic individualism, and an unduly abstracting subscription of agency to universalizing moral perspectives. Such general points gain their urgency in particular cases, of course. Regarding Eliot's Farebrother, for instance, his case appears to exhibit liberalism's emphasis on the agent's fundamentally voluntaristic sociality, and he also epitomizes the liberal agent's abstraction of himself—and, presumably, of others—from particularity. Farebrother, that is, is acting as he would have all persons act under the circumstances. Critics of liberalism following the likes of Michael Sandel might well deem Farebrother an "empty self," just as Kant's categorical imperative seems to imply an "empty formalism."[25]

Against such current critiques of liberalism, I propose a regulative perspective to allow for a measured affirmation of liberalism. I have already offered a distinction between Dorothea Brooke's regulative liberality and Farebrother's rather more disquieting substantive liberalism. This distinction between regulative and substantive liberalism recalls a Kantian vocabulary, whereby *regulative* ideas stand opposed to *constitutive* knowledge. Very generally, the regulative turns on how we think, on how relations and ideas of existence factor into human experience; the constitutive turns on what we think, on what we bring into the phenomenology of human experience and engage as matter for cognitive appropriation.[26] We regulate our conduct in mathematical theory with reference to an idea of infinity, for example, although we cannot in fact literalize that idea as an object of knowledge in the same way that we can many other ideas. The regulative function implies a kind of formalism, in the end, in that it bears on the a priori conditions of possibility for the entertaining of an idea such as infinity. But to speak of an empty formalism in this context is to overstate the regulative perspective's pretensions to a substantive character. The language of "emptiness," in other words, presupposes a valuation of content (or substance) over form. By the end of this chapter, I mean to call into question the authority of that valuation and to revise the distinction on which it relies.

To the extent that Eliot invites us to literalize Farebrother's character to our minds, we are, as I have argued, perhaps bound to find him a bit flat. That is so, I suggested, precisely because his characterization is too narrowed in the direction of a concretized or substantive liberal agency. That this narrowed liberal agency is not the whole story about liberal agency is suggested already within Eliot's novel, however, once one allows that there is, between Dorothea Brooke and Farebrother, a kind of family resemblance in matters moral and ethical. Each character is heavily marked by qualities of tolerant judgment and respect. And the more compelling face of liberal aspiration, over against liberal substantiation, is at hand in the richer appeal that Dorothea seems destined to mount to most readers. This speculation can seem tenuous, of course. So I will seek to make my proposal more answerable to some powerful critiques of liberalism by looking directly in this section to those critiques.

Although diverse in many respects, communitarians and many feminists and multiculturalists have in common a sense that liberalism valorizes an abstract regime of rights-based individualism that does not properly credit thickly constituted selves and specific collective identities. The universalizing morality of liberalism is opposed, in such critiques, to various particularized ethical and cultural values, needs, and substantive ideas of the good. Years of debate along these lines have normalized some concessions on all sides. John Rawls, who revived deontological (duty-based) moral liberalism in the 1970s, has updated his thinking to allow for respects in which moral agents are necessarily informed by their traditions and social placements. Thus he mitigates his earlier tendency to argue from a universalizing conception of all moral agents in an "original position" by allowing, in his later work, for meaningfully plural "comprehensive doctrines" that might still get along by means of "overlapping consensus."[27] Meanwhile, communitarians such as Michael Walzer and Charles Taylor seem willing to allow that the idea of individual rights is not exactly modernity's most pernicious spawn. To that extent they mitigate their tendency to anathematize universalization as an absolute detriment to authentic and wholesome subjectivity.[28]

But hard cases still bedevil those arguments, such as Seyla Benhabib's *Situating the Self*, that have tried to bridge the differences between liberalism on the one hand and communitarian and feminist argumentation on the other. Benhabib goes some way toward defending liberalism in its Habermasian register by drawing on the intersubjectivity presupposed by Habermas's notion of communicative ethics and assimilating it to an Arendtian set of precepts, congenial to communitarians, about difference-based public dialogue as a constitutive factor in the making of genuine political subjectivity. But Benhabib, laudably pressing her point to its limits, also has to concede that one should deem phenomena such as sadomasochism wrong, because such practices inescapably collide with "principles of moral respect and egalitarian reciprocity."[29] For Benhabib, then, the community that might gather itself around the erotics of sadomasochism is, in effect, declared beyond the pale on the basis of an a priori claim about right conduct, understood as that which can pass the test of universalization.

To detail my own intervention into this ethical terrain, I will undertake a reading of Uday Singh Mehta's recent *Liberalism and Empire*, which argues that liberalism tends inherently to imperialism, understood as a project of domination made justifiable to liberals themselves on grounds of perceived cultural superiority.[30] Mehta's argument draws on and exemplifies communitarian critique, in which liberalism inherently threatens to erase identities based in a sense of social difference and particularity. With its concern to reveal an imperialistic urge "internal" to liberalism (8, 20), Mehta's work also exemplifies a widespread gambit in current critiques of liberalism, which see in it programmatic condescension to non-Western forms of life.[31] I select Mehta's text for a number of reasons, as my reading will show, but I should declare at the outset that my largest concern bears not simply nor even primarily on the context of imperialism that Mehta takes as his primary theme. One might equally look to argumentation that sees in liberalism a programmatic Western masculinity disposed to consign femaleness to animality or unreason, or a programmatic racism that styles Africans or other nonwhite populations as uncivilized and not yet ready for enlightenment or autonomy. Ideally, I would reconsider characterizations of liberalism in all these contexts separately. As my view to Mehta will suggest, however, such reconsideration needs to take a long and careful look at the rhetoric of agency at hand in particular lines of arguments, and a wide-ranging reconsideration of liberalism in that respect would amount to a detour too large for this study to accommodate reasonably. Therefore, I suggest that my reading of Mehta be taken as one step in such a direction. And here my special concern is to show how his line of argumentation admits a coherence problem, as a result of the communitarian and pragmatist thinking that grounds his standpoint.

I grant Mehta's claim that the classical liberal tradition—especially its English lineage from Locke through Bentham and the two Mills—systematically discounted liberalism's ostensible concerns with freedoms and rights when confronted with the challenges of Empire in India. Liberals did so by wielding a rhetoric of cultivation in its most disquieting aspect. They rationalized domination of India by infantilizing the culture and by relegating its religious forms to superstition. Thus John Stuart Mill can argue that the Indian populace was not yet civilized enough to sustain a representative government of the sort that Anglo-European contexts merit. Likewise, there was little question of viewing Indian religious observance in the light deemed appropriate for British dissenting Protestants or even Catholics, because liberals viewed Indian religion as irrationality and madness (35–36, 90). Mehta's historical claims are strong and salutary, and by no means do I wish to deny the human costs of imperialistic culture. I contest his claim, however, that this argument says anything generally damning about liberalism as such, except insofar as one assimilates liberalism to an extreme of universalization and rationalism that figures like J. S. Mill, in particular, never advocated.

Mehta's picture of cultural difference is at the root of the problems I mean to identify. Fundamentally at issue for Mehta is the failure of British liberals to relate sympathetically to the "unfamiliar": "In the empire, the epistemological commitments of liberalism to rationality and the progress that it was deemed to imply constantly trumped its commitments to democracy, consensual government, limitations on the legitimate power of the state, and even toleration. Moreover, it is the epistemological commitments that are symptomatic of a narrowness in which the challenge of understanding an unfamiliar world, with multiple singularities, forms of living, and experiencing life, is most starkly betrayed by liberals"(36). In this view, then, liberals betray the prospect of "understanding an unfamiliar world" for reasons internal to their liberalism. Mehta's claim might well be regarded as quite sound. For liberalism—both in its messy historical forms and in its most careful theoretical elaborations—finally comes down to a stipulation that some forms of living are tolerable and others are beyond the pale. Where Mehta's argument falters, however, is in enlisting Edmund Burke as an alternative historical figure who encounters the unfamiliar in a more creditable fashion.

Typically classed among political conservatives and vilified by nineteenth-century liberals for his alarmism at the French Revolution, Burke is nonetheless understood by Mehta to have promoted a truer liberality, documented especially in his speeches opposing British entanglements in India. Refusing to package India as the object of a knowing and superior Western gaze, Burke urges a hands-off approach that looks now like prescient good sense. Burke's advantage, as Mehta most often gives it forth, lies not in having a better or more adequate conception of India's difference but in having a more appropriate sense of "humility," an unwillingness, finally, to presume that an unfamiliar culture could securely be deemed backward and in need of alignment with British cultural forms: "For Burke, in contrast with both the Mills, the significance of experience and the forms of life of which they are a part is not provisional on their incorporation in a rationalist teleology. Reason, freedom, and individuality, as nineteenth-century liberals understood them, are not, for Burke, the arbiters of the significance of these forms of life; when they are assumed to be such arbiters, he is aware that it is usually by relying on an implicit alliance with political and other forms of power"(21).

For many literary and cultural historians, Mehta's anathematizing of reason will recall Horkheimer and Adorno's vision of Enlightenment reason as the culprit in the flattening out of myth, nature, and human experience as such.[32] But Mehta draws most directly on communitarian and neo-pragmatist thinking to support his general claims. Pragmatism serves Mehta's needs because its hostility to a priori reason seems to map congenially onto his own critique of imperialistic liberalism. In words quoted approvingly by Mehta, Richard Rorty contends that "solidarity has to be constructed out of little pieces, rather than found already waiting, in the form of an urlanguage which all of us recognize when we hear it" (21). And for Mehta himself, rationalistic liberalism characteristically "specifies in advance of the encounter with the 'facts' of history the general structure of what it would mean for facts to hang together 'rationally,' and only thus could they have meaning" (18). Because Burke lacks the liberals' overweening faith in the adequacy of any a priori mental equipment, he "can see and imagine a form of life in India that is not of necessity in need of imperial superintendence" (215).

Here Mehta would have us accept what I see as a contradictory picture of Burke's relation to the unfamiliar. At issue, then, is not simply who Burke was but whether we as readers can take home any convincing picture of critical agency and sociality in the kind of figure that Mehta makes Burke out to be. The instability in Mehta's argumentation can be gleaned already when we isolate the agency of Burke in Mehta's language and then seek to distinguish that agency clearly from the style of agency apparently claimed by liberals. Here are several examples of Mehta's language, with my emphasis in each case, all regarding Burke: "His thought *is pitched* at a level that *takes seriously* the sentiments, feelings, and attachments through which peoples are, and aspire to be, 'at home' " (21); "Burke *exposes himself and enters dialogue* with the unfamiliar and accepts the possible risks of that encounter" (22); "Another people's independence, as Burke prophetically foresaw, is always the limiting point of our vision—the darkness that reason does not illuminate" (39); "Through his attention to the local, Burke *is in a position to see the integrity*—literally that which holds things together—of lives that perhaps share nothing more than the fact that they are all constituted by the unavoidable engagement with the local" (41).

To judge by these characterizations, it is much to Burke's credit that he is more open-minded and respectful than liberals. Burke wields a kind of tactical critical agency that issues in an ethical posture valorized by Mehta. Mehta's passive-verb formulations—to the effect that Burke's "thought is pitched" so as to treat the unfamiliar affirmatively—clearly imply a degree of responsible choice on Burke's part. And more active phrasings—as when Burke "exposes himself and enters dialogue"—lend further substance to the view that Burke is, as it were on principle, choosing to run a risk. Because Mehta's language is hardly unusual in current critical argumentation, it might seem odd that I single it out so deliberately. But it is precisely my point that current academic writing systematically underreads the implicit logic of agency in such phrasings.

The problems that follow on such underreading are most crucially apparent in Mehta's recourse to the phrase "forms of life," invoked insistently throughout his argument. The phrase is associated principally with Ludwig Wittgenstein's late philosophy, but Mehta draws primarily on Richard Rorty's appropriations. Rorty, with much other recent pragmatist scholarship, has seen a welcome support in Wittgenstein's antimetaphysical points about language games as constitutive of discourse. Pragmatists declare that one cannot stand outside of practice to ask extrinsically about its warrants or value, and Wittgenstein's ideas of language games and forms of life seem congruent and authoritative. But both Mehta and (until recently) Rorty himself violate Wittgenstein's usage by mistaking—or at least vacillating deeply on—the respects in which one form of life can relate in any principled way to another form of life.

Regarding Burke's relations to the unfamiliar, Mehta styles him in two different ways. Sometimes Burke seems to be registering the Indian difference to a degree that allows him to understand that British imperial dominion is not proper to it. At other times, however, Mehta styles Burke as acting upon a more general perspective about communication—namely, that true communication involves running the risk of an opacity that characterizes the encounter of different forms of life. Presumably, in this latter view, the Indian form of life is simply opaque to Burke and, for that reason, comes across as intractably other. The one view conjures ideas of cultural affirmation versus negation, while we could say, to borrow from J. L. Austin's language of speech acts, that the other view conjures felicity versus infelicity.[33] It is the first of these relations to the unfamiliar that Mehta has in mind, it seems, when he commends the "deep, and even reverent humility that Burke feels in the face of differences—cultural, economic, and political" (164).

Here is the problematic step in Mehta's argument, for this value of "reverent humility" goes well beyond anything that can find secure authority in Wittgenstein. To my mind, the most relevant argumentation in Wittgenstein turns on the distinction of sense and nonsense, because the difference between one language game and another is there most directly at issue. Says Wittgenstein, "When a sentence is called senseless, it is not as it were its sense that is senseless. But a combination of words is being excluded from the language, withdrawn from circulation."[34] Because Mehta's argument invokes Wittgenstein only in passing—albeit at decisive junctures—we have no compelling reason to digress at length into Wittgenstein. Perhaps it can suffice if I translate Wittgenstein's remark (and, perforce, reverse it) by suggesting that Mehta has this to say: "When liberals call another form of life uncultivated, it is the sense of that culture that they disdain and violate." Wittgenstein, in my view, would say something very different: to call another form of life uncultivated is precisely *not* to reject its sense per se but instead to regard its form as uncirculatable for some reason that cannot be specified within one's own form of life.

Wittgenstein's perspectives cohere with some elements of Mehta's project, insofar as Mehta is simply taking Wittgenstein to mean that communication can falter in engaging other forms of life. In this view, forms of life might well differ in such a way as to make any Habermasian ideal-speech situation look very much in need of amendment.[35] The problem in Mehta's argument, however, is that the Wittgensteinian view cannot lend any positive content or rationale to a practice of reverent humility in the face of difference. Indeed, it seems much more appropriate to assimilate that dimension of Mehta's argument to the profoundly liberal conception of universal respect that Mehta is supposedly targeting.

Here Mehta's recourse to Richard Rorty becomes key. Rorty seems, on the face of it, a more appropriate figure for Mehta's purposes than Wittgenstein, because Rorty so actively promotes a specifically antifoundationalist liberalism. Provided this kind of liberalism can be rationalized, it might stake out a space whereby some general ethical precepts can take hold, even as we also stand clear of the transcendentalizng embarrassments of Rawlsian deontological liberalism and Habermasian discourse ethics. For Rorty, such a precept would be the abjuring of cruelty; for Mehta, reverent humility in the face of different forms of life. But as Alice Crary has argued in a careful essay on debates over Wittgenstein's relevance to political theory, the Rorty of *Consequences of Pragmatism* (Mehta's Rorty) has been disavowed in some key respects by the Rorty of more recent vintage, and on matters that seem to impinge on Mehta's concerns.[36] In a 1993 essay, Rorty cedes the mistakenness of the vocabulary he employed in earlier works, where he was prone to dismiss philosophical controversies over distinctions such as realism and antirealism, or emotion and cognition. He remains convinced as to the nullity of those debates, but now he says that he should not have argued his point by declaring that those debates were mistaken and mired in "pseudo-problems." For this later Rorty, a pragmatist should only speak "of distinctions whose employment has proved to lead nowhere, proved to be more trouble than they were worth. For pragmatists, the question should always be, 'What use is it?' rather than 'Is it real?' Criticism of other philosophers' distinctions and problematics should charge relative inutility rather than 'meaninglessness' or 'illusion' or 'incoherence.' "[37] Rorty is allowing, in other words, that one is bound to invoke an inappropriate analytic logic when contending against an idea, or a debate over ideas, by understanding it to be mistaken and concluding that one should or must therefore abandon it. The pragmatically relevant issue is one of relative inutility.

If Mehta were to take on board the change that Rorty has admitted, it would have the effect of disabling claims that turn on issues like truth or appropriateness *in any general sense*. Just as late Rorty comes to see that he cannot license his early scorn for philosophical pseudoproblems without taking up the very rhetoric of truth that he was purporting to supersede, Mehta's critique of liberalism cannot grant ethical or moral content to reverent humility or imperialist condescension without taking up what finally looks very much like liberalism's universalization of respect. To resist Mehta's valuations of reverent humility is not, of course, to offer an apologia for nineteenth-century British imperialist chauvinism. It seems impossible to read the liberals' infantilization of Indian culture as anything but a deployment of British power along the lines of something very different from universal respect. My reading in Mehta's argument is directed toward his claim that liberalism *expresses* itself, rather than *contradicts* itself, in asserting a relation of imperialistic dominance in the face of unfamiliarity.

I submit, instead, that Burke and the liberals are essentially alike in assuming a relation of *judgment* over against the Indians. Burke judges British cultivation to be inappropriate to India, while nineteenth-century liberals generally judged it to be appropriate and justified. But in seeking to distinguish Burke and the liberals, Mehta is driven to bifurcate the idea of *judgment* in a way that finally lacks any clear conceptual foundation. He consistently criticizes liberalism as "judgmental" (17–18, 79) while at the same time commending the hermeneutic richness that Hans-Georg Gadamer extols under the rubric of "prejudice" (21–23, 41). In other words, the difference between vilified judgment and valorized prejudice—the latter term simply means a priori judgment—remains ill defined. It is important to allow that the distinction might have some rhetorical warrants, and indeed Rorty's argumentation has increasingly moved toward the stance that philosophical work is nothing but rhetorical work. But Mehta argues his concerns through a combination of historicist and philosophical voices that indicate a desire on his part to call upon a foundation in truth rather than persuasion simply. In the end, the differences between Burke and the nineteenth-century liberals lie principally in the divergent practical effects that their judgments could be assumed to have, if or when those judgments were to find realization in British policy. It is not any thoroughgoing reverence or humility that redeems Burke but the congruence of his hands-off position with our current anti-imperialistic norms. And that anti-imperialism, I contend, is best rationalized as a value of generalized rights rather than of cultural specificity, respect rather than recognition.

Thus we can see how communitarian and pragmatist critiques of liberalism tend to falter in related but distinguishable ways. Communitarianism insists that human flourishing proceeds not from the realization of a generalized humanity and respect for such humanity, but from a particularized sociality that deserves recognition. In lodging this claim, however, communitarianism inevitably will either betray itself through a categorical value of respect or neglect the prospect that communities, in their specific traditions and values, can generate substantial and potentially problematic prescriptions regarding conduct. I have already argued Mehta's involvement in the first of these alternatives, whereby a general and liberal valuation of respect for others seems crucial to the cogency of his claims. He approximates the second alternative as well when he casts humility as the precondition for understanding cultural contexts that imperious liberalism would consign to backwardness. Mehta faults liberalism for its obliviousness to "what the stranger is deeply and hence not provisionally *invested* in." Included among potential deep investments are "religious piety" and the possibility of accepting a position in "an imperfectly mobile and traditional hierarchy" (27). In the Victorian sociopolitical context, as we will see in this chapter's final section, Mehta's terms were also employed in Tory and other traditionalist perspectives that were increasingly viewing liberalism as a pernicious devaluation of prereflective obedience, leading liberals to be deaf to the authority of social tradition and revealed religion.

At issue, it seems, is whether liberal agency is better viewed as a corrosive threat to authentic community or as the premise that makes sense of individuality within community. Arguing pointedly for the first view—and accepting the salutariness and appropriateness of communitarian prescriptions—Charles Taylor justifies the logic whereby French-speaking Quebec *mandates* that people who are ethnically Francophone instruct their children in French rather than English.[38] Extrapolating on this kind of logic, K. Anthony Appiah makes plainer its difficult consequences. Writing as a black homosexual male, Appiah proposes the analogy of a communitarian demand that Appiah organize his identity around his race and/or sexuality, each of which is clearly marginalized and threatened by the dominant American culture and therefore in need of recognition. Such a demand, prescriptive for reasons internal to communitarianism, points up for Appiah the blurriness of the line between "the politics of recognition and the politics of compulsion."[39]

The pragmatist strain tends, in turn, to underread what I am calling a regulative aspiration to critical self-reflection in moral agency. In general, pragmatists contend on more or less analytic grounds that there is no getting outside practice. And the point is hard to dispute if we take this claim on its own terms by asking whether a substantial agent can stand outside its own world of possibles. By what Archimedean leverage point, we want to ask, could the agent get outside, and on what ground would the agent then stand? While there is room to wonder about the appropriateness of the metaphors here—of space, of leverage, even of gravity in the image of standing *on* something—I accept the powerful nature of these questions. What is striking, however, is how routinely pragmatist argumentation allows for something a bit more.

In the closing words of his "Lecture on Ethics," to take one example, Wittgenstein has this to say about the nonsensicalness of talk *about* ethics:

I see now that these nonsensical expressions were not nonsensical because I had not yet found the correct expressions, but that their nonsensicality was their very essence. For all I wanted to do with them was just *to go beyond* the world and that is to say beyond significant language. My whole tendency and I believe the tendency of all men who ever tried to write or talk about Ethics or Religion was to run against the boundaries of language. This running against the walls of our cage is perfectly, absolutely hopeless. Ethics so far as it springs from the desire to say something about the ultimate meaning of life, the absolute good, the absolute valuable, can be no science. What it says does not add to our knowledge in any sense. But it is a document of a tendency in the human mind which I personally cannot help respecting deeply and I would not for my life ridicule it.[40]

Alongside the familiar late-Wittgensteinian perspectives that have seemed so congenial to pragmatists—the repudiation of going beyond the world, understood as an "absolutely hopeless" and unprogressive enterprise—we find Wittgenstein admitting his own engagement, and that of many others, in precisely that enterprise. Ethics documents "a tendency in the human mind" that Wittgenstein "cannot help respecting deeply."[41]

A philosophical case for liberal agency as a regulative ideal seems fully compatible with the viewpoint outlined here by Wittgenstein, whose language explicitly invokes the key liberal terms of human nature and respect. We may recall here that Kant never argued the obviously incorrect point that people invariably and inevitably act according to universalizable moral principles, nor did he argue for any substantiality in the transcendental moral agent. Instead, he proposed that the human experiential apparatus carries with it a tendency to ask questions and to posit relations beyond those that can be determined within human ratiocination. Kant's point is not that we can self-consciously *be beyond* what Wittgenstein calls here our "cage." Instead, Kant tells of our capacity—and, as Wittgenstein has it, our tendency—to make it our business to strain against the boundaries of phenomenal experience. Kant parlays this idea of essential striving or aspiration, already present in matters of epistemology, into an idea of humanity's essential *interest* in universalizable moral action. Granted, we cannot "be" outside of practice. The difference between antifoundationalist pragmatism and deontological liberalism evaporates, however, once both standpoints stake out common ground in an idea of human nature and its tendency to extrapractical aspiration.

But finding contradiction in nonliberal lines of thought—even finding an in-
cipient liberalism in those lines of thought—is something very different from
establishing the strength of liberalism itself. In turning now to a more positive
argument, I mean to advance a generally Kantian perspective. In some respects, I credit a Habermasian view that recuperates Kantian moral rationalism by purporting to do without Kant's tendencies to ahistorical and
schematically transcendental assumptions about human subjectivity. Habermas transfigures Kant's analytical argumentation, which focused on the a priori logic of conscious experience, by arguing instead from the practical logic of
communicative action, which for Habermas has socially significant entail-
ments (for instance, a concern for respectful consensus-seeking).[42] As will be
apparent especially in my argumentation concerning Oscar Wilde, himself a
favorite of poststructuralist theorists, I share with Habermas a sense that poststructuralist argumentation enters shaky ground when it seeks to warrant itself
along the lines of any specific sociopolitical values. It is not that the values of
most such authors are hard to glean, but that their argumentation typically
evinces what Habermas calls a "crypto-normativity" by valorizing terms such
as *rupture, resistance* and *revolution* without acknowledging the normative appeal
and indeed the tendentially liberal values (such as autonomy and fairness) that
undergird poststructuralist claims to political and ethical relevance.[43]

On the question of normativity, and outside the widely debated terms of
Habermas's communicative argumentation, the philosopher Christine Korsgaard has argued even more directly for the conceptual perspective that I am
taking up. In this view, liberal many-sidedness instantiates an agency constituted by critical self-reflection. "The human mind is self-consciousness," says
Korsgaard, "in the sense that it is essentially reflective." In such accounts as
Korsgaard's, we should note, the capacity for reflection is not a property that
we might assign to particular individuals and withhold from others—not a personal quality such as thoughtfulness or meditativeness, that is—but instead it
names an elementary capacity for self-inspection or distancing that enables
people to pose questions to themselves. In this sense, as Korsgaard notes, reflection concerns, not thoughtfulness, but "the structure of our minds that
makes thoughtfulness possible."[44] This is to say, the important matter of cultivating thoughtfulness—much at issue for J. S. Mill and Matthew Arnold in my
upcoming discussion—stands apart in Korsgaard's account from those conditions of possibility that she identifies, for better or for worse, with humanness
as such. This step will be, I take it, the crucial one for critics of liberalism in its
Kantian guise, for here is the universalization that my own argument accepts
but that argumentation such as we see in Mehta is probably still disposed to see
as essentially imperialist.

Korsgaard views normative thinking as a regulative function, as an agential
investment that is practically coextensive with valued identity as such, and
therefore as something common to all the discursive communities canvased in

my argument, from Kantians to communitarians, pragmatists, and even post-structuralists (to the extent that they can be said to promote anything loosely construed as a kind of identity or enacted value). Her comment on communitarianism is compact and telling for my purposes:

It is urged by communitarians that people need to conceive themselves as members of smaller communities, essentially tied to particular others and traditions. This is an argument about how we human beings need to constitute our practical identities, and if it is successful what it establishes is a *universal* fact, namely that our practical identities must be constituted in part by particular ties and commitments. The liberal who wants to include everyone will now argue from that fact. And the communitarian himself, having reflected and reached this conclusion, now has a conception of his own identity which is universal: he is an animal that needs to live in community. (118–19)

The communitarian, as Korsgaard goes on to elaborate, can be understood to argue for two different aspects of selfhood—a subjective experience and an objectification of experience as such. In the first place, there is the subject who simply needs a specific communal attachment, or attachments. At the same time, reflecting on him- or herself more objectively, this subject contends that he or she is a *kind* of creature in need of ties to *some* community or other. This latter, more objective self-assessment implies a normativistic universalization along these lines: "respect the needs of people to be embedded in traditions." That universalization seems entailed even in those arguments meant to serve the first, more subjective and prereflectively figured image of communitarian personhood.

Many readers in contemporary literary and cultural studies will find this argument disquieting. Universality seems like a buzzword for neoconservative political orientations, and normativity, while perhaps nobody's buzzword, seems bound up with a will to prescriptiveness that, in turn, seems likely to rationalize privileges and exclusions making up the status quo. History makes such concerns unsurprising. But history also shows that ideas and vocabularies can be put to widely varying and even contradictory uses. In the Western intellectual tradition, the language of voluntarism has often coexisted with forms of sociality that underscore heavily the authority of reigning kings and other established authorities. From the other direction, we can note that the Puritan vision of predestination, ostensibly a grim determinism, coincided with radical revolutionary action in respect to earthly authority. We can find a recent instance of this general point in Stanley Fish's account of the far right's co-optation of "magic words" like fairness and justice, now put to new service in the dismantling of affirmative action.[45] It is by no means clear that terms like *normativity* and *universalization* are presently amenable to what would amount to a reverse hijacking by the left. But I do contend that current academic and cultural circumstances warrant renewed thoughtfulness concerning the claims of normativity and universalization on progressive interests in literary and cultural studies.

Many-Sidedness as a Form of Life

I return now to specifically mid-Victorian reference points by mounting a consideration of "many-sidedness," understood as a personal disposition to consider alternative vantage points in private and public issues. Many-sidedness is one facet of the period's discourse of *character*, a term that found popular consideration by the likes of Samuel Smiles and theoretical elaboration in the works of liberals such as Herbert Spencer, T. H. Green, and John Stuart Mill.[46] In my view, the aspiration to many-sidedness epitomizes the period's liberal ideal of cultivated agency. At once an idea of much interest conceptually and a matter of sustained and locatable debate throughout the 1860s, the idea of many-sidedness will let me historicize the general discussion of liberal agency offered in the previous section.

To begin, however, I want to clarify the conceptual problem that motivates and underlies this historical discussion: from what vantage point can there be more than one "form of life"? Notwithstanding the fact that Wittgenstein and his followers typically speak in the plural—of *forms* of life, that is—it is not clear for whom forms of life can be plural, if a form of life is interpreted as something immune to meaningfully "external" criticism. This immunity is generally argued from an analytical or practical perspective, through a twofold claim: that external criticism cannot gain meaningful purchase on the internal workings of a form of life; and that people within a given form of life, in turn, cannot themselves attain to a meaningfully external position. Of course, the notion of immunity can also be argued, as in Mehta's study, in a way that appears saturated with a view of ethical propriety. In that light, "judging" another form of life is understood to be not so much impossible as it is ethically regrettable. In any case, my general suggestion is that the liberal standpoint of critical self-reflection simply is that standpoint in which forms of life can be meaningfully pluralized. By contrast, the communitarian perspective—as viewed in the foregoing section—seemed to falter in one of two ways, either by taking on board what I am calling liberal generalizations about respect, or by embracing a kind of prescriptiveness in which, as Appiah had it, the line between recognition and compulsion becomes worrisomely blurred. The aspiration to a meaningful pluralization of life-forms is fraught with practical difficulties, to be sure. There will be, essentially, much room for self-deception or hypocrisy. My point is hardly that these dangers can be theorized away, but instead that we will be the worse off in allowing the pretense (or, worse, the reality) of refusing such pluralization's claims on our collective interests.

As a historical matter, in turn, my point in what follows is that the idea of many-sidedness was very much in the air in the 1860s, and due to then-current sociopolitical developments in the ascendancy of Victorian liberalism. I will briefly indicate some of the political conditions in a moment, and this study's third chapter takes a more detailed approach to them. Now I need only fore-

warn that writers at this time seldom invoke many-sidedness in explicitly political terms. Instead, they call on more depoliticized perspectives. This is so, very
likely, because of the tendency of Victorian liberals to treat politics as the effect of accumulated individual ethical stances, thus underlining in yet another
way the methodological individualism that I referenced at this chapter's outset.
An inquiry into specifically mid-Victorian treatments of many-sidedness must
therefore cast a wide topical net.

Consider, for instance, William Gladstone's account of the heroic age of ancient Greece, in which he recalls a time when hale youth would bring "many-
sided intelligence" to bear in their own cultivation.[47] The term, as Gladstone
surely knew, is a formulaic marker for Homer's Odysseus, an individual understood to earn that description for his expression of various personal features
indicated in the Greek *polutropos*: from "wide travels" and "resourcefulness" to
"wiliness" and "guile."[48] To the extent that this spectrum of meanings suggests
cosmopolitanism on one end and bad faith on the other, it seems that *many-
sidedness* had already built into it some of the practical tensions that this study
explores in the mid-Victorian rhetoric of cultivation. For cultivation, too, can
equally name a kind of noble elevation above provincial conditions and also a
kind of hegemonic ruse. And once we view the stakes of many-sidedness in this
light, it is the least of surprises to find that Gladstone's commentary on the
Greeks was written during the Parliamentary recesses of 1867 and 1868—just
as the Liberal party took over after the first election under the new Reform Bill,
in other words, and just as Gladstone was taking up his most illustrious years
as prime minister.

These years are at once the pinnacle and the crisis-point of Victorian political liberalism. The period of the Second Reform Bill brought with it not
merely an expansion of the franchise into the reaches of working males but
also, in Gladstone's ministry of 1868–74, a remarkable array of liberalizing
legislative acts. Historically significant political acts affected higher and elementary education, the civil service, the army, trades unions, the rights of Irish
Catholics, and much more. A new marketplace of viewpoints was on the way,
and the cultivation of viewpoints was therefore a pervasive concern for those
who could fear the impending effects of uncultivated social and political
agents, whether of the working-class male variety or of the hidebound middle-
class liberal variety that Matthew Arnold bemoaned.

At this point I should recall as well an earlier reference to many-sidedness at
the end of my reading in Eliot. That reference reveals a widespread uncertainty in mid-Victorian debate about the agential bearing of many-sidedness:
"What men gain in manysidedness, it is said, they are losing in vigor."[49] In
these mid-Victorian years, the idea of vigor is seldom far from a gendered
characterization, whereby it lines up with manliness. To the extent that many-
sidedness saps vigor, therefore, many-sidedness stands opposed to manliness.
The problem confronting liberals like Mill and Arnold would seem to be how,

under these cultural circumstances, to present many-sidedness as the new vigor. And in fact that is part of the mission my reading will uncover in them. But each writer's tendencies to contradiction come to bear on this matter as well. For Mill, it turns out, many-sidedness does not relate at all clearly to genius, and thus we need to parse the distinction of genius and many-sidedness more carefully in order to understand the forms of valorized individuality actually at hand in Mill's argumentation. For Arnold, the tension shows up in the wobbly work of his Hellenic ideal, which he presents variously as a complementary equal to Hebraising agency or as the enabling and superior expression of human agency *tout court*.

GENIUS AND MANY-SIDEDNESS IN JOHN STUART MILL

Especially in the guise of characterology and ethology, ideas of cultivation pervade Mill's writings, and with the widely noted effect of suggesting or even demonstrating deep tensions in his thinking. Very generally, the division reflects Mill's concern, on the one hand, to confirm aspects of a utilitarianism that construes humans as agents oriented toward maximizing collective pleasure, even as he also tries, on the other hand, to set base and cultivated pleasures apart and to "declare the pleasures derived from the higher faculties to be preferable *in kind*, apart from the question of intensity, to those of which the animal nature, disjoined from the higher faculties, is susceptible."[50] The anxiety that haunts projects such as Mill's turns on the prospect that many people or classes of people—the crowd, the public, the masses, women, those of other races—might be finally committed to a one-sided animal nature after all. I. M. Greengarten's well-argued treatment of T. H. Green, another key exponent of Victorian intellectual liberalism, makes clear that this anxiety pervades Victorian liberal culture at this time.[51] It is one thing to promote and esteem cultivation, quite another to count on it.

A remark from *On Liberty* points to this tension. There Mill tells, "[I]n the human mind, one-sidedness has always been the rule, and many-sidedness the exception" (252). In this brief for many-sidedness, Mill advocates an exceptionalism, a cultivated subjectivity above and beyond the norm. Even some ostensibly liberal values, such as respect and fairness, seem threatened by the celebration of a many-sidedness that, as Mill underlines, is far from the norm. Is not Mill here inviting his readership to look down on the one-sided figure and, if need be, to take that injunction even to the point of looking down on oneself, should one-sidedness seem there to obtain? Then again, how can we literalize a situation whereby a one-sided person looks *at* him- or herself, if we take *looking at* to imply an act of reflective self-distancing? Such objectification of the self would obviate, if only in the simplest sense, the prospect of one-sidedness.

These questions only deepen with further reading, and it is not my goal here to iron out Mill's viewpoint. But I do mean to clarify a point about Mill's supposed relation to liberal culture. He is widely taken to be the preeminent liberal theorist of the nineteenth century, commonly placed between Kant and Rawls in theoretical accounts of liberalism. In closer historical terms, Mill is the preferred Victorian liberal spokesman: more humane than Herbert Spencer, more systematic than Matthew Arnold, and more rhetorically available than T. H. Green. His *On Liberty*, in particular, is held to be a classically liberal statement for its celebration of individuality over collectivity. Taking all these commonplaces for granted, what I want to show here is that we under-read Mill and liberal culture as well when we fail to distinguish between his two forms of individual exceptionalism: genius and many-sidedness.

Mill himself tends to underread this difference, and thus we might have here one more face of the so-called two-Mills problem, whereby he one day wakes up a Coleridgean romantic, only to wake up the next day a Benthamite utilitarian. We can grant the romantic character of genius, I think, but it is not clear that many-sidedness implies utilitarianism, unless we view many-sidedness, not as a subjective property, but as a description of representative government. In this last view, argued by Mill in *Considerations on Representative Government*, individuals factor into his argument as "one-sided," and the value of representative government, in turn, emerges in its guarantee that multiple viewpoints will be brought into conversation and debate. Mill argues along utilitarian lines for the value of the resulting many-sidedness: we all profit when our blindnesses are exposed systematically to other views.[52] But my account brings out Mill's image of many-sidedness as a subjective feature of at least some individuals. My point will be that Mill's liberalism cannot be fully captured as a romantic or atomistic individualism so long as his thinking also privileges a many-sidedness that finally stands apart from the heroic individuality of the *genius*.

In the third chapter of *On Liberty*, entitled "Of Individuality, as One of the Elements of Well-Being," Mill dwells at some length on genius. What emerges is his conflicted interest in taking up romantically charged ideas of original agency but in ensuring, also, that a social ethic of tolerance and considered judgment emerge from these ideas rather than stand in conflict with them. Mill proceeds from a recommendation that society provide the needed environment for the flourishing of genius: "Genius can only breathe freely in an *atmosphere* of freedom. Persons of genius are, *ex vi termini* [by definition], more individual than any other people—less capable, consequently, of fitting themselves, without hurtful compression, into any of the moulds which society provides in order to save its members the trouble of forming their own character" (267–68). Here individuality is not an absolute but a relative quality, with the genius being "more individual" than all the rest. But what does it mean for a given person who is not a genius to look up to this supremely self-evaluated and valued individual in the way that Mill is urging? Two prospects open up: Mill's

readers are either invited to strive for that value and move along some continuum toward genius; or they are invited to recognize that they are not and cannot be geniuses, and the recognition of that latter fact would seem to enjoin
simply a state of admiration for the real genius. Each alternative implies a state
of agency, but with this difference: the first alternative—one of striving toward
an ideal of genius—would seem to figure the more empowered and optimistic
vision of agency, and it finds expression in widely scattered liberal-democratic
utopianisms from William Godwin's theories to Mill's own time;[53] the second
alternative appears abject by comparison, in that the accomplishment of that
second "agent" looks much like a feat of resignation, a consigning of the self
to limitation or shortcoming.

The special complexity of Mill's rhetoric of genius turns on the incapacity
of his argument clearly to occupy one or the other of these tendencies. Mill
put great stock in his theories of self-development.[54] At the same time, his argumentation leaves unclear how broadly the prospect of self-development pertains. Mill is clearly not understanding his readership as a collection of
geniuses, so his rhetorical situation in *On Liberty* seems to consist in a challenge
of enjoining readers at once to exalt this ideal of individual genius and to
maintain, at the same time, an attitude of critical self-assessment. Mill's ensuing discussion makes plainer a looming tension:

> People think genius a fine thing if it enables a man to write an exciting poem, or paint
> a picture. But in its true sense, that of originality in thought and action, though no one
> says that it is not a thing to be admired, nearly all, at heart, think that they can do very
> well without it. Unhappily this is too natural to be wondered at. Originality is the one
> thing which unoriginal minds cannot feel the use of. They cannot see what it is to do
> for them: how should they? If they could see what it would do for them it would not be
> originality. The first service which originality has to render them, is that of opening
> their eyes: which being once fully done, they would have a chance of being themselves
> original. (268)

Mill implicitly challenges his readers to declare an identification either with the
unoriginal or the original mind. To the extent that it seems implausible that
someone would cast his or her vote on the side of the unoriginal mind, Mill's
remarks spotlight not merely the elitism that many readers have seen in his
overall posture but suggest as well that readers of Mill are themselves being
asked to enlist themselves in that elitism—to disdain, that is, the way that
"nearly all" people think and to see themselves as rising or risen, by means of
intelligent reflection, above the obtuse herd. Mill's concern is that "the general
tendency of things throughout the world is to render mediocrity the ascendant
power among mankind." "At present," he observes, "individuals are lost in the
crowd" (268). Even pleasure is scripted for those who "like in crowds" (265).
And for the figure who lets his environment "choose his plan of life for him,"
there is "no need of any other faculty than the ape-like one of imitation" (262).

But neither is it so clear that Mill—in recommending originality and genius—is making even an elitist sense. He suggests that unoriginal minds are incapable of seeing what originality could do for them, and he goes so far as to say that whatever unoriginal minds can comprehend must be, by definition, not an instance of originality. This leaves it quite uncertain how we are to picture the substantive realization of the "opening" of "their eyes" that originality somehow delivers as a "first service" to unoriginal minds. If unoriginal minds cannot comprehend originality at all, then by what means does originality gain enough purchase on unoriginal minds to open their eyes? This figure of speech—this opening of eyes—implies a dawning of comprehension that Mill has just said cannot actually transpire in the unoriginal mind.

Mill's tangled logic of originality parlays itself into a tangled logic of enlightened liberal agency more generally. These words follow immediately on the quotation given above: "Meanwhile, recollecting that nothing was ever yet done which some one was not the first to do, and that all good things which exist are the fruits of originality, let them [unoriginal minds] be modest enough to believe that there is something still left for it to accomplish, and assure themselves that they are more in need of originality, the less they are conscious of the want" (268). To embrace the "modesty" called for here, one would have to refuse or bracket one's own viewpoint to a profound extent. As literary critics writing in a neopragmatist vein have made clear in recent decades, there is something practically bizarre in asking people, as Mill here does, to give credit to a need in inverse proportion to their sense of actually experiencing that need.[55] Whether we regard this prospect as impossible or merely peculiar, it seems that it actually constitutes a precarious but consistently asserted vision of agency that is, in turn, fundamental to the liberal aspiration of Mill's overall argument.

Other passages in *On Liberty* make this point plainer. Mill argues, for instance, that even in those cases when society holds views that are already substantially "true," it is important to keep the channels open, as it were, to dissenting and therefore false views. It is not simply that false views might well have a grain of truth in them (Mill does allow that, too), but, more importantly, that only complacency and finally outright forgetting of a given truth's authority can follow on shielding the truth from competing viewpoints. Here is the social equivalent of the savvy rhetorician's concern to understand the opposition's viewpoint in its fullest strengths, so as better to serve his or her own argument against that opposition viewpoint. "Ninety-nine in a hundred of what are called educated men," says Mill, are in poor position to "argue fluently for their own opinions. Their conclusion may be true, but it might be false for anything they *know*; they have never thrown themselves into the position of those who think differently from them" (245; my emphasis). I emphasize the word *know* here to make plain that Mill is placing clear weight on knowing truth as opposed simply to voicing it in an unwitting or experimental fashion.

The crux for my argument can now be brought more plainly to light, for at this point, the question of the substantiality—as opposed to the regulative operations—of a critical liberal agency is coming to a head. Concerning this one-in-a-hundred person who throws himself "into the position of those who think differently," do we regard this person as *knowing* what those others think? Mill's answer is, of course, that one can know, not only what one thinks, but also what a different way of thinking might look like. This is a point at which many-sidedness seems logically to be at issue.

Reasons for puzzlement at this many-sidedness are not hard to find. I have already canvased the kinds of objections typical of pragmatist thinkers, for whom Mill's ambition to be in "the position of those who think differently" is not only a contradiction in terms but also the signal mistake of much modern philosophical idealism and rationalism. Another line of criticism can best be viewed through Nietzsche's *On the Genealogy of Morals* (1887), which seems a worthwhile reference at this point on conceptual and loosely historical grounds. Nietzsche was not concerned to theorize liberalism per se, but his sharp critique of procedural objectivity and moral rationalism is clearly on target in any assessment of liberal many-sidedness. Nietzsche's most condensed passage on what has been called his perspectivism contains this admonition, following on his description of the modern philosopher's ascetic ideal as a perverse will to self-contradiction: "But precisely because we seek knowledge, let us not be ungrateful to such resolute reversals of accustomed perspectives and valuations with which the spirit has, with apparent mischievousness and futility, raged against itself for so long: to see differently in this way for once, to *want* to see differently, is no small discipline and preparation of the intellect for its future "objectivity."[56] As in Wittgenstein's message concerning ethics, Nietzsche's language spots out a kind of "futility" in the aspiration to see outside one's own perspectives in any radical sense. But he also, again like Wittgenstein, grants an operative character and a sort of affective constancy to this aspiration. The difference between "to see differently" and "to *want* to see differently" is one that Nietzsche underscores verbally and syntactically, and he recognizes fully that an entire discipline of self-distancing grounds itself in the desire to orient moral and epistemological projects along such lines. Although it is typical in many contexts to contrast Nietzschean dionysianism with the Millite valorization of cultivated character, the crucial matter in this context is the larger similarity in these two thinkers, both theorists of self-making in a world shorn of idealism.

Mill's call is plainly to some kind of difference-seeing, in any case, and the crucial point here is that we have no evidence to suggest that this capacity or disposition applies to the genius. Is the genius "many-sided"? Mill's argumentation actually points to the contrary. Genius looks like a radically individuated, self-actualizing agency that is potentially quite one-sided. The genius's proper work is simply to be "more individual" than all the rest. Many-sidedness, in turn, comes to look like a species of modesty and self-denial, the nongenius's ideal condition in due observance of the genius, for whom the distinction of many-sidedness and one-sidedness really seems more or less moot. But neither is it clear that Mill means to argue such a point. Indeed, it is hard not to assume that he would have resisted my line of interpretation. The situation recalls the terms that Steven Knapp brings to Samuel Taylor Coleridge's own tangled rhetoric of genius: in Knapp's account, Coleridge wants the term *genius* to indicate at once an extreme instance of enthusiastic investment and a point of balance or mediation between enthusiasm and fanaticism.[57] While ideas of enthusiasm and fanaticism have little play in Mill's account, the tension between genius as extreme and genius as consummate mediation is fully in play. Mill's thinking enacts an incessant oscillation between two antithetical values: on the one hand, a vision of genius, understood as a heroics of individuality; and on the other hand, a practice of liberal many-sidedness, a kind of tolerance and cosmopolitanism that has to be understood itself as another kind of accomplishment.

This second form of heroism—this liberal heroics of self-management—is key to the present study's conceptual and historical claims. It seems clear that Mill clings to a value of genius that is insecurely readable in terms of his value of many-sidedness. It likewise seems clear that judging Mill's overall vision of liberal individuality entails something more than reading a kind of atomistic individualism from his celebration of genius. For genius turns out to be a different thing than cultivated many-sidedness. Mill's very logic, as I noted earlier, leaves uncertain whether the expansive consciousness of the genuinely original genius can put down roots in the unoriginal mind. It seems that originality, or genius, will be appreciated only by an agent constituted through a open-minded quality of many-sidedness that Mill has said is hardly typical in the population generally.

At this point, Mill's terms seem in many respects to mirror a tripartite scheme of sociopolitical classification. We can employ the terms of Matthew Arnold, to whom I will turn in a moment. Genius looks aristocratic, many-sidedness looks middle-class, and one-sidedness looks like the disposition of the populace. The faultiness of that mapping seems clearest in its implication that the typical middle-class figure is, for Mill, many-sided. Even in this faulty mapping, however, we remain with Matthew Arnold's terms. Arnold clearly but rather casually employs the term *middle-class* in two registers: it signifies both a dully materialistic and rigidly pious mind-set and a socioeconomic portion, with which Arnold himself identifies, in which self-cultivation is the promise of future progress.

LIBERAL CULTURE IN MATTHEW ARNOLD

Numerous features of Matthew Arnold's work echo points explored above in connection with Eliot and Mill. We can view Farebrother's and Dorothea's respective cultivations of self, for example, in the light of Arnold's distinction between the best self and the ordinary self. Likewise, we can recall Mill's rhetoric of genius in noting that Arnold, too, brings the term on board to a similarly destabilizing effect—notably, when he insists that a "genius" such as the middle-class reformist John Bright has to be viewed outside class terms, because "so far as a man has genius he tends to take himself out of the category of class altogether, and to become simply a man."[58] More generally, Arnoldian disinterestedness and self-distancing stake out important problems for liberal theory and—as Amanda Anderson has recently shown in a discussion embracing Eliot, Mill, and Arnold—the Arnoldian account partially anticipates recent thinking among cosmopolitanism theorists, who seek to relate and preserve values both of universalism and embodiment.[59] Eliot, Mill, and Arnold cohere in their efforts to value a cultivated subjectivity, answerable to the demands of a new conception of individuality as something internally validated and self-consciously rationalized. This demand for inwardness, while surely related to Protestant valuations of reflection and personalized commitment, can be seen from the mid-Victorian years onward in the light of a secularization that increasingly defines cultural projects called liberal.

To see Arnold's version of the specific standpoint problems examined above in connection with Millite many-sidedness and genius, we do best to examine his distinction between Hebraising and Hellenizing agency, elaborated most fully in the fourth chapter of *Culture and Anarchy*. Hebraising and Hellenizing are both ways of thinking and acting that aim finally at human perfection, according to Arnold, but they mark out more or less opposite paths to that end. For Arnold, Hebraising thought celebrates strict conscience, seriousness, earnestness, obedience, and the regulation of conduct, all viewed as Hebraic for their salience in the Judeo-Christian heritage and, most pertinently for England, in Protestantism. And Hellenizing thought, associated with the ancient Greek culture of inquiry and also with the Renaissance, celebrates intellectual free play and spontaneity of thought, consciousness in its variety rather than conscience in its strictness, and an open-ended concern to "see things as they really are." This last phrase, recast and reasserted in numerous key works by Arnold, recalls in spirit J. S. Mill's celebration of the will to follow one's understanding to whatever conclusions it may lead. The tension in Arnold's usage emerges in the following contradiction. On the one hand, he often styles Hebraising and Hellenizing modes as valuable equivalently in their own ways, and as equivalently concerned with their goal of human perfection. On the other hand, Arnold quite clearly has his most affirmative things to say about

Hellenizing, and for reasons that seem to go beyond his own consistent effort to explain that privileging in merely situational terms.

Arnold's argument is, of course, richly embroiled in social debates current in the period surrounding the passage of the Second Reform Bill, including those Liberal party actions taken in the Reform Bill's immediate aftermath. For Arnold, contemporary action-minded liberals such as Frederic Harrison and John Bright are promoting a thoughtless politics of sham progressiveness in such areas as the disestablishment of the Irish Church, the Real Estate Intestacy Act, free-trade policies, and more. His complaint is that the English in general are prone to value doing over thinking, and that current Liberal practitioners are recklessly playing to that disposition by taking legislative actions in advance of any clear understanding of how and why those legislative actions answer to criteria of thoughtful justification rather than a knee-jerk appetite for doing. It is in this contextual sense, Arnold frequently declares, that Hellenizing has its claims on our interest: "Now, and for us, it is a time to Hellenise, and to praise knowing; for we have Hebraised too much, and have over-valued doing" (255).

It is this sense of contemporary action as profoundly unwise that drives Arnold, strikingly, to prescribe "cultivated inaction" as the most constructive attitude toward his historical moment's social and political challenges (191, 220). His ideal of cultivation contends against three foes: the haughtiness of the aristocracy, the dull materialism and stiff religiosity of the Hebraising middle classes, and the mindlessness of the masses who would translate rights of doing as one likes into rights of "smashing as one likes" (119). Arnold contends that the dangers of unwise action—at this particular historical juncture— outweigh the dangers of inaction. And cultivated inaction, in turn, presumably marks an advance on simple inaction because, in cultivation, some light of thinking (Hellenism) might eventually clarify whatever wise and constructive courses of action were at hand.

Arnold's situational explanation for his privileging of Hellenism becomes problematic, however, when we try at all seriously to distinguish Hebraising and Hellenizing, whether as choices marking out distinct lines of action or even as complementary but opposed aspects of a more encompassing subjective agency. The problems repeat many of those discussed above in respect to many-sidedness and the inhabiting of other standpoints than one's own. In one characteristic passage, following an account of the Puritan's fatal tendency to imagine his strictness of religious conscience as the "one thing needful" in human life, Arnold contrasts Hellenism and Hebraism in general: "And as the force which encourages us to stand staunch and fast by the rule and ground we have is Hebraism, so the force which encourages us to go back upon this rule, and to try the very ground upon which we appear to stand, is Hellenism,—a turn for giving our consciousness free play and enlarging its range. And what

I say is, not that Hellenism is always for everybody more wanted than Hebraism, but that . . . at this particular moment, and for the great majority of
us . . . it is more wanted"(181). Here Hellenism is that which impels us to "try
the very ground" of our conduct rather than follow mechanically whatever
"rule and ground" we happen to possess. Arnold is speaking without much regard to the content or the specific outcome of this rethinking. Such abstraction
from content—in the form of a celebration of disinterestedness—features
often in Arnold's argumentation. Here we have his version of Mill's open-
ended valuation of anything that might count as thinking differently.

This is where the notion of "cultivated inaction" becomes suggestive in ways
that seem to go well beyond Arnold's probable intentions. His self-
understanding is fairly clear: throughout *Culture and Anarchy*, Arnold sees himself as embattled on two sides, with Conservatives on the one side whose
hostility to thoughtful change he abhors, and Liberals on the other side whose
openness to thoughtless change he likewise abhors. He says of himself, "I am
a Liberal, yet I am a Liberal tempered by experience, reflection, and re-
nouncement, and I am, above all, a believer in culture" (88). Thus his answer
to Liberal charges that cultivated inaction amounts to "Conservative scepti-
cism." Once we recall, however, that Arnold's Hellenism is functionally equivalent to the impetus to culture—that value to which he hews "above all"—it
becomes harder to remain by his earlier, even-handed theorization of the difference between Hebraism and Hellenism. In rebutting charges from liberals
and conservatives that his points are unduly serviceable to the other side's concerns, Arnold avers that,

in truth, the free spontaneous play of consciousness with which culture tries to float our
stock habits of thinking and acting, is by its very nature, as has been said, disinterested.
Sometimes the result of floating them may be agreeable to this party, sometimes to that;
now it may be welcome to our so-called Liberals, now to our so-called Conservatives;
but what culture seeks is, above all, to float them, to prevent their being stiff and stark
pieces of petrifaction any longer. It is mere Hebraising, if we stop short, and refuse to
let our consciousness play freely, whenever we or our friends do not happen to like what
it discovers to us. (220)

Once he puts the term *Hebraising* to this service, he cannot finally sustain his
claim that Hellenizing stands back from an interested relation to the distinction of Liberal and Conservative culture. What Arnold cannot fully admit is
his persistent investment in a subjectivist authorization of right thinking and
right action, as opposed to culturally conservative argumentation, which privileges forms of external authority, the hierarchical conception of social strata,
and, finally, traditional realist theology.

Arnold declares plainly enough at many points that he means by culture "an
endeavor to come at reason and the will of God by means of reading, observing and thinking" (12). But God finally has no clear role within the purview of
culture when Arnold is ready elsewhere to credit this distinction: "Religion

says: *The Kingdom of God is within you*; and culture, in like manner, places human perfection in an *internal* condition, in the growth and predominance of our humanity proper, as distinguished from our animality" (94). As the impulse to self-perfecting called culture is, in Arnold's argument, the same thing as the impulse of Hellenism, we have to regard Hellenism as an autonomous ethos in respect to the reality of God's kingdom. Of course, a similarity in the two dispensations can be found in the common reliance of culture and religion on one or another idea of transcendence. My reading of Eliot's Farebrother touched on this view by suggesting that his liberal heroics—his "imitation of heroism"—is a secularized appropriation of transcendence as an element of the self. My point here becomes something more than spotting out another Victorian drama of faith and doubt, however, when we recall Arnold's distinction of Liberal and Conservative sentiments and their bearing on Hellenizing spontaneity.

Liberal culture, as Arnold portrays it, has two significant "others": one of them is Conservatism; the other, action-minded middle-class Liberalism. His value of Hellenism, primarily in service to a "many-sided perfecting of man's powers" (185), stands apart from the unduly prescriptive domain of Conservative inaction, on the one hand, and from the unduly unreflective domain of action-minded Liberalism, on the other. And in keeping with the *Saturday Review* commentary referenced above—where gains in many-sidedness were carrying with them perceived losses in manly vigor—Arnold himself associates Hellenism with a failure to act decisively. It is "liable to fail in moral strength and earnestness," and "sometimes deficient in intensity, when intensity is required" (184). We have arrived at the seedbed of modern aestheticism once we grasp the fact that Arnoldian differences from both Conservative culture and activist Liberalism lie here, insofar as cultivated inaction comes to look, in Arnold's rendering, like a standing mode of life, a refusal to settle on any one view and a resolution instead to proclaim the "floating" of views a highest value.

Action-minded Liberals such as Frederic Harrison perceived Arnold's patience in the face of inaction—provided it be cultivated inaction—and found in that patience a worrisome air of inexhaustableness. This inexhaustableness would come to be embraced as such by many late Victorian artists and critics, who take up this strategic suspension of pressing realities in their construction of the aesthetic sensibility, itself a strategy of active refusal. I will develop this point in the following section of this chapter and, later, in my discussion of Wilde. To conclude this section, however, I need to return briefly to Arnold's traffic in this idea of looking at things from many sides.

For Arnold, culture "enables us to look at the ins and the outs of things . . . , without hatred and without partiality, and with a disposition to see the good in everybody all around" (127). Similar images of mobile versus immobile perspective run throughout his argument, with culture always on the side of mobility and opposite "fanaticism" (104). Culture "will not let us rivet our faith upon any one man and his doings. It makes us see not only his good side, but also how much in him was of necessity limited and transient; nay, it even feels a pleasure, a sense of increased freedom and of an ampler future, in so doing" (110). In dilating on this last point, Arnold rather starkly reverses the value of trying "to see the good in everybody all around." He recalls a time "when I was under the influence" of Benjamin Franklin's immense example, a circumstance of subjection alleviated only when Arnold came across what he regarded as Franklin's clearly small-minded reading of a passage in Job. Says Arnold, "I well remember how, when I first read that, I drew a deep sigh of relief, and said to myself: 'After all, there is a stretch of humanity beyond Franklin's victorious good sense'" (110–11). Arnold repeats his point in recalling his encounter with Jeremy Bentham's claim that Socrates and Plato "were talking nonsense under pretence of teaching wisdom and morality": "From the moment of reading that," says Arnold, "I am delivered from the bondage of reading Bentham! the fanaticism of his adherents can touch me no longer. I feel the inadequacy of his mind and ideas for supplying the rule of human society, for perfection" (111).

It is not surprising that culture lets Arnold toggle blithely from a project of seeking the good in everybody to one of taking pleasure in the bad, given Arnold's notorious and self-conscious indifference to systematic exposition. As Amanda Anderson's reading of Arnoldian cosmopolitanism also shows, the surprising point here is the individualist subjectivism to be found at the root of Arnold's thinking, a result that stands at odds with his reputation today as an objective-minded precursor to an aestheticist impressionism ostensibly set up to oppose him.[60]

The effect of Arnoldian subjectivism can be brought out clearly if we compare his thinking to John Locke's influential account of many-sided deliberation. For Locke, too, human liberty resides in our ability to suspend impulses and desires and instead to "examine them on all sides, and weigh them with others." Problems arise, says Locke, when "we engage too soon, before due examination" of our options.[61] As in Arnold's account, liberty of thought obtains here as an active suspension of desires, a moment of inaction. But for Locke this situation only persists until such time as the critical examination is concluded, whereupon the will is in fact determined to action. Arnold's terms suggest something rather the reverse: Arnold is initially, in each case that he discusses, in "bondage" to another, whether Franklin, Bentham, or Benthamites, and then he experiences the comeuppance of this other as an intellectual release for himself ad infinitum. Where Locke moves toward determination, Arnold moves away. Of course, one might generously suppose that Arnold's examination of Franklin or Bentham concluded with a "determined action"—namely, to disregard them as high authorities—but the fact remains that Arnold styles these moments as scenes of "pleasure" in "increased freedom." Critics in Arnold's own time fully anticipated a verdict often delivered today, to the effect that Arnold's aspiration to a best self seems all too like a service to the pleasures of his ordinary self.

Many-Sidedness and Liberal Agency

In this chapter's next and final section, we will see how Arnold's ordinary self could look at this time like nothing other than a specifically liberal self as well, evocative of a new literary liberalism. Before turning to that effort at tethering liberal and aesthetic agency, however, I will try to spell out, at the conceptual level, what we can and cannot take away from the foregoing consideration of many-sidedness.

In neither Mill's nor Arnold's case does many-sidedness emerge as an especially coherent or predictable stance. Mill presupposes the existence of many-sidedness and clearly valorizes it, but he fails to consider at all carefully the subjective or social conditions under which many-sidedness might be cultivated, apparently because his temperament and perhaps simply the rhetorical work of *On Liberty* disposed him to privilege instead a quasi-romantic opposition of exceptional genius and unthinking custom, the latter enforced through the tyranny of the majority. More so than Mill, Arnold seems concerned to articulate a value of subjective many-sidedness in his Hellenic ideal, but we find problems there when he vacillates between seeing this ideal as a form of life and seeing this ideal as a means of standing above and outside any particular form of life. Given that many-sidedness, in my account, is another name for the agential aspiration proper to liberal subjectivity, the foregoing uncertainties pose a challenge for my argument overall. Our choices here might look to be two. On the one hand, we could see in liberal agency itself a certain incoherence and lack of consistent outcomes, in which case Mill and Arnold, in their confusions, might be taken to have reflected a condition that applies necessarily to the value of many-sidedness. On the other hand, we could seek in many-sidedness some kind of coherent tendency that Mill and Arnold distort for reasons having nothing to do with their aspiration to internalize and strategically engage multiple viewpoints and forms of life.

These two alternatives are, however, distorting in their simplicity. The so-called incoherence of many-sidedness in these instances might more charitably be taken as a reflection of what I earlier called the inherent precariousness of the self-conception underlying liberal agency. Thus I accept to that extent the first line of explanation above, whereby Mill and Arnold get tangled in their terms inevitably, because many-sidedness is inherently an indeterminate and volatile stance. This understanding gives some credence to the ironic prospect, obviously aversive to various notions of common sense, of a stance-less stance. In spelling out this view, I accept a further point, as well, that we cannot establish the claims of liberal agency on completely sure and concrete footing—although I think, as well, that it would be foolish to disdain clarifying efforts in that direction. By way of rationalizing as much as possible the ironic position of liberal many-sidedness, I have proposed that we see its cogency as a regulative aspiration. At issue finally, for us, is whether and how we will grant credence to a notion of strategically mobile and meaningfully pluralist viewpoint. If a positive "proof" of that regulative aspiration's cogency seems to be intrinsically impossible, perhaps a kind of negative confirmation can emerge through the Kantian-style critique that I offered earlier in this chapter. Systematically, arguments about human agency and sociality that set themselves up in opposition to liberalism's privileging of critical self-consciousness tend to admit, in one form or another, elements of agential reflection with debts to the liberal model of critical agency. This is the light in which we can and should view such matters as the "respect" that Wittgenstein voices for that "tendency in the human mind" to run against the walls of our own language games, our own forms of life.

Toward a Liberal Aestheticism

The second half of this study offers my detailed cases in late Victorian aestheticist culture. But I can outline already my basic claim that the artists and writers understood then and now as aestheticists promoted a fusion of art and life with conceptual and historical debts to liberal culture's evolving discourses of autonomy and self-culture. Critical discussions over the last century have hardly failed to notice this point, but those discussions have often epitomized, in so doing, one or both of two problematic critical moves. Sometimes they reduce aesthetic agency to bourgeois subjectivity, in keeping with a related critique of liberalism. More often, in what looks like an effort to distance their claims from "vulgar" economism or determinism, modern critics give credence to aesthetic representation as a scene whereby social contradictions find expression and awaken utopian or otherwise progressive critical thought. The first and more deterministic of these views actually has few contemporary exponents, although one could take Pierre Bourdieu's *Distinction* to have such a view at its base. Something more like the latter approach informs Bourdieu's later work on aesthetic culture, culminating in *The Rules of Art*, and works by Fredric Jameson and Terry Eagleton, to name two other key authorities.[62]

Related to this last critical tradition is a set of arguments that aim to split the difference between deterministic and utopian conceptions of aesthetic activity by granting to certain artists a privileged place in commodity culture. In this view, artistic projects in the period leading into and out of modernism can express a doubleness in keeping with commodity culture's confused thinking about the nature and the sources of value.[63] I engage such arguments in this study's second part, so here I will simply assert that neither commodification theory nor neo-Marxist critical utopianism spell out a cogent alternative to what I have been calling the liberal aspiration to critical self-consciousness. Such arguments often position the artist finally as a knowing agent, in which case those arguments cohere with and confirm the perspective I am offering. At other times, these arguments take too much for granted how categories of contradiction and social tension function, leading critics to underread the properly liberal character of that indignation presumed to follow on a perception of exploitative and indefensible social relations.

In what follows, I will be arguing a narrower historical claim that a liberal rhetoric of agency came to inform much of the period's aesthetic culture. It did not do so without contestation, however, and we can see this contestation and take the measure of its historical and theoretical stakes by looking to an 1874 omnibus review article that canvases works by Arnold, Thomas Carlyle, Walter Pater, and J. A. Symonds, figures gathered derisively by the reviewer under a banner of "literary Liberalism."[64] The review's author was the staunchly conservative poet and critic W. J. Courthope, who would go on in the 1890s to be professor of poetry at Oxford. Courthope's relative invisibility to most literary-historical scholarship today is one sign of the linkage between broadly liberal and aesthetic culture. As regards the canon formation of high literary culture and modernism, the next hundred years had a sound drubbing in store for Courthope's style of literary conservatism. But few figures can be so useful to my present purposes as Courthope, so keenly perceptive was he of literary liberalism as a threat to conservative understandings of sociality and the social work of literature.

Toward the conclusion of his comments on Arnold—whose *Culture and Anarchy* was discussed in company with Arnold's *St. Paul and Protestantism* (1869) and *Literature and Dogma* (1873)—Courthope tenders this condemnation:

If we once concede the position of Protagoras that all truth is relative to the individual, it follows as a matter of course, that the prime object of education should be to cultivate individual perception. And this is just what Mr. Arnold wants. The great secret of life, in his eyes, is to give an air of philosophy to the commonplace, "to let," as he says, our "consciousness play freely round our present operations and the stock notions on which they are founded, so as to show what these are like, and how related to the intelligible laws of things, and auxiliary to true human perfection." Of course, this *modus operandi* results in a science of style. All Mr. Arnold's skill is expended on giving an apparently general character to his own personal perceptions by crystallising them in precise forms of expression. (410)

My argument's perspective on Victorian liberal culture brings out a neglected integrity in Courthope's collocation of literary figures. Neglected, insofar as present-day literary critics seldom find cause to cast Carlyle as a liberal—likewise Ruskin, whom Courthope views in the same light, although not formally reviewing his works here—and generally prefer to explore differences between these figures. Granting the useful work of our more commonplace lines of discussion today, I want to accept Courthope's much broader claim, as well, that these writers work from a common vantage point in which revealed religion has lost much of its authority as literal truth.[65] Carlyle early noted, in 1831, that literature seemed destined to become the "main stem" of his century's religious impulse, having ever been a "branch" of religious expression before.[66] All these figures proffer a life of letters as their means of articulating a self in this new dispensation. Priests of culture, they aimed in common to superintend on the cultivation of new tastes, rites, and authorities—a natural supernaturalism.

This point has already been finely argued by Linda Dowling.[67] For Dowling, we misunderstand Victorian aesthetic culture if we see there a withdrawal from contemporary politics. Figures such as those named by Courthope embraced a vision of universal human responsiveness to beauty—a vision handed down from the eighteenth-century Whig aesthetic writings of the third Earl of Shaftesbury—even as they also confronted, in their own historical moment, an oblivion or recalcitrance in the *demos* respecting the difference between higher and lower aesthetic pleasures. In this way, what Dowling calls the "vulgarization" of art—art's democratization, that is—became at once a desideratum and a calamity for the likes of Carlyle, Ruskin, Walter Pater, William Morris, and Oscar Wilde. The increasing untenableness of prior religious and metaphysical anchorings of value made it difficult for aesthetes to rationalize their elevated taste as a service to the greater good rather than merely to an elite disposition. I endorse Dowling's claims to this extent but also seek to expand on her narrative, which focuses on a very small set of mid- and late Victorian Oxonians. She leaves out other aspects of Victorian aesthetic practice, not to mention most of liberal culture as it took shape outside the imaginations of her selected literary figures. This segment of my discussion, however, very much accepts Dowling's term and confirms her view of Victorian aestheticism as a kind of ontic agony.

Arnold's particular gesture, as Courthope mockingly notes, lay in giving up on literal truth in religion and trying to salvage instead a metaphoric and historicized truth. Courthope deplores Arnold's implication, for example, that St. Paul's moment was not historically advanced enough to have allowed St. Paul or his contemporaries a full understanding of the specifically figurative truth in the story of Christ's resurrection. Says Courthope, "It is, of course, true that St. Paul speaks of Christ's death and resurrection in the metaphorical sense expounded by Mr. Arnold; but is it not obvious that the whole force of the metaphor is derived from a belief in the actual fact?" (398). The salience of religious contention in liberal culture will play a role in a later stage of this study, when I seek to account for the diversity of public feeling in respect to the Tichborne imposture. There we see that the progressive liberal viewpoint tended to construe the largely working-class crowds, duped by the Claimant, as minions of a naively conceived faithfulness, made possible by the absence in those crowds of a "trained intellect." For now I want to emphasize another perspective on the difference between Courthope's viewpoint and the literary liberalism he condemns. At stake are two different accounts of those verdicts or beliefs that a "trained intellect" might be expected to produce or admit. The accounts differ, very generally, in what they take to authorize belief and conduct, whether the traditionalist appeal to extrahuman authority or the newer liberal conception of self-authorization, with its tendencies to self-conscious individualism and impressionism.

The historical interest of Courthope's argument lies in his perception that literary liberalism boils down to a cultural intervention. What Arnoldian culture has to offer, according to Courthope, is a solipsistic individualism, veiled or candid, with little claim to our belief in its authenticity or its connection to any ground of value outside individualistic decision. As I noted earlier in connection with Eliot's characterization of Farebrother's moral rationalism as an "imitation of heroism," the language of authenticity is consistently at stake in connection with the liberal viewpoint, and in such a way as to align liberalism generally with the inauthentic. This was so in Eliot's case, of course, not because of some covert nihilism on her part, but because this inauthenticity is what we finally have to call the new authenticity in a humanist culture working out still its relation to previous cultural constructions of authenticity, chiefly the religious. In Courthope's case, the language of authenticity emerges in his claim that Arnoldian cultivation is a fraud. Regarding "the groundwork of true Culture," in turn, Courthope offers a paean to traditionalism that carries a broadly conceptual interest for my argument as well. For even as Courthope's terms reflect the religious contestation of his moment, they also anticipate features that I isolated earlier in both the communitarian and pragmatist objections to liberalism. In spelling out what he takes to be the wholesome alternative to liberal culture, Courthope writes, "The praise of being 'natural' we ascribe to those who, with unconscious grace, without consideration of effect, perform the duties and maintain the dignity proper to their condition in society. The standards of honour, courtesy politeness, refinement,—all that is comprised in that sense of what is due to others as well as to ourselves, which we call by the name of good breeding, and which is the result of complex traditions, and continuous development, these qualities are as far above the manufacture of art as they are beyond the reach of analysis" (415).

Courthope's twofold ambition is to put modern art and literature in its place and to hold traditional sources and signs of value "beyond the reach of analysis." His language anticipates communitarianism in its sense that liberal culture's judgmentalism threatens the integrity of a traditional system of social relations in which people find themselves and learn their place. His language anticipates certain aspects of pragmatism in its resistance to the prospect that rational self-consciousness has any legitimate office in the radical interrogation of the contexts within which we find "what is due to others as well as to ourselves." Any defense of liberal culture over against the kind of critique offered by Courthope—or by communitarians and pragmatists—seems to have this question as its burden: in what way can liberal agency answer the concern for foundations when religious or otherwise traditionalist accounts of foundations are no more workable than the pragmatist end-run around the question of foundations?

My suggestion is that liberal agency in its regulative aspect offers crucial recourse in this direction and that we can get a handle on this point by recalling Courthope's complaint that Arnold's posture can only generate a "science of style." The complaint implies an opposition of style and content, or of style and substance. In a way that should recall for us the communitarian condemnation of the liberal agent as an empty self, Courthope's project is to portray literary liberalism as bereft of content/substance. Courthope's transition at this point to Walter Pater's then-recent volume *The Renaissance* (1873) is to be expected. Indeed, Courthope heads directly into an extended quotation from Pater's hothouse prose-poetical meditation on the Mona Lisa. Says Pater, in part:

The presence that rose thus so strangely beside the waters, is expressive of what in the ways of a thousand years men had come to desire. Hers is the head upon which all "the ends of the world are come," and the eyelids are a little weary. . . . All the thought and experience of the world have etched and moulded there, in that which they have of power to refine and make expressive the outward form, the animalism of Greece, the lust of Rome, the reverie of the Middle Age, with its spiritual ambition and its imaginative loves, the return of the Pagan world, the sins of the Borgias.[68]

Indicting not the floweriness of Pater's language but its character as reasoning, Courthope complains that Pater's style of criticism "assumes a knowledge in the critic of motives [Leonardo's and the represented Lady Lisa's] which are beyond the reach of evidence," adding that "there is no justification for calling that criticism which is in fact pure romance" (411). The problem, for Courthope, is the "quackery and imposture"—again, the language of authenticity—served by a regime in which critics "reject the natural standards of common sense in favour of private perceptions" (412).

Courthope's resistant response is hardly eccentric, nor even is his view that Pater's excesses should be chalked up finally to the influence of John Ruskin.[69] While Courthope purports to object on something like procedural grounds to Pater's critical ethos, his review also reflects a specific contention between his traditionalist conception of human agency and another conception of agency, newly circulatable under the rubric of literary or aesthetic liberalism. Courthope is most truly exercised not by Pater's affronts to reasoning and evidence, that is, but by literary Liberalism's generally secularized conceptions of value and conduct. It is horror at the broadly liberal specter of subjectively self-authorizing agency that animates Courthope's argument. In this sense, Pater's Mona Lisa, upon whose head "all the ends of the world are come," is a provocative concretization of the Kantian humanized kingdom of ends.[70]

Clearly, saying that she is so does not make it so in any substantial sense. But the provocation in Paterian aestheticism lies in this pretension to feed a modern spirit of impressionistic flourishing through his own version of an Arnoldian science of style.

Such an aspiration's bearing on the present discussion's regulative account of liberal agency can be brought to some clearer light if we look briefly to an account of style proffered a few years ago by Charles Altieri.[71] His "expressivist" theory of subjective agency implies a kind of answer to Courthope's concerns, which themselves parallel the communitarian and pragmatist critiques examined above. Where Courthope deplores literary liberalism's usurpation of substance by style, latter-day critics of liberalism deplore its arid proceduralism and its empty formalism. Altieri's concern is not exactly to spot out a content or substance behind liberal agency that somehow has eluded the grasp of liberalism's critics. Better to see Altieri's gambit as one of disputing the presumptive authority of the distinction between form and content, or style and substance, as readers like Courthope have tended to construe that distinction.

A concern to mediate between two broadly opposed and increasingly deadlocked accounts of agency drives Altieri's argument. He tells that structuralist and social-constructivist viewpoints, on the one hand, unduly determine agency through their privileging of deep structures and social codes as explanatory matrices. And poststructuralist gestures, on the other hand, have normalized a vision of agency "as an irreducibly indeterminate principle of free play . . . that cannot be confined within any categories of the understanding" (1). Where the first account tends to understand agency as an illusion or proxy, the second account identifies agency only by submitting it to what can seem like another kind of impoverishment, whereby agency cannot correlate richly to social values or even other agents. Altieri argues that an expressivist tradition of thought, with sources in Spinoza, Hegel, and Wittgenstein, might provide useful conceptual resources in this terrain. In that tradition the project is not to submit selves—whether one's own self or that of others—to an antecedent knowledge or description of what selfhood must, or should, be. Instead, selves are things made on the go, through processes of articulation that work with and from available social routines. "Expression" therefore indicates, in such an account as Altieri's, not the representation of some truth that lay previously within the agential interior. Instead, expression names the bringing into being of something legible but also potentially new—new even to the agent. Altieri draws much of this view from the later Wittgenstein, for whom, also, agency is an immanently worked out articulation rather than a metaphysically or rationalistically grounded affair. This view makes sense of an intentionality that does not draw on naively essentializing claims about interiority or deep subjectivity. And this prospect bears on, among many other things, what we might take the word *style* to mean.

Regarding Pater's style, we can ask now what is at stake when he takes the Mona Lisa to be "expressive" of modern philosophy's key product, namely "an idea of humanity as wrought upon by, and summing up in itself, all modes of thought and life" (99). For Courthope, as we have seen, what is immediately at stake in this ecumenical invitation is whether or not a rampant impressionism (or perspectivism) is going to overrun literary culture and Victorian society perhaps with it. In no uncertain terms, Courthope implies that a cultivated disposition along Pater's epicene lines portends a weakening in the men of the nation, no doubt an invitation to the recently rampant Prussians. (Courthope ends his essay by arguing that the supposedly backward and dully Hebraising traditional English temper, not prone to "constant self-analysis," was after all good enough to produce "the men who won at Trafalgar and Waterloo" [415].) All these concerns for manliness and national heroics stand more or less opposed to a broadly construed and historically new formulation of aesthetic liberal heroics, which has, among its features, a more cosmopolitan ambition to blend individuality and universalization in the cauldron of aesthetic style.

Altieri's account of style opens up a way to suggest that Pater's writings articulate an aestheticist authorial agency related to, but not exactly determined by, an entire sociohistorical context. Recall Courthope's objection to Pater's impressionism: in disputing that the Mona Lisa in fact "expresses" the sweep of human experience, Courthope and his kind are engaged in an effort to foreclose on the very kind of expressive agency that Pater means to articulate. There is a willfulness to Pater's style, after all, a determination to express himself above and beyond his supposed object of inquiry. And even if Pater's particular mode can look like a "wilful weakness"—Henry James's characterization, on the way to allowing that Pater was "divinely uncommon"[72]—it nonetheless constitutes a kind of assertion of the imagination that is organized around what we can view as two roughly opposed ambitions. On the one hand, Pater ascribes to the Mona Lisa not so much an otherworldly as a many-worldly expressiveness. In so doing, Pater expresses his own aestheticist form of the broadly liberal ambition toward many-sidedness. In his account of the Mona Lisa, that is, he posits a consummation of "modern" philosophy's conception of humanity. On the other hand, over against this universalization, Pater "expresses" in no uncertain terms the radical singularity of his impressionism. This singularity is, famously, declared in his "Conclusion" to the *Renaissance*, where experience is a tale of "isolation, each mind keeping as a solitary prisoner its own dream of a world." The result is, for Pater, an idea of the self as a "wisp constantly re-forming itself on the stream," in a "strange, perpetual, weaving and unweaving."[73]

What kind of agency that stream of reformations might imply becomes more graspable once we imagine a person to *be* what his or her style *does*. In that view, the expressivist vision of style that Altieri adumbrates has been embraced and even, in a sense, substantialized. But in what sense substantialized? It will not do to posit a relation of correspondence between a transcendental agent, on the one hand, and that agent's exteriorized representation (or misrepresentation), understood as evidence of the agent's transcendental ground. Kant appears to posit such a relation, of course, when he distinguishes transcendental and empirical dimensions of human agency. In his account, however, it is only our empirical self that we are in any position to observe or to interrogate as an object of thought. Our transcendental self is all the while outside objectification and, indeed, has to be viewed as the condition of possibility for any observation whatsoever.[74] Critique simply yields up our operative and transcendentalizing assumption that freedom of will applies to us as agents. In distinguishing a substantive and a regulative agency, my concern has been to promote the idea of a quality of agency to be claimed and debated in the doing rather than in the being. Sheerly as an issue of theory, the "being" of transcendental agency can be bracketed as an issue once one concentrates instead on the operative character of an expressive "doing." What distinguishes liberal agency, then, is its character as a form of life that engages meaningfully with the idea of plural forms of life. Liberal subjectivity declares a habitation in a critical position from which various positions—even positioning in general—can be thought. To declare a place in that habitat is to lay claim to what I have suggested is a distinctively liberal aspiration to manysidedness, a vision to which, as Pater has it, "all the ends of the world" are a matter of interest and concern.

It will hardly do, of course, to credit Pater with summing up in himself all modes of thought aesthetic. Differences between Pater, D. G. Rossetti, and Wilde—the selection of aestheticist figures treated in this study—are more than notable, and a wave of recent work is showing how previously neglected women aesthetes were themselves looking to literature and the arts as means of articulating female agency within the contingencies of fin-de-siècle gender and market relations.[75] Much less can Paterian style be understood to express Victorian liberal culture in all its diversity. When George Eliot saw Pater's *Renaissance*, she deemed it "quite poisonous in its false principles of criticism and its false principles of life.[76] (Wilde, of course, found it deliciously poisonous.) This chapter's work has been to tell a very general story about liberal agency's migration into aesthetic agency, in part to make a case, and in part to prepare the way for further demonstration, that reductive or overly casual accounts of human agency in current literary-critical work have obscured the richness of individual and collective engagements with the idea of agency in Victorian Britain.

In seeking to confront the variety of those engagements, the following chapters do not aim primarily to collapse liberal agency and aestheticism into one category, although the discussion continually references overlappings in these

terms. The reader might best view the following chapters, then, as semiau-
tonomous essays in their respective contexts, efforts to understand the salience,
and assess the various effects, of modern critical self-consciousness in specific
historical frames.

Chapter 2

Reflections of Agency in Ruskin's Venice

John Ruskin's place in Victorian liberal culture is no simple call. One tradition of reception, both popular and academic, views Ruskin as a progressive spirit and even as a protosocialist on the basis of several key elements of his work. In "The Nature of Gothic," the most influential portion of his monumental cultural history *The Stones of Venice* (1851, 1853), Ruskin condemns the modern world's repetitive and dehumanizing modes of labor, and he extols an alternative program to recover the creativity, authenticity, and exuberant workmanship epitomized in Gothic architecture.[1] In *Unto this Last* (1860), he offers a presciently radical critique of political economy and recommends social reforms such as a fixed minimum wage and workmen's compensation. Mid-Victorians often deemed him insane for tendering such views, which ran counter to the laissez-faire tendencies of most self-described liberals even as those same views offended many conservative sensibilities as well. With the rise of organized socialism in the 1880s, however, Ruskin's reputation as a sagacious progressive took hold, leading the socialist William Morris to reprint "The Nature of Gothic" in pamphlet form as a manifesto for the Arts and Crafts movement.[2] Meanwhile, Ruskin's own self-descriptions present him differently—as an heir to Tory conservatism, a figure powerfully imbued with a sense that values of tradition and hierarchy trump values of individualistic flourishing, human equality, or social progress. Like Thomas Carlyle, another sage marginalized by trends in mid-Victorian intellectual and political life, Ruskin typically denigrated key liberal values such as reflective distance and tolerance, seeing them as pernicious hindrances to honest and immediate vitalism. Given his disposition to construe liberal many-sidedness as weakness or indolence, he has to be read as one of democratic and liberal culture's competing others.[3] As Robert Hewison has pointed out, nobly correcting his own earlier oversight of this point, the principal task of Ruskinian workers is to live with a vigorous but satisfied sense of their proper place, not to revel in self-asserting individuality.[4]

In engaging this particular complexity I mean to contribute to recent work that emphasizes Ruskin's self-conscious modernity, a characterization that carries with it, here at least, a commitment to reading specific paradoxes or tensions in his thinking as constitutive.[5] This vantage point encourages us, for example, to see even his apparently backward-looking projects—most critics cite the medieval-flavored Guild of St. George—in the light of positive assertion and instructive anxiety. His contemporary liberal critics, such as Leslie Stephen and John Morley, dismissed his thinking as an antiprogressive determination to recover a feudal world.[6] But Ruskin's rhetoric of individuality finally reflects the same problems that those more conventionally liberal-minded Victorians were also working through. A preliminary point to make here—a point that I touch upon again in the next chapter—is that mid-Victorian liberal culture reflects an agony of religious thinking at a time when such thinking was embattled on several fronts. Ruskin famously disavows his Evangelicism midway in his career, for instance, deeming it rigidly doctrinaire, and he begins at that time to develop views that some of his contemporaries would style as atheistic. But Ruskin's actual tack from this point onward is to maintain a roughly pantheistic viewpoint, one that lets him draw what he wants out of religion (an anchor for authority) while disowning everything he does not want (the rigid formalism of schools).

The constant in Ruskin's thought is a determination to ground assessments of value and beauty in terms that transcend but also inform the contingency of human affairs. And in that sense, he might be said to oppose the secular-humanist authorization increasingly adopted by liberal intellectuals. As I argued in the previous chapter, however, liberal agency itself is defined by aspirations to self-transcendence, from George Eliot's portrait of liberal heroics to Matthew Arnold's understanding of Hellenism as a process of cosmopolitan self-extraction from the ordinary self. In this chapter, I look to Ruskin with a sense both of his difference from liberal culture and of his imbrication with it. After the previous chapter's more conventional line of Victorian liberals, I try here and in the next chapter to bring a wider lens to mid-Victorian imaginings of individuality and the aesthetic sensibility. Ruskin is a telling case, insofar as his career is a fitful transition into a liberal culture that had more claims on his own thinking than he liked to admit. A critic of monumental striving, Ruskin inevitably expresses elements of the modern critical individualism that he ostensibly deplores.

I approach Ruskin by way of his lifelong relation to the city of Venice. For in the very particular city of Venice, Ruskin found his most intensive focusing point for a much more general concern about what it means to be particular. Ruskin saw in Venice—in its grandeur and in its decline—an image of himself. Or, to be more precise, he saw an image of his own conflicted feelings about individuality and agency. Ruskin's obsession with Venice is therefore hardly reducible to a romantic taste for dreamy gondola rides and picturesque decrepitude. In 1841, early in his career, Ruskin does remark of Venice, "It is the Paradise of cities."[7] But critics have long known that his engagement with this paradise would be driven more often by a sadder sense of the place as a paradise lost. It is exactly in that mixed feeling, however, that this city came to play its enormous role in Ruskin's life. Dinah Birch has noted how the "Fall, the loss of Paradise, is Ruskin's great theme," and she concludes that all his varied arguments and passions amount to a "long composite narrative of the Fall."[8] Once we allow that the Fall itself poses a problem of human agency—a problem of the relation between human disobedience and providence—we are arrived at something like an adequate view of Ruskin's cathexis.

The following discussion therefore elaborates a version of a freedom/determinism drama, chiefly by close reading in some neglected portions of *Stones*. My account spotlights a tension in Ruskin's understanding of his critical objects, which seem to him, on the one hand, to be constructed and determinable by more or less universal laws and, on the other, to be staging points for a more individualized free expression. Focusing on three aspects of Ruskin's exposition, I show how his account reiterates this dramatization of agency even in seemingly distinct contexts. The three contexts are, in effect, nested: at the broadest level, we have Ruskin's account of the origin and the power of the city of Venice itself; next, his discussion of Venice's expression of itself through architecture; and finally, his sense of the Venetian artist Tintoretto. In each account, Ruskin's rhetoric evinces a conflicted sense of modern subjectivity and liberal agency. A brief concluding section considers how the contradictory character of his thinking has served as much to establish his claims on modern interest as to subvert them. In this respect, I set Ruskin forth in much the same light that I will explore in later chapters through Dante Gabriel Rossetti and, especially, Oscar Wilde.

Originating Venice

Of all works in the conventional ambit of literary history, *Stones* might well rank supreme as a monumentalizing of an object—namely, Venice—that actually monumentalizes an interpreting subject—namely, Ruskin. It is common to hear that Ruskin's emotionally charged method, in *Stones* and elsewhere, reflects a kind of rampant but unacknowledged subjectivism, and that prospect apparently weighed on Ruskin's mind as well. The epigraph to each volume of his *Modern Painters* is a passage from Wordsworth's *The Excursion* in which the quintessential reflective poet attempts to head off a charge that his image of human Soul is no more than "a mirror that reflects / To proud Self-love her own intelligence" (4:978–92).[9] Ruskin, like Wordsworth, protests too much about the objective justifications underwriting his subjective procedures, and we can well suppose in each case that these concerns to refute allegations of self-involvement are motivated by a sense that perhaps undue self-involvement is a problem after all. My central concern is not to cast him as a narcissist, however, nor exactly to spare him from such diagnosis. Instead, I mean to examine the form that his projection takes and to ask what it is about Venice that rendered it suitable as a screen onto which Ruskin could project his complex and embattled sense of human agency. The conceptual and rhetorical aspects of his argumentation make clear that Ruskin would own to himself, at some level, every quality that he attributes to Venice—the grandeur, the imperilment, the sense of decline. The form of identification most crucial to my larger argument, however, turns on Ruskin's sense of Venice as a monumental fusion of contending and even antithetical influences. In his identification with that fusion, Ruskin reveals his stake in the rhetoric of many-sidedness that I offered in Chapter 1 as a distinctive concern for mid-Victorian liberal culture.

In the chapter that opens volume 2 of *Stones*, the first volume to look in detail at the development of Venice and its architecture, Ruskin recalls the "olden days of travelling" (10:1) when people used to approach Venice slowly and scenically by boat rather than, as they had come to do, on rails: "the noble landscape of approach to her can now be seen no more, or seen only by a glance as the engine slackens its rushing on the iron line" (10:7). This chapter is subsequently organized, however, not to foreground his well-known aversion to the mindless efficiency of modernity—that is the work of his next and more famous chapter, "The Nature of Gothic." Ruskin's actual starting point in his treatment of Venice turns instead on the individuality of Venice, the nature of Venice. And the terms through which he conjures that nature map onto the terms through which he figures human agency.

As a displaced account of his own affective concerns, Ruskin's Venice amounts to a pathetic fallacy, a subjectivity projected onto objects.[10] But Ruskin is at pains to distinguish his treatment of Venice from those typically at hand in the "Venice of modern fiction and drama" (10:8), all picturesque decay and diffused lighting, Lord Byron's "fair city of the heart."[11] For Ruskin, Venice can only be known from a patient excavation, an inquiry into "the humility of her origin" (10:7) as a city arisen in highly improbable circumstances and marvelously adapted to those circumstances. For Ruskin, Venice's "wonderfulness cannot be grasped by the indolence of imagination, but only after frank inquiry into the true nature of that wild and solitary scene, whose restless tides and trembling sands did indeed shelter the birth of the city, but long denied her dominion" (10:9).

Such inspection involves viewing Venice in the light of its adaptation to its particular physical and cultural circumstances, a discussion that leads inevitably into the issues of agency that organize, I argue, all his key points of interest in Venice. Built entirely apart from a mainland, Ruskin notes, Venice arose on numerous islands in a lagoon formed as part of an alluvial plane: "the main fact with which we have to do is the gradual transport, by the Po and its great collateral rivers, of vast masses of the finer sediments to the sea" (10:10). His elaborate citation of the physical circumstances that challenged and, in a related sense, enabled Venice reflects procedure of explanation handed down from Locke's empiricism and then being practiced by another notable theorist of origins and adaptation, Charles Darwin. There could be no Venice, he observes, were it not for a host of special facts: the uniform shallowness of the waterways between islands made possible the consistent use of gondola transports while at the same time it made impossible any attack from large warships that would have required deeper waters; the exact and unusually narrow range of the tides, about three feet, meant that the waterways are at times largely evacuated (thus washing away sewage, an effect not possible in other parts of the Mediterranean where tidal fluctuations are sometimes absent), but the tides also never fluctuated so widely as to require buildings to be set high on pilings (thus only could Venetians effect reliable, convenient, and graceful water-level access to their buildings). In the laws of nature, "there was indeed a preparation, and *the only preparation possible*, for the founding" of Venice (10:15).

To press his account further, however, Ruskin has to encroach ever more fully on a conceptual aporia. On the one hand, he emphasizes that Venice is a monument to its own formation by a specific physical situation. In this light, Venice's particular form expresses a general rule that cities—like individuals and cultures—are in thrall to the constraint of material circumstance, and for us to understand Venice, we must simply understand its subscription to this outlying rule. Ruskin's appeal is also, however, to our interest in Venice's accomplishment of a kind of singularity, and in that latter appeal lies a spectral celebration of radical individuality and purposive agency. Venice is, in this light, a parable of its own exceptionalism and individuality. Ruskin generally deplored individualism as a species of fatuous pride, of course—thus his remarkable distaste for the Renaissance, which earns his all-but-wholesale scorn chiefly by virtue of its exaltation of individuality. But his underlying interest in the idea of individualism can be glimpsed at all turns—glimpsed especially, as I will soon show, in his disavowals.

But first it is well to allow that the passage cited above is not necessarily in conflict with itself, in that Venice can be understood at once as an effect of its surroundings and as a unique particular. Venice can be unique, that is, entirely in line with its physical circumstances, which are themselves unique. The problem arises, however, in the general work to which Ruskin wishes to put his particular case. J. B. Bullen has characterized Ruskin's intellectual procedures overall as a "synecdochic method," meaning that Ruskin habitually strives to treat particulars as indices to larger wholes.[12] In *Stones*, Ruskin aims to set Venice's particularity as a case in a larger point concerning the rise and fall of civic vision. And for Ruskin's claim to be cogent, he has to be embrace a notion that Venice might have been otherwise than it has been, and that other places, as well, might be otherwise than they are. Where there is no choosing, there can be no purposive action, no responsibility or morality. Thus for Venice to mean what Ruskin wants it to mean, Ruskin must admit a precarious and sometimes contradictory picture of its supposed agency.

On the one hand, then, we have Ruskin's diagnosis of Venice as a parable of formation by circumstance and, on the other, an ideal of Venice as a singularity with its own purposive agency. Ruskin's negotiation with this conflict is plainer to see in the original reflections that lay behind his published passage's formulations. In 1851 he had written much the same observations to his father, explaining how the uniform depth of the canals and the exact range of the tides enable Venice to function as it does. Ruskin went on to indicate the divided and even incoherent sense of Venice that I've been explicating:

> When people first discover the peculiar adaptations of an animal or plant to its position, they are apt to exclaim—What wonderful preparation for the existence of this little creature! Whereas, if they knew more of the Universe, they would begin to understand that everything in existence was put in the place it was fit for, and the mere fact of its existence proved that it was in its right place. And so one might look over Europe and see how each town takes its natural position and becomes prosperous if it happens to understand that position, and take due advantage of it; and one might say generally, Genoa grows up in the place for Genoa, and Rotterdam in that for Rotterdam, and Venice in that for Venice. But I am almost disposed to admit a sort of special providence for Venice. The tide at this end of the Adriatic is a mystery no philosopher has explained. The structure of the mouths of the Brenta and Adige is unexampled in the history of Geology. It seems that just in the centre of Europe, and at the point where the influence of East and West, of the old and new world, were to meet, preparation was made for a city which was to unite the energy of the one with the splendour of the other (10:15 n. 1)

Ruskin's distinction here—between places that seem prepared for their creatures and creatures that seem to have been placed where they are "right"—falters once we see that, precisely in his examples, the cities that he mentions need in some sense to "understand" and "take due advantage" of their circumstances. Such *understanding* and *taking of advantage* indicate a force of judgment and tactical mobility that implies something apart from a providential basis for success. Here the success is based on accomplishment and overcoming through the agency of the particular entity. What is more, Ruskin's special feeling for Venice in this agential light is clear. The incapacity of philosophers and of geological historians to "explain" Venice seems to have been for Ruskin, in the end, a matter of some relief, for Venice's intractability to explanation secures for it an aesthetic richness that would be destroyed by any reduction to mechanistic explanation. His letter to his father announces his disposition "to admit a sort of special providence for Venice" forthrightly, but the process of writing and polishing his thought for *The Stones of Venice* obscures that disposition. What motivates and regulates his disavowal is an anxiety on his part concerning agency, an uncertainty about the relation between a "special providence" and particular or individualized acts of understanding and response.[13]

And if Ruskin's divided thinking about agency tends to be papered over in the polishing of his expression, the division emerges again as contradiction in the larger levels of his exposition. And the contradiction tends to arise exactly at his key characterizations of Venice itself. Consider two passages from the opening chapter of the first volume of *Stones*, which have in common the task of assessing Venice's distinctive role in history. The passages are separated by only eight pages, a proximity worth noting as a warrant for my close attention to a subtle but instructive difference there in play.

The contradiction turns on this question: are we to see in Venice a force of historical change or merely an incidental location for such change? Ruskin says both, and I will be arguing that this contradiction mirrors—and is determined by—a related contradiction informing Ruskin's own self-conception as a critical agent. In the first passage, we have Venice as the merely incidental locus of forces properly outside itself. It is a meeting point of distinct cultural agencies, here called Lombard, signifying the northern influences centered in modern-day Austria and Hungary, and Arab, signifying Byzantine influences, which varied geographically but were centered in the Balkan peninsula and Asia Minor. The passage has the additional advantage for my discussion of preparing the way for my upcoming attentions to the Ducal Palace in Venice:

> The work of the Lombard was to give hardihood and system to the enervated body and enfeebled mind of Christendom; that of the Arab was to punish idolatry, and to proclaim the spirituality of worship. The Lombard covered every church which he built with the sculptured representations of bodily exercises—hunting and war. The Arab banished all imagination of creature form from his temples and proclaimed from his minarets, "There is no god but God." Opposite in their character and mission, alike in their magnificence of energy, they came from the North and from the South, the glacier torrent and the lava stream: they met and contended over the wreck of the Roman empire; and the very center of the struggle, the point of pause of both, the dead water of the opposite eddies, charged with embayed fragments of the Roman wreck, is VENICE.
> The Ducal palace of Venice contains the three elements in exactly equal proportions—the Roman, Lombard, and Arab. It is the central building of the world. (9:38)

Here Venice's specific character is not at issue; instead, the city is the happenstance locus of contending outside forces, the decayed fragments of a defunct Roman empire serving as the stage for an energetic collision of the Lombard and Arab agencies. To the extent that these outlying forces define Venice in its distinctive importance, the image of the city emerges in relative weakness here as "the dead water of the opposite eddies."

This connotation of weakness has dissipated eight pages later, however, to be replaced by an image of Venice as a motive force of its own:

> Now Venice, as she was once the most religious, was in her fall the most corrupt of European states; and as she was *in her strength the centre* of the pure currents of Christian architecture, so she is in her decline *the source of the Renaissance*. It was the originality and splendour of the palaces of Vicenza and Venice which gave this school its eminence in the eyes of Europe; and the dying city, magnificent in her dissipation, and graceful in her follies, obtained wider worship in her decrepitude than in her youth, and sank from the midst of her admirers into the grave.
> It is in Venice, therefore, and in Venice only, that effectual blows can be struck at this pestilent art of the Renaissance. Destroy its claims to admiration there, and it can as-

sert them nowhere else. This therefore will be the final purpose of the following essay.(9:46–47; my emphasis)

We find already the familiar components of Ruskin's larger effort to paint Venice as an emblem and warning to modernity. It is a tragic fusion of magnificence and decline. Then, too, its decline is a matter of religious and moral character. And, finally, Ruskin's own project takes shape as an active assault on the common wisdom of his own modernity, which is itself all too ready to celebrate the impious individualism underlying "the pestilent art of the Renaissance." In marked contrast to his immediately prior characterization of Venice, however, Ruskin's characterization here turns on a sense of the city's strength and potency. Venice, we are now told, was a strong center, a scene of originality and splendor that seduced Europe and served as the origin or "source" for the Renaissance. Venice matters because its specific character attracts, compels, and seduces.[14] Venice, here, is an object of desire because it is an agent of historical change. These characterizations map fully onto one prevalent idea of individual agency in the modern period—that of an individualism that can take aggressive or entrepreneurial forms and that finds its everyday expression in the faith that the individual is master and owner of his or her fate.

The contrast between these two images of Venice was notable enough to Ruskin himself that he added a footnote on the matter some decades later, in an 1879 edition of *Stones*. His note enters following his remark, in the course of the later passage that had told of Venice as a "source" and "centre" in her strength. His note is a confession: "I am ashamed of having been so entrapped by my own metaphor. Look back to §24. She [Venice] was the centre of Christian art only as the place of slack water between two currents. I confuse that notion here, with the central power of a fountain in a pool (9:47). Ruskin would have us see this confusion as an effect of metaphor usurping logic, and he sees this usurpation as a passing embarrassment, "noteworthy" in a literal sense but also inconsequential. Some fifteen or twenty years ago, a deconstructive critic might have relished both the unhinging effect of metaphor here and Ruskin's desire to discount the havoc it creates in his larger claims.[15] Indeed, Ruskin's effort to minimize this tangled point's importance seems meaningful. But I suggest that the unhinging effect of metaphor here signals, not a radical indeterminacy to which linguistic representation as such is heir, but a determinable aspect of Ruskin's critical agency. Ruskin's adjustments to his point reflect features of liberal agency that I earlier described as precarious, as regulative rather than substantive. At issue here is a kind of interpretive mobility, played out through ongoing efforts of judgment and assessment. And while no single citation can in itself substantiate my larger speculation— namely, that Ruskin's procedure is at times a liberal many-sidedness loathe to speak its name—the point can be made plainer after further documentation of this move in his readings of Venice.

Agency into Architecture

The key rhetorical division in Ruskin's account of Venetian architecture turns on an antagonism between individual expression and a sense of the agent's subscription to outlying norms and protocols. To make this point I will concentrate on two rather underread segments of his writing in *Stones*. First I show how Ruskin's exposition of architectural theory enacts a drama of agency as a complex construct. Next, I focus on his treatment of the Ducal Palace of Venice to show how his key example wins its privileged role in *Stones* because that example fuels Ruskin's own processes of identification with his critical objects.

The first volume of *Stones* offers a general outline of architectural theory. Here Ruskin establishes the conceptual foundation for his historical narrative of specifically Venetian architecture in the second and third volumes. His chapters in the first volume consider walls, arches, roofs, and so forth in two distinct aspects. In the volume's first division, treating *construction*, Ruskin discusses elements of architecture in terms of more or less objective issues of strength, so that, for example, one must judge walls and columns in terms of quantifiable stresses they must manage. In the second division, treating *ornamentation*, the key issue is beauty, not strength (9:64), and Ruskin treats all the same elements of architecture anew with an aesthetic concern in mind. Only in the second division, when qualities of judgment, imagination, and invention come explicitly into play, does Ruskin find cause to theorize the agency proper to the worker and the architect. But the value of invention is something that Ruskin must extol with caution so as not to let it become equivalent to a fancifulness that could, in the end, look like license and immorality. In this respect, the forms of ornament and decoration are approached as expressions of potentially moral or immoral action.

Ruskin's treatment of capitals and cornices will here illustrate the conceptual and finally emotional tensions driving his thought. Capitals and cornices are related by virtue of his organization of architectural elements: capitals sit on columns or, as Ruskin has it, "shafts," and cornices sit on walls or "wall veils"; the two forms are kin in that both perform the function of gathering force from above and focusing it strategically on a surface below. (Thus, for Ruskin, a line of columns is but a redistributed version of a wall.) The imperatives of construction set some of the terms, mandating a fundamental form and two branches of variation (9:93; Figure 2). The fundamental form (a) must answer objective requirements of construction: its lower end must be narrowed to concentrate weight exactly on the wall or column that supports it, and its upper end must be broadened to distribute force onto a greater area, so as not

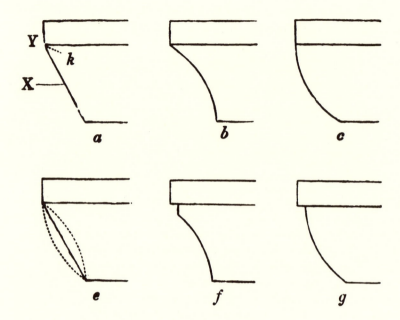

2. Convex and concave cornices from John Ruskin, *The Stones of Venice* I. In John Ruskin, *The Works of John Ruskin*, ed. E. T. Cook and Alexander Wedderburn, 39 vols. (London: George Allen, 1903–12), 9:93.

to threaten a puncturing of the roof material. The straight diagonal line describes a "fundamental" cornice by virtue, it would seem, of Ruskin's assumption that a straight line is basic.[16] Two different forms evolve from this basic one: a concave form (b), adapted to the more efficient sloughing off of rain, and a convex form (c), adapted to the greater loading of weight from above.

Invention has a sharply limited role in these three forms of capitals, variation being confined to concave and convex shapes that are themselves determined not by aesthetic but functional needs. But when Ruskin recurs later in this first volume to the decorative treatment of this architectural feature, capitals become staging points for a drama of good and bad conduct on the part of sculptors. For Ruskin, decorating the recess of the concave form requires a degree of forethought and geometrical planning that is not required by the convex form, where the rough material bulges out plainly and can be treated much as one might treat a stand-alone block of stone. Thus workmanship for the concave cornice or capital tends to be precise and masterfully controlled while the convex form tends to be irregular and rude. Characteristically, Ruskin then proceeds from this empirical claim to a speculation concerning the distinct visions of human agency here in play. After noting that "we shall not fail to find balancing qualities in both" forms, he distinguishes their effects firmly:

The severity of the disciplinarian [concave] capital represses the power of the imagi-nation; it gradually degenerates into Formalism; and the indolence which cannot es-cape from its stern demand of accurate workmanship, seeks refuge in copyism of established forms, and loses itself at last in lifeless mechanism. The license of the other [convex capital], though often abused, permits full exercise to the imagination: the mind of the sculptor, unshackled by the niceties of chiselling, wanders over its orbed field in endless fantasy; and, when generous as well as powerful, repays the liberty which has been granted to it with interest, by developing through the utmost wildness and ful-ness of its thoughts, an order as much more noble than the mechanical symmetry of the opponent school, as the domain which it regulates is vaster. (9:382)

Notwithstanding his initial concern to admit "balancing qualities" in each form, this passage culminates in a plainly unbalanced preference for the imag-inative potential of the convex form, which now takes the place of a certain ideal of action—imaginative but still, in some hard to specify sense, not exces-sive. The maneuver here recalls the pretension we saw in Matthew Arnold to speak of balancing qualities in both Hebraism and Hellenism, even as he clearly privileges, in fact, the spontaneity and free play of Hellenism. Ruskin soon makes clear how fully he means to generalize about human action through this unlikely battle of the capitals: "we now find, that these two great and real orders are representative of the two great influences which must for ever divide the heart of man: the one of Lawful Discipline, with its perfection and order, but its danger of degeneracy into Formalism; the other, of lawful Freedom, with its vigour and variety, but its danger of degeneracy into Licen-tiousness" (9:383; Figure 3).

Thus do details of architecture stage for Ruskin the conditions of the human psyche in general. In treating the various shapes of arches, to take an-other instance, he argues, "The arch line is the moral character of the arch, and the adverse forces are its temptations" (9:156). Architecture for Ruskin is instinct with dramatic interest. His discussion of decorative variation draws even more emphatically on a conception of proper human action. Already in *Modern Painters* 2, Ruskin had offered the general argument that nature's beauty is constituted, in part, by its expression of God's choice that nature operate lawfully rather than arbitrarily.[17] In that account, beauty is a function of self-restraining liberty (9:304), originally God's condition but now also the prerog-ative of human agents who can find in self-restrained liberty a middle ground between sterile formalism and decadent license. In *Stones* I, Ruskin tenders his account of beautiful action in terms of architectural decoration: "Now, corre-spondingly, we find that when these natural objects are to become subjects of the art of man, their perfect treatment is an image of the perfection of *human* action: a voluntary submission to divine law" (9:304). Human action generates

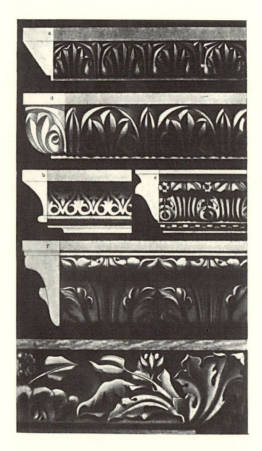

3. Cornice decoration from *Stones* I. In Ruskin, *Works*, 9: facing 365. Ruskin discusses the decorative styles in these cornices at length (9:365–72). Among other points, he contrasts the vitality and naturalness of the topmost cornices (*a, d*) with the lifeless copyism of that at middle left (*b*) (9:368–69). All three, in turn, reflect Byzantine influences, thus earlier forms than the lowest two (*f, g*), which are fully developed Gothic forms. The bottommost epitomizes for Ruskin the Lombardic-Gothic form, "Lombardic vitality restrained by classical models" (9:366). Of that cornice, he notes, "That is Protestantism,—a slight touch of Dissent, hardly amounting to schism, in those falling leaves, but true life in the whole of it" (9:371).

beauty when the agent chooses lawfulness, miming the autonomy of a law-choosing God.

Ruskin values most highly, therefore, those ideas that preserve individual choice and general rule at once. In fact, the finest "image of human action" in decoration has to include the "special infringement of a general law" (9:305). He illustrates his point with reference to the decoration work of one Venetian

4. Byzantine arch, woodcut from Ruskin, *Stones* II. In Ruskin, *Works*, 10:293.

building, and while Ruskin's woodcut—offered in the next volume of *Stones* to illustrate a different matter (10:293)—does not make this point's details plain, it is worth reproducing here because a sense of the perfect symmetry of the rounded arch is also part of the story that Ruskin needs to tell (Figure 4). For the arch's detailed carving is "a most curious instance . . . composed of a wreath of flower-work—a constant Byzantine design—with an animal in each coil; the whole enclosed between two fillets. Not the shake of an ear, the tip of a tail, overpasses this appointed line, through a series of some five-and-twenty or thirty animals; until, on a sudden, and by mutual consent, two little beasts (not looking, for the rest, more rampant than the others), on one side each, lay their small paws across the enclosing fillet at exactly the same point of its course, and thus break the continuity of its line" (9:305). Ruskin argues that a decorative pattern's "expression" of human action "is heightened, rather than diminished, when some portion of the design slightly breaks the law to which the rest is subjected" (9:304). It would seem that what "heightens" this expression is nothing other than our own propensity to be interested in images of agency. Recall how we are supposed to be interested in the two forms of cornices—the convex, tending to license, and the concave, tending to rigid formalism—because in their divergent tendencies "these two great and real orders are representative of" our self-understandings as agents. The interest of this Byzantine arch likewise depends on its status as an image of contested terms in balance, the perfect roundness of the arch and the continuous framing line of the fillets figuring the rule to which rampant creatures are subject, but not absolutely.

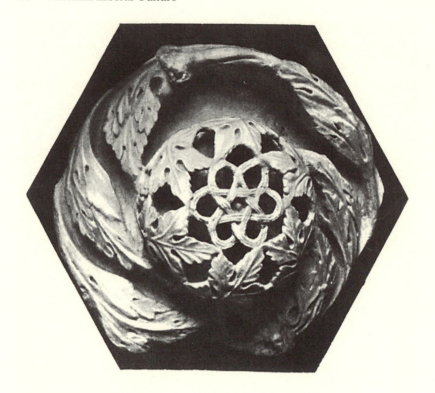

5. An 1852 Ruskin cast from Venetian architecture, probably a globe from the architrave of St. Mark's Cathedral. Currently in the Collection of the Guild of St George, Sheffield Galleries & Museums Trust. In Ruskin, *Works*, 30: facing 188.

A phenomenal labor of note-taking and sketching lay behind Ruskin's approach to such points—he was flat on his back drawing cathedral vaults, hanging from ladders, sitting on scaffolds, generally oblivious to amused passers-by as he accumulated his register of details and facts. His ideal, in effect, was to count each stone of Venice, and behind these painstaking efforts, as I have argued, lay his concern to reflect on the nature and the sources of human agency. In the remainder of this section, I will be suggesting further that Ruskin's counting of capitals and stones also reflects his charged engagement with the liberal methodological individualism noted at this study's outset—a view of collectivity in which the individual is fundamental, in which the collectivity is in the end but a collection of individuals. It is at this level that we can seem most plainly how Ruskin took into his own thinking those energies of liberal affect that he would most often disavow in direct confrontation.

Ruskin's traffic in parts and pieces is most tangible in his several hundred ar-

6. A Ruskin cast from Venetian architecture (1852). Currently in the collection of the Guild of St George, Sheffield Galleries & Museums Trust. In Ruskin, *Works*, 30: facing 188.

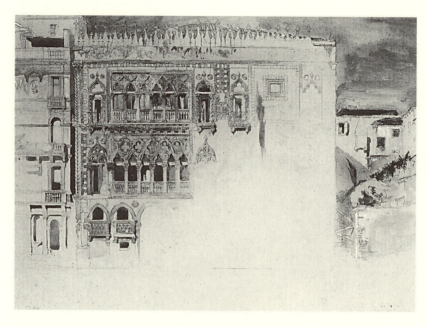

7. John Ruskin, the drawing *Casa D'Oro* (1845). By permission of the Ruskin Foundation (Ruskin Library, Lancaster).

chitectural casts (Figures 5-6). His declared motive in amassing the collection was to record details of architecture for posterity, for Venice was indeed literally falling apart. The decrepit and crumbling nature of Venice had long been a key part of its picturesque appeal for Grand Tourists, of course, but Ruskin's sense of the city's decline is more idiosyncratic and intimate. In an 1845 letter to his father, he relates a poignant scene attending his effort to draw a Venetian façade: "You cannot imagine what an unhappy day I spent yesterday before the Casa d'Oro, vainly attempting to draw it while the workmen were hammering it down before my face."[18] As the incompleteness of that picture poignantly conveys, these recording efforts were far from sufficient in Ruskin's eyes, and indeed they were staging points for an anxious sense of his agential powers (Figure 7). In another letter to his father from 1848, following a failed effort to draw a restored porch of a cathedral in Abbeville, Normandy, he writes, "I seem born to conceive what I cannot execute, recommend what I cannot obtain, and mourn over what I cannot save" (8:xxix). Exactly as he entered into his immense effort for *Stones*, then, Ruskin felt a sense of his actions canceled, his aspirations thwarted. In 1852, while developing the second and third volumes of *The Stones of Venice*, Ruskin began taking his plaster casts. As in so many of his critical objects, Ruskin saw himself as an agent in the casts.

They mirrored him in at once preserving originals and mourning their loss, and in this they mirrored broader cultural debates over what aesthetic agency involves—a cross-current of tradition and the individual talent, for example, in which originality reflects at once a placement within tradition and a supervention of it.

Another facet of Ruskin's interest in the casts turns on their nature as studies of parts—details of capitals from the Ducal Palace, grotesque visages from St. Mark's, individual panels from the church at Murano. In rendering architecture through parts rather than wholes, the casts recall a theme that troubled Ruskin in his working habits at this time. An 1845 letter to his father has Ruskin declaring about one Venetian landmark building, "I am thoroughly thrown on my back with the Palazzo Foscari—don't know what the deuce to do with it. I have all its measures & mouldings, & that is something, but I can't get on with the general view."[19] When introducing his *Examples of the Architecture of Venice*, a work conceived as an illustrative companion to *Stones*, Ruskin preemptively explains that his work will seldom render a whole view of any given building.[20] His rush to explanation looks like a rationalizing defense of his fragmentary mode of illustration, but as his earlier letter to his father showed, he was also struggling with a sense of inability in rendering wholes to his satisfaction. Ruskin's father, John James Ruskin, writing in 1846 to a long-time friend, delivers a mixed judgement of his son's fragmentary procedure, a judgement no doubt communicated to Ruskin himself. John James writes that the younger Ruskin's latest inquiries were "gathered in scraps hardly wrought, for he is drawing perpetually, but no drawings such as in former days you and I might compliment in the usual way by saying it deserved a frame; but fragments of everything from a Cupola to a Cart-wheel, but in such bits that it is to the common eye a mass of Hieroglyphics—all true—truth itself, but truth in Mosaic" (8:xxiii).

That Ruskin's concern with fragments reflects the deepest currents of his critical nature and his methods is a claim underlying several modern accounts of him.[21] This sense seems implicit in J. B. Bullen's characterization of Ruskin's procedure as a "synecdochic method." In a passage from *Stones* II, Ruskin justifies his decision to draw merely a fragment from one of the archivolts at St. Mark's Cathedral by saying, after a characteristic passage of appreciative description, that our "decision of the respective merits of modern and of Byzantine architecture may be allowed to rest on this fragment of St. Mark's alone" (10:116–17; the plate faces 10:115). *Stones* as a whole depends on a sense that Venice does not merely suggest but indeed embodies the rise and fall of Western art over a thousand-year period. Ruskin's plaster casts combine intimacy with their originals and a clear distance from them, and in this sense they serve a disposition in Ruskin to think, if anxiously, about the relations of wholes and parts. In seeming, for Ruskin, to touch something beyond their minute particularity, the casts mime a key challenge of modern liberal agency, insofar as such agents look to find in individual action something at once particular and more broadly intersubjective or social.

The overarching issue in Ruskin's divided standpoint is whether the casts might bear their own value as such or whether their value is properly confined to their service as means to some other and greater end in representation or instruction. Formulated in this way, the issue mirrors a predicament facing modern agents disposed to comprehend themselves as agents. The idea of bearing one's own value lines up with the more or less romantic vision of self-creation and self-authorization, while the definition of value according to one's service to projects and schemes of value lines up with ideas of traditionalism, communitarian identity, and intersubjective ideas. And to look at Ruskin's actual engagements with the casts, as also with engraving and photography, we see conflicted views that trace back to his concern with this divided standpoint on the sources of value.

For notwithstanding Ruskin's affection for the casts, he also felt driven at many times to set some limits on their status as objects. Two divergent lines of thinking run throughout Ruskin's engagement with the casts. The casts are marvelous, but their proper use must be confined to study. They are to record fact and inform knowledge, but they are not to take the place of originals nor to be the basis for any full aesthetic response. They may instruct but had better not delight. Ruskin's affection for the casts in themselves therefore sits alongside a concern to circumscribe or regulate their claim on our interest.[22] And when copies threaten to recall originals to a degree that might be disturbingly satisfactory, we are looking at another version of George Eliot's "imitation of heroism," which sometimes looks in modern times like a truer or more proper mastery.

Venetian architecture's dramatization of agency is most fully argued in Ruskin's treatment of the Ducal Palace, that "central building of the world" (9:38). In volume 2 Ruskin devotes a lengthy chapter to the building "which at once consummates and embodies the entire system of the Gothic architecture of Venice—the Ducal Palace" (10:327). The pervasive contestation in his thinking between various concepts of agency is already apparent here in his distinction between consummation and embodiment, ideas that he sets up in deceptively casual apposition. For to consummate is to act in such a way as to complete something; to embody, in Ruskin's apparent sense, is not so much to act as to be, but with a certain significance granted to that being. To embody the "entire system of Gothic architecture," for example, is not merely to lend substance to an example but instead to establish a categorical essence through a particular form. Seen in this light, Ruskin's chapter on the Ducal Palace clearly evinces the synecdochic impetus in his thinking.

In an 1852 letter to his father, Ruskin dilates on his concern to proceed in this manner: "The fact is the whole book will be a kind of 'great moral of the

Ducal Palace of Venice. . . . And so I shall give many a scattered description of a moulding here and an arch there, but they will be mere notes to the account of the Rise and Fall of the Ducal Palace, and that account itself will be sub-servient to the showing of the causes and consequences of the rise and all of Art in Europe" (10:327 n. 1). The resulting chapter on the Ducal Palace has hardly been a favorite among readers, and it seems that the unifying effect that Ruskin foresaw his scattered descriptions accomplishing has gone generally lost. Ruskin would follow most modern readers by allowing, in his later life, that another chapter in *Stones* II, "The Nature of Gothic," was the program-matic heart of his three volumes. But his original sense of this Ducal Palace chapter's centrality was surely motivated by his awareness that here, more than in any other chapter of the work, he was staging his interest in the conjunction of particularity and generality. The chapter's scattered particulars are anxious signals, bids to consummate a generality through an accumulating registration of particulars. And that sort of project has a claim on Ruskin's interest in its appearance of miming a predicament of modern agency, itself a tale of par-ticulars alternately sensing fulfillment and dissolution in the claims of general essences on their sense of particularity.

Very early in his discussion of the Ducal Palace, Ruskin focuses on an asym-metry of the windows on the side of the Palace that confronts us directly in his woodcut illustration (Figure 8). The two windows on the right sit lower than the four corresponding windows to the left, in what Ruskin calls "one of the most remarkable instances I know of the daring sacrifice of symmetry to con-venience."[23] This arrangement reflects successive stages of building in the Ducal Palace: the two lower windows belong to an older part of the building arranged in four stories, while the higher windows correspond to a later part of the building, designed as a grand meeting chamber for the Venetian Sen-ate. Due to an interior difference in the number of floors in each section—the entire height of the later section was given over to the meeting chamber—placing the four later windows in line with the earlier two would have rendered the new windows rather low within the Senate hall, compromising their serv-ice to the interior in several respects:

The ceiling of the new room was to be adorned by the paintings of the best masters in Venice, and it became of great importance to raise the light near that gorgeous roof as well as to keep the tone of illumination in the Council Chamber serene; and therefore to introduce light rather in simple masses than in many broken streams. A modern ar-chitect, terrified at the idea of violating external symmetry, would have sacrificed both the pictures and the peace of the Council. He would have placed the larger windows at the same level with the other two, and have introduced above them smaller windows, like those of the upper story in the older building, as if that upper building had been continued along the façade. But the old Venetian thought of the honour of the paint-ings, and the comfort of the Senate, before his own reputation. He unhesitatingly raised the windows to their proper position with reference to the interior of the chamber, and

8. John Ruskin, bird's-eye view, woodcut, of the Ducal Palace, Venice. From *Stones* II. In Ruskin, *Works*, 10:331.

suffered the external appearance to take care of itself. And I believe the whole pile rather gains than loses in effect by the variation thus obtained in the spaces of the wall above and below the windows. (10:334–35)

Although Ruskin is careful to recount how this asymmetry is motivated by practical concerns for interior lighting, his chief pleasure is in the resulting aesthetic effect of the exterior's asymmetry. His drawing *The Gothic Facade of the Ducal Palace* (1852) is framed not only to detail the Gothic section of the palace's sea face but to preserve a sense of the distinctive window placement (Figure 9). His aesthetic judgment that "the whole pile rather gains than loses in effect by the variation" appears to illustrate his well-known concern to affirm a vision of skilled and boldly decisive thought in the creative work of persons such as craftsmen and architects. And this view, of course, amounts to a celebration of robust and salutary agency. Ruskin appreciates the Ducal Palace as a form that discounts and outstrips rigid formalism. This characterization of the Palace is a veiled statement of his own ideal of self-reflecting agency, whereby the agent manages complex challenges without being overcome or obscured by them.

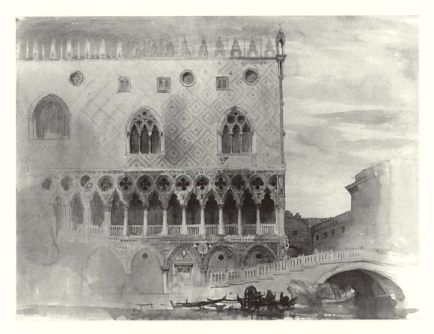

9. John Ruskin, *The Gothic Facade of the Ducal Palace* (1852). By permission of the Ashmolean Museum, Oxford.

A later passage from the famous chapter "The Nature of Gothic" dilates on the position from which Ruskin's favor for the Ducal Palace windows appears to proceed:

And it is one of the chief virtues of the Gothic builders, that they never suffered ideas of outside symmetries and consistencies to interfere with the real use and value of what they did. If they wanted a window, they opened one; a room, they added one; a buttress, they built one; utterly regardless of any established conventionalities of external appearance, knowing (as indeed it always happened) that such daring interruptions of the formal plan would rather give additional interest to its symmetry than injure it. So that in the best times of gothic, a useless window would rather have been opened for the sake of the surprise, than a useful one forbidden for the sake of symmetry. Every successive architect, employed upon a great work, built the pieces he added in his own way, utterly regardless of the style adopted by his predecessors; and if two towers were raised in nominal correspondence at the sides of a cathedral front, one was nearly sure to be different from the other, and in each the style at the top to be different from the style at the bottom. (10:212)

Ruskin appears to relish the freedoms that he can attribute to the individual builders here: "If they wanted a window, they opened one; a room, they added one," and so forth. The "wanting" here on display operates, it seems, as a playful spontaneity. Each builder can proceed "in his own way, utterly regardless of the style adopted by his predecessors." This view of designing agency looks, from a distance, exactly like the kind of heedless individualism that Ruskin would condemn in Renaissance designers. The variation and changefulness in Gothic architecture is a more or less objective matter in embodying a complex but nonetheless aesthetically harmonious whole. Such complexity in harmony maps exactly onto a modern ideal of self.

For Ruskin, the Ducal Palace was not simply excellent of its kind but transformative of subsequent building in Venice, and his language in rendering this point conjures the Ducal Palace as if it were a Carlylean ideal of heroic agency. The Ducal Palace, that is, cast its surroundings into renewed order after its own image: "Under every condition of importance, through every variation of size, the forms and mode of decoration of all the features were universally alike; not servily alike, but fraternally; not with the sameness of coins cast from one mould, but with the likeness of members of one family" (10:311). Notice that Ruskin's terms insist on the singular character of the Ducal Palace and also on its capacity to disseminate a consciousness of form and feeling that finds expression—indeed, that constitutes the expression—in all of ensuing Venetian Gothic architecture. Ruskin is careful to style this influence in such a way that the ensuing architecture is not exactly subjugated or evacuated of its own vitality: the buildings after the Ducal Palace are "not servily alike, but fraternally," and they reflect their original inspiration "not with the sameness of coins" but with a family likeness that includes, in some undecidable admixture, both common and singular identity. Ruskin's aspiration to credit the Ducal Palace with this complex identity is decisive to his general interest in it.

That point will become plainer if we recall now his characterization of the Ducal Palace from volume 1 of *Stones*, quoted above as it was appended to one of Ruskin's climactic proclamations about Venice generally. There, Venice was "the very center of the struggle" between Arab and Lombard powers, each working their image forth out of the "embayed fragments of the Roman wreck." Ruskin's conclusion: "The Ducal palace of Venice contains the three elements in exactly equal proportions—the Roman, Lombard, and Arab. It is the central building of the world" (9:38). His terms appear to suggest that the centrality of the Ducal Palace consists in its rendering of "exactly equal proportions" of three distinct elements, namely, the Roman, Lombard, and Arab. This rhetoric of *exactness* seems to be motivated by a concern on his part to pretend that his conclusions are grounded in empirical observation of the building's objectively reckonable elements. And to an extent his observations are so grounded: one can indeed offer as an objective fact that the Palace exhibits Byzantine color patterns, Gothic decoration, and classical columns. But to insist that their proportions are exactly equal is to invoke a language of precision precisely where that language can only be hortatory.

The consummate aesthetic effect that Ruskin asserts here in fact pertains more to his sense of self than to his ostensible object. The Ducal Palace wins Ruskin's admiration not in its passive reflection of three outside agencies but in its capacity to conjure for him an active management and balancing of such contending forces. The Ducal Palace is not an emblem of Venice's thralldom to circumstance but of its negotiation of circumstance, a negotiation that is marked by magnificence, imagination, power of influence, and epochal force of conviction. So while the building indeed "represents" the assorted forces that it manages, its *interest* for Ruskin lies in a richer substrate of response: it represents a vision of agency as transformative power. And it does so in terms that mirror an image of self, including residual uncertainties about that image's plausibility and its consequences, that Ruskin obsessively engaged.

Ruskin and Tintoretto

> *"There is none like him*—none.*"*
>
> —*Ruskin on Tintoretto, in an 1870 letter to Charles Eliot Norton*[24]

> *I must speak a few words about myself, to-day, before entering on our subject. I should not venture to say anything to you of Scott, or of any other great man, unless I knew myself to be in closer sympathy with them than you can generally be yourselves; but observe, in claiming this sympathy I do not claim the least approach to any equality of power. I had sympathy with Tintoret, with Scott, with Turner, with Carlyle—as a child with its father or mother, not as friend with friend. What they feel, I, in a feeble and inferior way, feel also, what they are, I can tell you, because in a poor and weak way I am like them—of their race—but no match for them.*
>
> —*From an unused manuscript passage for Ruskin's 1873 letters on Walter Scott in* Fors Clavigera[25]

These remarks, both drawn from Ruskin's later writings in the 1870s, make clear the writer's enduring sense that he is in no position to equal the power of Jacopo Robusti (1519–94), the quintessentially Venetian artist commonly called Tintoretto or, as Ruskin has it, Tintoret. But as ever, we do well to unpack the nuances of Ruskin's language. To say of Tintoretto that there was "none like him" is, in this case, to make a claim for the artist's originality, understood as a radical singularity. In the other epigraph, however, we see Ruskin announcing a sense of identification with Tintoretto, along with some other figures who are well known as heroes for Ruskin.[26] So the two remarks suggest two antithetical claims: first, that no one was like Tintoretto; second, that not only was someone like Tintoretto (if only in pale imitation), but that this someone is Ruskin himself, and what is more, that this sense of likeness grounds a sympathetic response that in turn authorizes Ruskin to present himself as a critic to his audience.

The antithesis I have drawn here is at once too formal and too coarse, so my concern in what follows is to detail how Ruskin's commentary on Tintoretto actually underscores rather than diminishes this antithesis. I aim to bring out Ruskin's ambivalence respecting Tintoretto's power, and to bring out what relation that power has to Ruskin's own sense of power. For in the abjection that Ruskin here avows lies also a kind of critical self-affirmation. It has been my effort so far to paint Ruskin's relation to Venice as complex and ambivalent. Without clarifying the complex feelings of identification and incapacity underlying Ruskin's uniform praise of Tintoretto, however, it might seem that his conflicted relation to Venice must be of a different sort than his admiring relation to Tintoretto. But I mean to align Venice and Tintoretto both as terms through which Ruskin practiced the form of modern self-imaging that is this study's larger concern.

Ruskin first encountered the works of Tintoretto during his 1845 trip to Italy, and the encounter informed much of his subsequent life, generating, among other things, *The Stones of Venice*. After renewing his attentions to Venice in the late 1860s, Ruskin praised Tintoretto over Michelangelo in the most hotly contested of his Oxford lectures as Slade Professor of Fine Art,[27] and in his several other works recalling the power of Venice, he usually associated that power with the Tintoretto's paintings.[28] Ruskin admired Tintoretto with an extravagance and consistency that he would bring to few other persons or things, and modern critics have typically classed this trait among his miscellaneous eccentricities—as when Tim Hilton, in his generally wonderful biography of Ruskin, oddly avers that the enormous size of Tintoretto's paintings blinded Ruskin to the clear superiority of Titian and left him to overrate Tintoretto forevermore as a memorial to his immoderate feelings on that occasion.[29]

Granting that a sort of fixation informs Ruskin's engagement with Tintoretto, I want to develop a specific account of its meaning. Here we have another context in which one of Ruskin's key critical objects becomes key to him insofar as it provides a staging point for a conflicted sense of his own agency. Ruskin's sense of awed submission to Tintoretto's example was in place from the start. He wrote to his father during the 1845 visit, "I have been quite overwhelmed to-day by a man whom I never dreamed of—Tintoret" (4:xxxvii). Writing again the next day: "I never was so utterly crushed to the earth before any human intellect as I was to-day—before Tintoret" (4:xxxviii). Striking here is the intimate and heartfelt character of this engagement. In this chapter's foregoing cases—that is, in Venice's genealogy and its architecture—Ruskin's engagement has every appearance of placing the dramatization of agency outside himself, holding it at arm's length. With Tintoretto, however, Ruskin's feelings of sympathy and identification come more sharply into focus and render a more specific sense of the internal stakes in his conflicted sense of agency.

Given Ruskin's reputation for idiosyncrasy and tendentiousness, we do well to note that he had actually adopted one already established position in a long-standing controversy in the assessment of Tintoretto. Although Ruskin occasionally asserts that Tintoretto was virtually unknown in England, the view that Tintoretto is an extreme figure had been fairly commonplace all the way from Ruskin's time back to Tintoretto's own time. In 1568, Giorgio Vasari offered a loose but vivid account of Tintoretto as one "in the matter of painting swift, resolute, fantastic, and extravagant, and the most extraordinary brain that the art of painting has ever produced."[30] Vasari's words here look like emphatic praise, but his general assessment is actually negative, on grounds that Tintoretto, for all his vigor and imagination, is too ill-mannered and irregular, working "in a fashion of his own and contrary to the use of other painters." Vasari condemned the painter especially for "working at haphazard and without design," noting that Tintoretto "at times has left as finished works sketches still so rough that the brush-strokes may be seen, done more by chance and vehemence than with judgment and design" (2:509). Of course, one should not discount the role here of another point of contestation—that of Tuscan versus Venetian art, with Vasari writing in Tuscany—but it seems fair to see in Vasari's account an aspect of a more general Renaissance viewpoint that celebrates the controlled management of passion and deplores immoderation.

The subsequent ups and downs of Tintoretto's reputation resolve into a historical narrative tracing how given critics or groups of critics are disposed to judge a figure who steps outside established boundaries and regards the passionate development of an idea as more crucial than refinement in detail and finish.[31] In the seventeenth and eighteenth centuries, Tintoretto's reputation declined precipitously, and exactly in keeping with progressively more elaborate academic investments in rationalism and then neoclassicism.[32] Toward the end of the eighteenth century and into the nineteenth, with a romantic reassessment underway, notable early influences on Ruskin would already be making emphatic claims for Tintoretto's merits. According to the artist Frederick Goodall, Samuel Rogers often recalled the artists (including Turner) who visited Italy after the fall of Napoleon and declared the work of Tintoretto to be their greatest experience there.[33] Ruskin's admiration of Tintoretto is to be understood, then, in the light of a larger historical shift toward romantic values. These values, in turn, are largely coextensive with a romantic celebration of originality and genius, embracing an ideal of individual striving and encouraging dubiousness about academic emphases on formalism, rules, and technical fluency.[34] Tintoretto's disregard for exact finish, then, was not something for Ruskin to dispute; on the contrary, it no doubt indicated for him a creative vigor and propulsiveness of exactly the sort he would celebrate in *Stones* and elsewhere.[35]

A typical burst from his 1845 letters to his father showcases Ruskin's sense of the artist's titanic power and, crucially for my argument, specifies Ruskin's construction of that power as vigorous overstepping: "Tintoret don't seem able to stretch himself until you give him a canvas forty feet square, and then—he lashes out like a leviathan, and heaven and earth come together. M. Angelo

10. Tintoretto, *Massacre of the Innocents* (1582/1587). Scuola di San Rocco, Venice. Image courtesy of Alinari / Art Resource, N.Y.

himself cannot hurl figures into space as he does, nor did M. Angelo ever paint space which would not look like a nutshell beside Tintoret's. Just imagine the audacity of the fellow—in his Massacre of the Innocents one of the mothers has hurled herself off a terrace to avoid the executioner and is falling head foremost and backwards—holding up the child still" (4:xxxviii; Figure 10).[36] Thus can Tintoretto, notwithstanding his historical location in a Renaissance that Ruskin otherwise deplored, be aligned in Ruskin's eyes with the vitality and the bold but principled expressiveness he admired in the Venetian Gothic.

Although my examples so far have shown the urgency in Ruskin's sense of Tintoretto's power, only a closer look at Ruskin's claims and his argumentative assumptions can show how this sense of urgency bears on any specific issues of agency. What sort of power is at issue in Ruskin's accounts? And if the power is styled as Tintoretto's, how does such power acquire and sustain a claim on Ruskin's interest?

An ideal focusing point for these questions is Ruskin's treatment of Tintoretto's *The Crucifixion* (1565; Figure 11), for we have here one of Ruskin's most careful discussions of a Tintoretto painting and, also, an instance in

11. Tintoretto, *The Crucifixion* (1565). Scuola di San Rocco, Venice. Image courtesy of Alinari / Art Resource, N.Y.

which Ruskin construes Tintoretto's aesthetic power in a less conventionally dynamic sense than in the foregoing examples, which might too easily seem like blind esteem for represented action. In the same letter of 1845 in which Ruskin marveled at the dynamism of Tintoretto's *Massacre of the Innocents*, he goes on to commend the artist's "touch of quiet thought in his awful Crucifixion. There is an *ass* in the distance, feeding on the remains of palm leaves. If that isn't a master's stroke, I know not what is" (4:xxxviii). When Ruskin's extended observations about Tintoretto take their first published form the following year in *Modern Painters* II (1846), he makes plainer the sort of power to be located in the image of the ass. There *The Crucifixion* constitutes "the most exquisite instance" of "The Imagination Penetrative," which proceeds not through effects of combination (the work of "the Imagination Associative") but instead through apprehension of inward essences (4:270). This "highest intellectual power of man" (4:251), underwritten for Ruskin by his faith in a truth beyond all merely logical presentation, seldom takes shape in art by focusing on external appearances. Instead, this imagination takes possession of meanings in an indirect but thereby all the more powerful manner. In assessing the historical and psychological conditions that sustain specific styles of readerly interest, it is important that we clarify how this idea of strength added through indirection gains its appeal. What is involved in supposing that something is won through such indirection?

That quality of indirection emerges for Ruskin in two elements of *The Crucifixion*: the rendering of Christ and the man on the ass. If painters commonly render the enormity of the crucifixion either through direct suggestions of Christ's "bodily agony, coarsely expressed by outward anatomical signs" or by trying to render Christ's serene expression, "that countenance inconceivable by man at any time" (4:270), Tintoretto departs from that routine, instead filling the painting with "various and impetuous muscular exertion" but casting Christ's body in "perfect repose.'" What is more, rather than render the countenance of Christ with a clarity that would be necessarily reductive, Tintoretto puts it into shade and suggests the Agony only through an ashen glow of light around Christ's head, a glow that is in fact poignantly outmatched by the light of the sunset in the background. With the image of the ass we find an even starker instance of effects that are simply rendered and, for Ruskin, thereby all the more richly adequate to the ideas at hand. The image, Ruskin explains, recalls the King of Zion, arrived on this scene on an ass five days prior. The king signals a witnessing of "this madness of the people" (4:271) during Christ's final days: "In the shadow behind the cross, a man, riding on an ass colt, looks back to the multitude, while he points with a rod to the Christ crucified. The ass is feeding on the *remnants* of *withered palm-leaves*" (4:271), such as were strewn before Christ as he entered Jerusalem several days before his crucifixion.

The painting was but one of many by Tintoretto that won Ruskin's lavish praise. (Several times, Ruskin called the enormous *Paradise* in the Ducal Palace the greatest picture in the world.[37]) The effort of response was for Ruskin a staging of his own interpretive agency. In his "Venetian Index" to *Stones*, conceived as a guide to travelers, Ruskin offers sixty-one detailed descriptions of Tintoretto works adorning the walls of the Scuola di San Rocco. Leaving *The Crucifixion* to the last, he simply says, "I must leave this picture to work its will on the spectator; for it is beyond all analysis, and above all praise" (11:428). At such points, Ruskin is announcing at once an inadequacy to his object and a considered perception of that object as something beyond his powers. It is crucial that we realize the general interest of this divided standpoint, this assessment that is not one. For there is more than a hint of the sublime in the stance Ruskin here occupies—more than a hint of that Kantian sublime, at least, defined as the heightened consciousness of one's own supersensible vocation, wrought from a sense of the limits of one's own cognitive organization.[38]

In *Praeterita* (1885–89), the fragmentary autobiography that was to be Ruskin's last characteristic statement, he touches powerfully on Venice and Tintoretto together. His fullest statement appears in his narration of the 1845–46 trip to Venice, in the company of his friend J. D. Harding. Ruskin's regrets about Venice are conjoined here with his abiding sense of Tintoretto's grandeur. Notwithstanding the seeming opposition of sentiments, however, the whole of the passage also reveals Ruskin's underlying sense that Venice and Tintoretto alike meant for him an imperilment of his original and proper agency:

It was only for Harding's sake that I went on to Venice, that year; and, for the first week there, neither of us thought of anything but the market and the fishing boats, and effects of light on the city and the sea; till, in the spare hour of one sunny but luckless day, the fancy took us to look into the Scuola di San Rocco. . . . very earnestly, I should have bid myself that day keep *out* of the School of St. Roch, had I known what was to come of my knocking at its door. But for that porter's opening, I should (so far as anyone can ever know what they should) have written, *The Stones of Chamouni*, instead of *The Stones of Venice*; . . . and I should have thought out in full distinctness and use what faculty I had of drawing the human face and form with true expression of their higher beauty.

But Tintoret swept me away at once into the "mare maggiore" of the schools of painting which crowned the power and perished in the fall of Venice; so forcing me into the study of the history of Venice herself; and through that into what else I have traced of told of the laws of national strength and virtue. I am happy of having done this so that the truth of it must stand; but it was not my own proper work; and even the sea-born strength of Venetian painting was beyond my granted fields of fruitful exertion. Its continuity and felicity became thenceforward impossible, and the measure of my immediate success irrevocably shortened. (35:371–72)

The language tells of powerlessness: Ruskin is led fatally astray by "fancy," "swept away," and forced into the study of Venice, all this resulting in an alienation from "my own proper work." For all of the differences in his often dour characterizations of Venice and his affirmations of Tintoretto, both terms come to seem, in such passages, like distinct faces of the same coin. His life, it seems, has been a tale of aesthetically charged hijacking, with Ruskin himself the victim, making do. What emerges here is a surprising conjunction of powerlessness and an idea of critical agency now styled as a *failure* of power. We have here something like what Charles Altieri has called, in the ostensibly quite different context of postmodernist self-conception, a "sublime of self-disgust," a heroism solidified through a kind of self-undoing called criticism.[39]

Today, this vertiginous assertion of a critical power that professes not to be power is called theory. The confluence of subjection and critical insight animates literary and cultural history since at least the Althusserian and poststructuralist moments. I look most carefully to these larger contexts in this study's final chapter, in connection with contemporary readings of Oscar Wilde. For the time being, I will suggest that a tendentially liberal conception of operative, purposive agency underlies moments when subjects reflect on their subjection or declare insight into their blindness. Wherever insights into blindness arrive as usable or useful, what subtends the argument is nothing other than a logic of reflective liberal agency—or as in the last Ruskin quotation, a related self-conception along the lines of a Kantian sublime. In Kant, of course, the nub of the issue is how our finite sensual apparatus relates to our capacity of reason, which can engage ideas like infinity that sense cannot. More generally at issue in my argument is who we must take ourselves to be when we style ourselves as navigating or acting strategically in the face of such basic contradictions concerning the location and the purview of critical reflection.

On Ruskin's Contradictions

> *Mostly, matters of any consequence are three-sided, or four-sided, or polygonal; and the trotting round a polygon is severe work for people any way stiff in their opinions. For myself, I am never satisfied that I have handled a subject properly till I have contradicted myself at least three times: but once must do for this evening.*
>
> —Ruskin, address to the Cambridge School of Art, 1858

Ironic here is Ruskin's embrace of contradiction as a matter of principle. Only by such means, he suggests, might one accomplish the variety of perspectives that together make up a more adequate objectivity. In urging this view, Ruskin implies a critique of the practical rationality enjoined by Enlightenment theory, for which *principle* and *self-contradiction* are impossible bedfellows. Several decades later, Nietzsche would tender a point much like Ruskin's, arguing influentially that recourse to multiple perspectives establishes the modern vision of objectivity.[40] But an essential problem in such views lies in how we are to understand the sort of insight here generated. And perhaps a conceptual affinity of Nietzsche and Ruskin has to be allowed on this point, in that each seems bound to rely on a conception of an underlying will that disdains values of consistency and dispassionate knowledge, extolling in their place a vitalism that trumps objective truth with subjective passion. Self-contradiction, in this light, emerges not simply as a resource for objectivity but also as a *sign* of vitality. And in that latter respect, I suggest, we can begin to specify how the appeal of these large figures—who, in the words of another such figure, Walt Whitman, "contain multitudes"—depends on our interest in a specific ideal of agency, understood as individual vitality gratified in its will by managing somehow the competing mandates and influences that inform that will. To spotlight Ruskin's engagement with a modern liberal ideal of original agency, I have looked in this chapter to his treatment of Venice at several levels: the genealogy of the city itself; its architecture as a drama of moral decision; and finally the artist Tintoretto, a figure that Ruskin identified with even as he wished also to paint Tintoretto as a creator without parallel or equal. We can ask some larger questions now about the critical accomplishment of Ruskin himself.

In Ruskin's own time, critics often spotted out contradictions in his work to support dismissive accounts of his thinking overall. It was said, for example, that his theories of art were incoherent in celebrating exact detail in the Pre-Raphaelites while also insisting on the greatness of Turner, whose washes of color do not call ideas of exactness and precision quickly to mind. Sometimes Ruskin responded to such charges by insisting that he had been misunderstood.[41] In the case of Turner, however, his point was generally that Turner himself had been misread. Ruskin averred that Turner's "truth to nature" was in fact indisputable, and even in a famous case where Turner removed Shakespeare's Juliet to Venice, Ruskin's defense insists on Turner's exact verisimilitude, with the rendering of Venice "accurate in every particular, even to the

12. Joseph Mallord William Turner, *Bridge of Sighs, Ducal Palace and Custom-House, Venice: Canaletti Painting* (exh. 1833). Clore Collection, Tate Gallery, London / Art Resource, N.Y.

number of divisions in the Gothic of the Doge's Palace" (3:637).[42] It is especially worth noting this defense of Turner in the light of my foregoing discussion of Ruskin and the Ducal Palace, for Turner's own Venetian images of the Ducal Palace never rendered the windows of the Palace exactly, and, what is more, he seems not even to have rendered them the same way from image to image. In *Bridge of Sighs, Ducal Palace and Custom-House, Venice: Canaletti Painting* (exh. 1833) we get the whole sea façade of the Ducal Palace, but there, three of the four raised windows are rendered on a lower level with the two original windows that are in fact the only low ones (Figure 12). In *Venice, the Bridge of Sighs* (exh. 1840), in turn, we get only half of the Palace's sea façade, but that is already enough to show that the windows are quite differently rendered, departing not only from the facts of the building but also from Turner's prior rendering of it (Figure 13). Of course, these points are unlikely to influence any current assessments of Turner or of Ruskin. But especially given that Ruskin's defense of Turner proceeds from an account of Turner's exactness and verisimilitude, it is worth asking how it happens that Turner's inexactness and failing verisimilitudes can seem ungermane to our assessment of Ruskin's thought. Here, I suggest, we are prone to find but another face of Ruskin's own

13. Joseph Mallord William Turner, *Venice, Bridge of Sighs* (exh. 1840). Clore Collection, Tate Gallery, London / Art Resource, N.Y.

ideal of robust variation, no longer a matter of Gothic idiom, however, but of Ruskin's own critical self-conception.

In our time, nothing unites affirmative readers of Ruskin more clearly than their cheerful attitude toward his propensity to self-contradiction. This attitude, while most apparent in settings such as academic conferences where more casual characterizations are apparent, can be traced in writings back to the revival of modern interest in Ruskin and has resulted lately in a widespread sense that his less orderly later writings, especially *Fors Clavigera*, are really his crowning achievement.[43] On the face of it, readerly pleasure in Ruskin's ambivalence and incoherence might seem odd, but several factors have worked to dispel even any sense of oddness here. Following on widespread familiarity with models of psychology descended from Freud, ambivalence and contradiction have come to seem more or less intrinsic to the human, or at least the modern Western, mind-set. What is more, values of common sense and logical consistency are ritually unmasked by post-Enlightenment theorists as the work of ideology or, in the case of deconstruction, as signals of a broader Western logocentrism to be rethought. These accounts, and others besides, dispose readers today to a forgiving and indeed potentially celebratory sense of Ruskin's contradictions, which can now be understood to reflect either his humanity or his heroic engagement with confusions and uncertainties that he has simply inherited from the culture at large.

There is more to say, however, about what might underlie the contemporary reception of Ruskin's contradictions. And it bears directly on ideas of critical agency at issue in the broadly modern context. I suggest that, just as Ruskin's relation to the complexities of Venice reflects his interest in an image of his own subjective agency as complex, our contemporary relation to Ruskin's contradictions in turn reflects our own aspirations and appetites as agents. If readers smile on Ruskin's contradictions, the smile signals an affectively powerful disposition toward a figure construed as at once embroiled in the terms he has to work with and aspiring to rise above those terms to some meaningful, perhaps strategic purpose. In that figure is a quintessence of liberal critical agency, and, as such, an object with which modern liberal agents might identify. In this view, Ruskin's self-conception is a scene of contradiction that we are disposed to preserve as such, the better to stage there our deepest uncertainties concerning the ultimate nature and purview of critical agency.

For all that, we might remain uncertain about the representative character of so idiosyncratic a figure as John Ruskin. One could even suppose that this dynamic of self-reflection and critical agency is specific to the elite, masculine social position of the Victorian sage. To give such uncertainties due consideration, the next chapter takes up a broader cultural fact, a preeminent Victorian cause célèbre.

Chapter 3

The Work of Imposture: The Victorian Public and the Tichborne Case

A true story: in 1866, one Arthur Orton, wayfaring son of an East London butcher, quits his life of small adventure in Australia to return to England and assume the identity of Sir Roger Tichborne, who was presumed lost at sea over a decade prior. Sir Roger's mother, the Dowager Lady Tichborne, recognizes him as her lost son, as do numerous friends and family servants who earlier knew Sir Roger. Most of the Tichborne family dismisses Orton as an impostor, however, and he eventually enters a civil action to gain possession of the Tichborne estate and baronetcy. The suit collapses after almost a year of testimony, whereupon the judge immediately brings criminal charges of perjury against the "Claimant" (as Orton has come to be popularly designated). After a second lengthy trial the Claimant is sentenced to fourteen years in prison. Massive public interest follows both trials. Beyond the general merriment over the Claimant's obesity—provocatively at odds with Sir Roger's slightness of build when he left England (Figures 14–15)—public interest is extravagantly divided. The case occasions much skepticism in the middle classes and "respectability," but an energetic popular movement takes shape on the Claimant's behalf, featuring mass demonstrations, fund-raising rallies, broadside wars, souvenirs, popular songs, and parliamentary petitions. Appearing in support of the Claimant are no fewer than three weekly newspapers, not counting an apparent impostor newspaper.[1] By 1884, however, when the Claimant is released from prison, the storm has run its course, and he becomes a show-hall curiosity. In 1898, the Claimant dies penniless in London. Thus a very rough synopsis of the exceedingly complex "Tichborne case."[2]

Several aspects of this bizarre case warrant its inclusion in the present study. To begin, supporters and detractors alike appear to have treated the Claimant as an object of narrative fascination and fitful identification, and thus he was a kind of literary object, a foil for reflections on social or ethical agency. Further, the sustained career of the imposture was understood at the time to showcase a roguish agency on his part. In that respect, the case offers another variant on the problems of originality and authenticity that mark out anxieties proper to liberal self-conception. The Claimant's imposture, as an intersubjec-

14. Sir Roger Charles Doughty Tichborne, daguerreotype taken in 1853, shortly after his departure from England. In Douglas Woodruff, *The Tichborne Claimant: A Victorian Mystery* (London: Hollis and Carter, 1957). By permission of Random House.

15. The Tichborne Claimant, photograph taken in 1872, about the time of his civil trial. In Douglas Woodruff, *The Tichborne Claimant: A Victorian Mystery* (London: Hollis and Carter, 1957). By permission of Random House.

tive parallel to forgery or replication, anticipates issues of authenticity and originality to be taken up in this study's subsequent cases from properly aesthetic culture. More generally, the imposture echoes uncannily the "imitation of heroism" I explored earlier in connection with George Eliot's Farebrother in *Middlemarch*.

All the same, the conceptual homologies across this study's cases will not be my primary focus in this chapter, nor will I engage continuing scholarly uncertainties concerning who the Tichborne Claimant really was. I aim here to show how the public investment in this case reflects discourses of power and agency at this historical moment, revealing issues much broader than those of a merely private family squabble. To read the case in these broader terms is to follow the Victorians themselves. The tendency for public discussions of the Tichborne case to expand into diatribes over such topics as law and class was marked enough that journalists regularly had to step back and remind themselves and their readers that here, in the end, "the simple and sole issue is identity."[3] The high stakes of this social contestation, and the adaptability of this case to a broad array of social debates, allowed the improbable figure of the Claimant to dominate Victorian popular consciousness from the end of the 1860s to the late 1870s. The case's best recent historian, Rohan McWilliam, sees the Tichborne Claimant as the rallying point for perhaps the most significant movement of popular agitation in Victorian Britain between the decline of Chartism in the 1840s and the rise of organized socialism in the 1880s.[4] Just as the O. J. Simpson trial in the mid-1990s gained most of its public attention through its readability in terms of racial tensions and modern celebrity culture, the Tichborne sensation indexed large-scale social concerns of its own moment.

For most of the twentieth century, those social concerns were read as class conflict, with the working classes supporting the Claimant and the upper classes doubting his claim. Indeed, during the Tichborne trials—and in the interval between, when the Claimant toured the country in a campaign to fund his defense—the populations that came out in his support drew mainly on the working classes, on the so-called labour-aristocracy of skilled artisans, and also on a fairly broad economic spectrum of the female population. When the Claimant visited the lower-class Millwall section of London on 6 July 1872, the entire district effectively shut down, so widespread was the interest there in his cause.[5] A similar shutdown of the more affluent Mayfair or Chelsea districts would have been out of the question. In recent decades, however, following a more general trend in historiography, scholars have treated the case less in terms of class and more in terms of popular politics, in an effort to comprehend axes of social agency such as gender, race, religion, and nation, all typically underplayed in traditional class analysis.[6]

Here I argue for liberal subjectivity as one such axis of identity, not reducible to economic terms however profoundly imbricated in them. Very generally, I correlate opposition to the Claimant with an affirmation of middle-class, cosmopolitan, increasingly secularist, broadly liberal, and preponderantly male cultural authority. I also suggest that what Rohan McWilliam has called the "curious pastiche"[7] of support for the Claimant can be rationalized to some extent by the tendency of that support to stand opposed to one or more of those foregoing rubrics—*not* middle-class, *not* cosmopolitan, *not* secularist, *not* broadly liberal, and/or *not* male. Beyond those merely negative characterizations, however, I also defend a positive claim: those supporting the Claimant characteristically proceed from an embattled perspective of natural law and morality, set over against an increasingly powerful and broadly liberal conception of value reliant on positivist and secular-materialist premises. In my account, then, the Tichborne case reveals a symbolically charged contest between an older conception of social order, allied with ideas of natural law and moral realism, and newer conceptions of social power and ethical agency expressive of liberal culture and its protocols of reflective and critical self-management.

By these means I hope to present mid-Victorian liberal agency as an idea in contention with other important ideas of social and ethical agency. The Tichborne case is appropriate for this purpose, because it so dramatically showcases the period's actual diversity of thought and viewpoint. Depending on where we look, we find apparently earnest sympathy for the Claimant; cynical pleasure in his rabble-rousing; outrage at his affronts to respectability and property; or disdain of the entire matter, with the latter sentiment often expressed through resentment at the story's acknowledged monopoly on everyday conversation. Even the kaleidoscopic variousness of mid-Victorian public culture consists of reckonable shapes and relations, however, and I aim to show how debates about the Claimant's subjective agency and his objective authenticity—is he or is he not the real Sir Roger?—consistently reflect identifiable public contestations over the distribution and the sanction of social power.

I begin with a selective summary of the case to convey the terms through which it gained such notoriety and to lay groundwork for the remainder of the chapter, which explores the rhetorical tactics and substantive commitments distinguishing opposition to the Claimant and support for him. Only by reading this case through these large and sometimes vaguely fathomed differences can we understand how Victorian mind-sets toward the Claimant became so bizarrely discrepant that each side was more or less obliged to construe the other side as mad or vicious. And in that respect, we encounter this case's greatest purchase on this study's most general issues—of standpoint, argument, evidence, many-sidedness versus one-sidedness, and cultivated versus uncultivated social agency.

Outline of the Tichborne Affair

The last undisputed appearance of Sir Roger Tichborne was in 1854, when he set sail from Brazil on the *Bella*. All aboard were presumed drowned when the ship disappeared on its way to Kingston Jamaica. But Sir Roger's mother never gave up on seeing her son alive. Ten years later she placed advertisements in papers, offering a reward for information as to his whereabouts. Her advertisement appeared in Australia as well, on a rumor that survivors of a shipwrecked *Bella* might have ended up that way. A solicitor in Sydney who had noted the local advertisement soon picked up on passing comments by a client, Tomas Castro, a butcher in the outback locale of Wagga Wagga. Castro had mentioned having some unclaimed properties back in England, and he also made a passing comment suggesting his involvement in a shipwreck. Upon further questioning, Castro allowed that he was indeed Sir Roger Tichborne, living (as was common enough at the time in Australia) under an assumed name. This man was to become the Claimant.

He explained that the *Bella* had sunk, leaving him and a handful of crew members to float in a lifeboat until they were picked up by a ship bound for Australia. His lowly occupation as a Wagga Wagga butcher was explained with reference to Sir Roger's apparently undoubted distaste for a life among his family and the Hampshire aristocrats, a distaste certified by his departure for unpredictable wanderings around the globe. Now communications with the Dowager Lady Tichborne were struck up and led to a meeting between her and the Claimant in Paris in January, 1867, whereupon the mother promptly recognized him as her son. For countless subsequent supporters of the Claimant, the mother's acceptance was the chief point lending credibility to his assertion of identity. Mother and son lived on in this way, as Lady Tichborne had wealth to sustain them both. But she had strained relations with the rest of the Tichborne family, which regarded her as a foreigner (she had been born in France) and an eccentric. It does seem that she was highly strung, and people later came to suspect either her motives or her sanity. After her death and in the heat of the public sensation, the mainstream press pulled no punches on this question: "whether or not the Claimant was Roger, the poor crazy old lady was determined to recognize him, even before she saw or knew anything about him."[8]

In any case, it came about in this way that the Claimant spent over a year living as Roger Tichborne without concerted challenge to his identity but also without acknowledgment from most of the Tichborne family. Things came to a head only after the death of Lady Tichborne in March 1868, whereupon questions of inheritance became urgent for the Claimant. After many travails and negotiations between the Claimant and the Tichborne family, the case finally came to trial as a civil action in 1871. The case was initiated by the Claimant himself, who pressed for restoration of the estates to him. The estates were at the time legally possessed by Sir Roger's young nephew, the child of Sir Roger's younger brother, who himself had died young in 1862; the Tichborne house was then occupied, however, by a tenant, Colonel Lushington, who was privately siding with the Claimant, so impressed was he with the Claimant's knowledge of the property that he felt him to be the real Sir Roger.

The civil trial ran from 10 May 1871 to 6 March 1872. Although the length of the trial was unprecedented, it was followed closely in almost all the daily and weekly newspapers, as was common enough with Victorian trials. I have already noted that interest in the case divided very roughly along class lines—with the laboring folk inclining to the Claimant and the wealthier establishment and respectability disposed against him—but popular discussion turned on numerous themes and on a colorful array of characters on both sides. Miscellaneous social antagonisms over speech, manners, and pastimes played a large role, as people debated whether the Claimant was vulgar or merely cavalier in the manner of insouciant privilege. (This debate all the while turned on an underlying question of whether years in the Australian bush would or would not affect the bearing of an authentic gentleman.) Also apparent was a sometimes virulent anti-Catholicism among many supporters of the Claimant, as the Tichborne family was Catholic, and the establishment's apparent preference for the family as against the Claimant came to look like one more alarming sign of Rome's foothold in the higher reaches of society.[9] Also, and hardly least, the public was fascinated by the Claimant's ever-increasing corpulence. For detractors, his great weight offered fodder for endless jokes and caricatures, which permeated conversation and the press. Already portly at 224 pounds upon leaving Australia in 1866, the Claimant weighed in at 388 pounds by the time of his civil trial in 1872.[10] To his supporters, the Claimant's weight signified a jolly disregard for thrift, self-discipline, industriousness, and other sanctimonious virtues that the Claimant could be esteemed for discounting.[11] Furthermore, people could ponder an ancient family curse that seemed to be finding here its fulfillment: a Lady Tichborne from the time of Henry II extracted a promise from her reluctant husband to contribute food to the local poor each year, and if this "Tichborne Dole" were to fail, so went her curse, so then would the Tichborne family line. Remarkably, the rather arcane details of the ancient curse started to be fulfilled after the tradition was abandoned in the 1790s.[12] And still another facet: a since-retired black servant to the Tichborne family, Andrew Bogle, prominently supported the Claimant, and people could debate the prospect that Bogle was feigning support for the Claimant to exact revenge on his erstwhile masters.

Through these and other themes, the Tichborne affair possessed everyday consciousness. Edward FitzGerald, translator of *The Rubáiyát*, could praise Anthony Trollope's *The Eustace Diamonds* by noting that the book was almost as interesting as the Tichborne case.[13] Novelists were, in fact, at work on Tichborne-inspired novels featuring lost heirs.[14] Himself among these writers,

16. "Tichborne v. Mudie's!" *Punch* 61 (25 November 1871): 220.

Trollope later had to allow, "We poor novelists had not, amongst us, the wit to invent such a grand plot as that!"[15] An illustration in *Punch* suggests that the Tichborne drama amounted to a "bad outlook for the lending libraries," so obsessed had the public become with their daily newspaper reading in the case (Figure 16). The plot thickened decisively when the Tichborne family uncovered evidence in Chile connecting the Claimant and a figure named Arthur Orton, and during the trial the family developed a charge that the Claimant was none other than Arthur Orton. So the issue came to assume this provocative shape: either the Claimant was a lost nobleman being cynically held from his birthright, or he was the scheming son of a Wapping butcher. And both of these alternatives—so starkly at odds as to seem like matter for a fable—gained remarkable substance through testimony supporting each side in the dispute.

Those who doubted the Claimant's identity as Sir Roger were incredulous that his supporters could look past the Claimant's obliviousness respecting key points of Sir Roger's life. The Claimant could not speak French, a language from Sir Roger's childhood; he was unable to distinguish ancient Greek from Latin, despite Sir Roger's training in classical languages at school; he initially mistook his own mother's Christian name; and, more vaguely but perhaps as decisively, he showed at best a spotty observance of gentle manners. On the other hand, supporters of the Claimant could point beyond Sir Roger's mother's belief in his claim and cite numerous other individuals who also recognized the Claimant as Sir Roger, including assorted persons in Hampshire and figures who knew Sir Roger from his brief period of military service. Such recognitions were not simply or even usually based on a sense that the visual evidence was conclusive. More often, the evidence lay in the fact that the Claimant knew things that only Sir Roger should have known. Anecdotes to this effect proliferated in the pro-Claimant press: "when Mr. Onslow first met the Claimant on his return to England in 1867, at a gentleman's house, (a shooting party) Mr. Onslow, mimicked [Sir Roger's father] Sir James Tichborne when a bird was killed, upon which the Claimant said, 'Ah! I see what you are at; you are taking off my poor father; but you ought to say "Really, really."'" This was a constant saying of Sir James Tichborne's."[16] What is more, many persons supporting the Claimant were, unlike the Tichborne family itself, beyond suspicion of self-interestedness, as they had no property at stake.

The end of the first trial came as a "non-suit," meaning that the Claimant's counsel dropped the claim without relinquishing the right to press the case again. The mainstream press tended to regard this conclusion as evidence of an imposture.[17] But even newspapers strongly opposed to the Claimant felt obliged to allow, in a widely circulated statement issued at the end of the first trial, that his "claim was supported by 85 witnesses, comprising his own mother, the family solicitor, one baronet, six magistrates, one general, three colonels, one major, two captains, 32 non-commissioned officers and privates, four clergymen, seven tenants of the estate, 16 servants of the family, and 12 general witnesses, who all swore to his identity. The claim was denied by the oaths of only 17 witnesses."[18]

As if these numbers did not already make the failure of the Claimant's case look a bit odd on the face of it—how, after all, did seventeen witnesses outweigh eighty-five?—several other aspects of the case's conclusion fired popular suspicion. Many found it strange that the attorney general, John Duke Coleridge, had offered himself as counsel against the Claimant. Not only was it uncommon for an attorney general to lead such civil actions, but the depth of Coleridge's emotional involvement in the case was plainly apparent to observers early on, especially in the caustic rhetoric of his cross-examinations and his epic summation, which lasted twenty-six days.[19] Still more suspicious was the "tattoo evidence." Late in the trial, a former friend of Sir Roger emerged to declare that the real Sir Roger was tattooed. As the Claimant was not tattooed, this evidence was supposedly conclusive. But it was derided by the Claimant's supporters, who saw here only a suspiciously delayed introduction of evidence that should naturally have been introduced early on. Thus arose a sense among supporters that this claim had simply been cooked up to order. Another problem was the jury, in which the Claimant's supporters saw landed prejudice, because one qualification for membership in the jury was the possession of substantial property. This jury indeed was credited with bringing about a sudden and, by some accounts, premature end to the civil trial: shortly after the tattoo evidence was offered, the jury foreman made a brief formal statement that "the Jury do not require any further evidence."[20] This development was understood by the Claimant's counsel, no doubt correctly, to foretell a loss for his side, and it was in this context that the Claimant's case was withdrawn as a non-suit.

In words that would come to seem mere wishful thinking, a reporter declared, "Now that we know—or at any rate think we know—who the claimant is, the public interest in the case seems to have died away, and in short time people will begin to wonder how they could ever have felt any curiosity about the matter at all."[21] As it turned out, the keenest expressions of public involvement were yet to come. The judge decided to turn the Claimant over for criminal trial on charges of forgery (later dropped) and perjury.[22] The judge was not alone in evincing a rather vindictive attitude toward the Claimant, and one more fact of the trial evidence seems to have played a key role in generating this animosity in the upper ranks and the respectable: in the course of the trial, the Claimant had committed the most ungentlemanly of disclosures by suggesting that he, as the youthful Sir Roger Tichborne, had sexual relations with his female cousin, who had been an informal fiancée prior to his departure. This woman, now the Lady Radcliffe, was actually present in court to hear this imputation tendered, and there was great venom among those who supposed the Claimant to be either a liar or a seducer willing to defame his ostensible cousin. The Claimant's supporters, in turn, accepted an alternative account, namely, that the Claimant's confidence on this matter was betrayed by his own counsel and that he was then legally obliged to tender the statement under oath.

The ensuing criminal trial, which ran from 23 April 1873 to 28 February 1874, offered little by way of substantially new evidence in the case. But from the very announcement that a criminal prosecution would be pursued, suspicions flared among those who felt that corrupt establishment interests were determined to crush this solitary and now bankrupt individual. A number of circumstances informed popular sentiment here. The purse of the state was opened freely to the prosecutors, so that more funds were available to support travel for far-off prosecution witnesses from Chile and Australia than were available for bringing in corresponding defense witnesses. Six of England's most highly regarded barristers were put on the task of prosecution. The judge himself, Chief Justice Sir Alexander Cockburn, was a notably stern judge in this era, and he was widely regarded as prejudiced against the Claimant even before the trial, a charge that seems to have been true.[23] Between the two trials, as supporters of the Claimant began to organize with speeches, demonstrations, and parliamentary petitions, the court of Queen's Bench charged key supporters with contempt. Each of the two MPs who spoke in defense of the Claimant was assessed a £100 fine, and later fines would follow for these individuals and others besides. A priest who had known the school-age Sir Roger

Tichborne, and who been one of the Claimant's respectably placed supporters in the civil trial, was unable to repeat his testimony in the criminal trial because he had in the interim been consigned to a lunatic asylum.

The Claimant's counsel in the criminal trial—an extraordinary eccentric
named Sir Edward Vaughan Hyde Kenealy—became a flashpoint all his own,
a figure through which popular sympathy could articulate itself, and a figure,
as well, that respectability could roundly deplore. Kenealy's professional credibility as a barrister combined powerfully with his proclivities as a demagogue
and intellectual agitator. He was much more inclined than the Claimant's previous counsel to dramatize the image of a corrupt state apparatus contraven-
ing a mother's recognition of her son. Kenealy also proved quite capable at
exposing genuinely problematic aspects of the prosecution's case. He had some
success in questioning the credibility of the person who had brought forth the
"tattoo evidence" in the first trial, and he made much hay out of a discovery
that several documents used by the prosecution, allegedly written by the
Claimant, were in fact forgeries perpetrated by a lay opponent to the Claimant
and furnished under false pretenses to the prosecution. Although he was an
able advocate in these and other respects, Kenealy's conduct was generally hyperbolic and contemptuous of state and law during and after the criminal trial.
Shortly after the criminal trial, he was disbarred, whereupon he founded the
Englishman, a Tichbornite newspaper that featured his railings against the system and landed him in still more hot water.[24] From the viewpoint of popular
support for the Claimant, however, Kenealy's status as pariah only added to his
luster, confirming his role as a righteous martyr to this antiestablishment cause.

The Claimant's conviction came down on Saturday, 28 February 1874, after
a half-hour's deliberation by the jury. Publishers had spent some months under
a judicial order of silence on the case, brought about by the immoderate rhetoric of the pro-Claimant press and the stumping campaign. Now all were free
to pronounce on the matter, and numberless statements appeared in newspapers and other ephemeral media.[25] This reflection on the sensation offers
one account of the case's bizarrely protracted course:

> The most prominent circumstances which appear to have held the juries so long in sus-
> pense . . . seem to have been the following: the recognition of the Claimant by his sup-
> posed mother; the number of acquaintances of the real Tichborne who swore by his
> identity with the Claimant, many of them being above suspicion of collusion; the num-
> ber of circumstances related by him which had unquestionably occurred to the real
> Tichborne, and which were supposed to be known only to him, and the coolness with
> which he bore a long and trying cross-examination. To this should be added an argu-
> ment urged by many, that an ignorant butcher would not have wit enough to invent or
> sustain the part of Roger Tichborne with such cleverness and vraisemblance.[26]

That statement might seem fairly judicious, given that the class condescension
in the last point is held at some distance from the writer's own persona. But the
statement is plainly wary of the Claimant's position, if only in the fact that the

length of the trial seems to be the point that demands explanation. Writers supporting the Claimant's position were much more likely to pose questions about the seeming inequitableness of public prosecutions. Why had such inordinate national expense and legal personage gone to this case when the government had recently refused to prosecute at all in a prominent embezzlement scandal?[27] And with perhaps another case in mind, a newspaper not otherwise disposed to side with the Claimant observed, "That the claimant should be prosecuted is an appropriate sequel . . . but we cannot help contrasting the readiness with which the Government steps in when a rich family is believed to be attacked by an obscure individual, and the disgraceful laxity evinced when a public prosecution is suggested of financial or Joint Stock Company rogues of good social position, who have robbed the share, or policyholders, of a large concern."[28]

My argument about mid-Victorian culture requires only as much of the narrative as I have laid out here, because social contestation over the Tichborne Claimant was already well constituted by the time of the interval between the two trials, when the Claimant went stumping about the country to raise funds for his defense in the criminal trial.[29] But it bears noting that the public sensation had hardly run its full course at this point. A mass movement in support of the Claimant persisted for several years, notably in annual Easter demonstrations at Hyde Park. The most hyperbolic of the Tichbornite newspapers, Kenealy's *Englishman*, did not appear at all until a few months after the criminal trial, and it ran until 1886. To judge by the number of Tichborne societies and the attendance at public demonstrations, the pinnacle of pro-Claimant feeling was in the year following the criminal conviction, and that support tapered only slowly throughout the 1870s.[30] But this same period also saw the splintering of support for the cause into varied and even incommensurable interests. The *Englishman* had become so much a staging point for Kenealy's own messianic program that the editors of the defunct *Tichborne Gazette* felt obliged to resume publication of their newspaper in order to preserve the question of "Sir Roger's cause" as such.[31] The Claimant himself, meanwhile, sat in prison until he was discharged in 1884. Upon his release, lukewarm popular support came his way, and even those holdouts who remained concerned to defend the rights of a sorely abused figure soon came to deplore the Claimant's role as a kind of sideshow freak, because he was appearing for money at music halls and variety shows. His claim on popular sympathy had outworn its welcome.

This relaxation of popular support and even of popular regard for the case no doubt reflects some general, essentially transhistorical, considerations: the public was exhausted and bored by the story, disinclined to fight a cause with no clear legal goal in sight, and so forth. But the Claimant's moment was distinctively a matter of the 1868–74 period, as well, and to that extent, his case was not so amenable to the terms of the 1880s. It seems like a striking coincidence, given this study's concerns with liberal agency, that the 1868–1874 period—embracing the death of Lady Tichborne at the beginning and the final conviction of the Claimant at the end—also marks out exactly the period of Gladstone's first ministry, by all accounts the high point of proper Victorian political liberalism. While the exactness of the chronological parallel is surely coincidental, I mean here to argue the substantial relevance to the Tichborne sensation of the political events in these years, especially as regards the attempted fusion of liberal morality and liberal public policy in the mid-Victorian period.

The Tichborne sensation becomes more graspable, that is, to the extent that we view its contentiousness in the light of this period's social and political trends, most importantly the progression from a decisive Liberal electoral triumph in 1868 to an equally decisive Liberal defeat in 1874. The early 1870s see newly clear fault lines developing between liberalism and various aspects of radicalism and conservatism. Gladstone's 1868 victory was credited largely to his image as a spokesperson for "the people," and the period of his ministry saw a remarkable sequence of Liberal legislative acts. But Gladstone's loss to Disraeli in 1874 is commonly credited to working-class disaffection following those very acts—it is said, for instance, that the Licensing Act of 1872 interfered with their drinking and that the Criminal Law Amendment Act of 1871 vitiated the protections for organized labor supposedly secured through the Trades Union Act of the same year. Even the Education Act of 1870 had sowed popular discontent for religious and financial reasons.[32] But another, much broader story seems to be at issue here as well. Shortly after Gladstone's 1874 defeat, a letter headed "The Difference Between Whiggism and Republicanism" appeared in *Reynolds's Newspaper*, and the figure signing Gracchus there can be taken to voice a rather widespread sentiment.[33] The letter argues that Bright's and Gladstone's fall from favor among the masses, and the recent Tory victory, are not due to the passage of liberal legislation, such as the Licensing Bill or the Education Act. Instead, the fall reflects a more general sense that these progressive statesmen have given up on proper Republicanism.[34]

Underlying this failure was popular displeasure with the increasing presence of the state in Victorian institutions and daily life, and the increasingly interventionist logic of liberalism. *Lloyd's Weekly London Newspaper*, directed at the lower-middle and working classes but also consistently cool on the Claimant, complains: "Have we settled with Government about Mr. Ayrton's Park Bill? Are we satisfied with the waste of public money which Mr. Gladstone is to be permitted to make for his army scheme?" This remark arises exactly in the context of a brief report about the Tichborne Claimant, who was then awaiting bail in anticipation of the criminal trial. For *Lloyd's*, the sensation is a distraction in the nation's political life: "Have we, in short, no serious work left to do; that we are provided with accounts of the manner in which 'the claimant'

17. "The Old Man of the Sea." *Punch* 61 (18 November 1871): 209.

stirs his gruel?"[35] An earlier *Punch* illustration made much the same point (Figures 17–18).

The Liberal party's success and the defeat alike were due to the changing relation of working-class and radicalist constituencies to the Liberal party in these years. Much as the Claimant lost favor with his support, the Liberal party effectively outwore its welcome, and with much the same working-class and radicalist constituencies.

Opposing the Claimant

Mainstream press accounts of the Claimant's case are often so snide and dismissive that it seems important as well as useful to begin with an example. The immediate context, in this example, is the conclusion of the Claimant's first trial:

For a time society has been relieved of a great burden. The man from over the sea has dropped from our shoulders. The one all-pervading presence has experienced at least a temporary eclipse. The large person from Wagga Wagga, whose fortunes had taken possession of the British tongue for more than a hundred days, has collapsed. The corpulent claimant, whose name has added a new terror to the English dinner-table, is for the time extinguished. The story which has been for so many months the choicest weapon in the armoury of boredom is closed. No more is the great TICHBORNE conundrum to puzzle the wisest. No more is the British citizen called upon, on peril of his reputation, to have an opinion between ORTON and TICHBORNE. Butcher or baronet has ceased to be the one topic of modern conversation. We breath again after that dreadful infliction. Men are able once more to talk freely without being compelled to say what they think of the TICHBORNE case. Mankind are no longer racked with the question as to whether the heir of that venerable but somewhat unpleasant Hampshire family did or did not go to the bottom in the Bella."[36]

The remainder of the article's opening paragraph—I offer about half of it here—reiterates with additional flourishes and pomp that the claimant has been forced to give up his case, that he is very fat, and that the public is free at last think about something other than his protracted trial. Such venom and immoderation are the rhetorical equivalents of a smoke that tells of fire. But what exactly is ablaze here?

To judge by the reporter's subsequent remarks, the debacle just passed highlights problems in the legal system as it was then constituted. It was a widespread refrain that such a case should not have taken so much time to decide. For the *Morning Post*, the Claimant's case had "always seemed a transparent fraud."[37] Another newspaper: "the TICHBORNE trial is certainly an instance of the necessity of keeping in reserve a power to check the prolixity of litigants."[38] Later in the article from which the long quotation above is drawn, this point takes the form of a piteous plea: "Is there no way by which the course of justice may be accelerated?"[39] After wading through that very reporter's sentences, however, we are well placed to note that the deplored prolixity of the litigants and the exultant prolixity of the reporter, while arrayed opposite each other, each reflect assertions of viewpoint and position that insist on themselves at length, and repetitiously, precisely because the cases are hardly as clear and simple as advocates on either side wish them to be. Respectability's assault on the Claimant needs to be read as an assertion of specific middle-class social-power forms and, concomitantly, as an attempt to put lower-class social forces on guard.

Generally, the greater a newspaper's or magazine's pretensions to speak from and to a middle-class perspective at this time, the more emphatic that pe-

18. "The Old Man of the Sea" (detail). The lower-right portion of the whole image has the Claimant distracting public attention from the key projects of Gladstone's Liberal administration, including Army Reform, the Education Act and—central to several of Gladstone's most controversial moves—Ireland. *Punch* 61 (18 November 1871): 209.

riodical's opposition to the Claimant. The *Pall Mall Gazette*, for example, was early and always dismissive of the Claimant. Although one of its writers was a cousin of the Tichborne family,[40] the nature of response to the Claimant in other newspapers and magazines suggests that the *Pall Mall Gazette*'s opposition was defined more by the magazine's social positioning than by any such coincidences of personal involvement. The *Times*, the *Daily Telegraph*, the *Standard*, the *Morning Post*, the *Illustrated London News* and, indeed, all newspapers with a mainstream, middle-class outlook reported on the Claimant in ways that suggest resistance to his case's merits.[41]

At times, the reportage was stridently oppositional: the Claimant was clearly "a low-born, vulgar, illiterate brute" and just as clearly not "the representative of one of the oldest families in England, who had confessedly received a liberal education, held a commission in her MAJESTY's service, and mixed, whilst a young man, in the best society."[42] At other times, reports would offer some pretense at open-mindedness but nonetheless indicate that the whole affair was a social headache or a dismal comment on the state of public action: "It is nearly time that the London daily papers should commence to have some mercy on their readers. Seven or eight columns a day for several months of the private affairs of the Tichborne family, this has been the regular quantum, and this has been kept up to the sacrifice of much more interesting and important matter."[43] Sometimes, opposition to the Claimant would take the form of ignoring incidents that spoke at all to his favor, and this was especially the case in the limited reportage concerning popular demonstrations on his behalf. When papers opposed to the Claimant reported at all on pro-Claimant rallies, they were prone to underline episodes in which the pro-Claimant crowds hissed down or expelled any skeptical individuals who dared to speak up.[44] The more serious organs of the working-class press—such as the *Bee Hive*, a proto-socialist trades union newspaper—generally ignored the sensation as well.[45] This latter point suggests that the more embedded a newspaper was in the practical political discourse of the time, the less likely the paper was to devote dispassionate attention, or any attention, to a cause perceived as renegade, impractical, and incredible in the bourgeois public sphere.

An article published anonymously by Walter Bagehot makes clear that the newly enfranchised working classes could factor explicitly into a moderate liberal understanding of the Tichborne sensation. Bagehot, a preeminent voice of self-inspection for the mid-Victorian Liberal middle class, emphatically opposes the sentiments of the Claimant's sympathizers. But his statement is also uncommonly judicious and usefully oriented toward substantive rather than merely invective discussion. Writing one year after the Claimant's criminal conviction, and less than two months after Kenealy's election to Parliament, Bagehot marvels at the ongoing support for the Claimant. He notes that the Tichborne crowds at a recent Hyde Park demonstration actually exceeded, in spirit of conviction and perhaps sheer size, the assemblies preceding the passage of the Second Reform Bill less than a decade earlier.[46] In this context, he notes further, "The belief—incredible as it must seem to all persons of trained intellectual powers—that Roger Tichborne has been excluded from his rights and thrown into prison by a Papistical conspiracy is much more potent than any mere feeling that a vote is a right, and that a poor man should have it as well as a rich man, which is what the demand of the masses for representative reform really came to eight or nine years ago. And this belief is plainly beyond the reach of argument or evidence."[47] Even while implying that the Tichbornites should reflect more self-critically on the bases of their convictions, Bagehot also credits the sincerity of feeling behind their grievances. He acknowledges "the secret, unformed, but potent conviction of many among the lower classes that the well-placed and well-to-do are in an eternal conspiracy against the poor, the weak and the humble. And this suspicion transfers itself from persons to things, till at the bottom of many minds among the artisans and labouring classes is to be found a settled habit of regarding the Law, the Legislature, the Executive Government, and the Church, as so many instruments for keeping them down in the world and fencing in the successful from all risks." Thus Bagehot diagnoses a syndrome in the "lower classes," consisting of recalcitrance, anti-intellectualism, and persecution complexes. And any review of Tichbornite engagement with the case's points of evidence reveals their steadfast refusal to credit materials that contravene their preferred interpretation—thus, for example, the Claimant's early mistake in recalling his mother's full name is disregarded as evidence against him while his mother's recognition of him as Sir Roger is pointed to as holy confirmation of his identity. So it seems fair to say that Bagehot's diagnosis has some basis in the facts: Tichbornites are not conspicuous for a reasoned and dispassionate relation to their cause.

On the other hand, when Bagehot ventriloquizes the sentiment of the "lower classes" here—the sentiment, namely, that state and church apparatuses are best understood as mechanisms serving the perpetuation of exploitative social relations—it is hard today not to recognize in their supposed "viewpoint" some of our contemporary commonplaces of critical social theory. Consider Althusser's treatment of the Church as a signal medium of ideological interpellation, Foucault's arguments about institutional conduits of liberal "governmentality," Bourdieu's diagnosis of aesthetic "taste" as a means of social discrimination and hegemony, and the New Historicism's conclusion that even constructions of individual agency tend to function as culturally determined "strategies of containment"; it is plain that many of the most influential critical paradigms of the last several decades affirm something much in keeping with what Bagehot would have us dismiss as lower-class "madness."[48] Although Bagehot uses the term *madness* in connection first merely with the electors of Stoke-upon-Trent who recently placed Kenealy in Parliament, he is also noting that "they are not alone in their madness." For Bagehot, if we may judge by a close inspection of his language, the issue in public regard for the Claimant is sometimes one of greater or lesser degrees of "trained intellectual powers"; at other times, he construes lower-class sympathy for the Claimant, or for Kenealy, as a matter of "madness."

In common English usage, the difference between being untrained and being insane is usually quite firm. While characterizing the lower classes in this Tichborne context, however, Bagehot oscillates between these two terms, because he is inclined to take very much for granted the normative force and the integrity of a principled, as opposed to an emotional, foundation for conduct. Both the untrained and the insane are equivalently unfit to judge, it seems, so the difference between the two is moot. He couches his concern for proper judgment in terms of the franchise debate from the previous decade. Recalling how the main objection then concerned the ignorance of the lower classes and their consequent unfitness to judge as voters, he insists now that their unruly sentimentality provides "an equally cogent objection." The lower classes "give anything that fastens on their emotions an altogether disproportionate significance. The fact that Lady Tichborne recognized the Claimant as her son is the one piece of testimony in the Orton case, that the lower orders are capable of appreciating, and this they consider conclusive. It is the sort of consideration they regard as *moral*."

Bagehot does not dilate on what he means by *moral*, but his remarks overall suggest that he means to distinguish conviction substantiated by reason and considered judgment from conviction substantiated by mere feeling. Bagehot sees the pro-Claimant population as addled emotionalists. Here we can note that the morality that can proceed from mere feeling is one or another version of emotivism, in which that which is good or right is understood to be equivalent to that which one affirms in feeling. Against the emotivist alternative, Bagehot holds out an ideal of considered judgment, a facility won through the training of intellect. Here, where critical reflection stands poised to raise us out of our thralldom to inchoate feeling, we have liberalism's dearest philosophical prospect. But in his construction of the pro-Claimant demonstrators as emotivists, Bagehot overlooks the more likely basis of pro-Claimant moral conviction, at least as the demonstrators themselves would more likely describe it.

Liberal moral psychology, whether in its Kantian elaboration or in the ideal of self-regulation pervading the mid-Victorian middle-class culture, styles moral conduct as a sort of heroic self-discipline. When Dickens's David Copperfield, for example, is infatuated with Dora Spenlow, he wonders whether a letter to her two aunts, the Misses Spenlow, might help him circumvent her father's injunction that he not speak to her. He puts this question to the exemplary Agnes, and she lays down a liberal precept, a program of self-regulation: "Perhaps it would be better only to consider whether it is right to do this; and if it is, to do it."[49] This sort of attitude surely does stand more or less opposed to the emotivist logic that Bagehot attributes to the Claimant's supporters, by which lights one would not ask what action is right but rather what action is welcome. But by putting reflection and deliberation at the root of moral decision, Agnes (like Bagehot) is not merely jettisoning naïve emotionalism. She is also questioning an ethic of immediate moral conviction that looms large among the Claimant's supporters. The Claimant's supporters, as I will soon try to show, more likely argued from a deep-seated sense of moral realism, a conviction that fact and value are conjoined matters and amenable as such to human perception. In contrast, the liberal standpoint valorizes procedures of rationalization and deliberation that issue in reflective and ultimately contingent commitments. So it is not exactly the case, at least in their self-construction, that pro-Claimant crowds thought that their feelings alone can determine what is moral. Bagehot describes them that way, however, because he ascribes to them a habitual failure to engage in reflection and self-bracketing.

Perhaps it reflects Bagehot's anxiety at the increasing sway of mass opinion that his concluding words foreground his anxiety about posterity's perception of the facts here. He observes ruefully that, given the enormity of the movement on behalf of the Claimant, future historians will be inclined to suppose "that the crowds who protested their belief in the rightful pretensions of the Claimant, had 'something to go upon.' Yet the history of this delusion shows that extensive contemporary belief may exist, may be a passion with hundreds of thousands of persons, not only without any foundation in reason, but in spite of the most complete, and, to any trained intellect, the most convincing refutation." Here, too, Bagehot sets the figure of the "trained intellect" in opposition to the pro-Claimant crowds. His Liberal political stance emerges in this warning to reckon with the newly meaningful fact of poorly educated masses in the British population. In his view, widespread sympathy for the Claimant and the subsequent election of Kenealy to Parliament each illustrate the absurdities that the British public must now contend with as a result of the increased role of working-class sentiment in the public sphere. It is very much a function of mid-Victorian political life that this circumstance would seem to have tendrils throughout social life. In these same years the Liberal but anti-democratic Robert Lowe was being widely cited for a sentiment he had voiced upon the passage of the Second Reform Bill: "We must now educate our new masters."[50] The agency behind Lowe's "we" is not exactly that of the propertied establishment. It is a liberal agency both in its self-conception and in its vision of cultivating Victorians.

Writers voicing working-class perspectives at this time had much to say about sanctimony and condescension underlying many of this period's projects of cultivation. The "journeyman engineer" Thomas Wright wrote in 1873 of the poor bedeviled by do-gooders: after bracing themselves for "the exceeding quantity and infinite variety of visitation and inquisition to which they are subjected," the poor are all the more soured by their knowledge that the philanthropists "come to the cottage in a manner in which they would never dream of approaching the mansion."[51] For Michael Roe, popular support for the Claimant plainly reflected popular hostility toward the encroachments of a hegemonic "respectability."[52] Thus supporting the Claimant could seem—to some people, at least—like snubbing the increasingly intrusive moralizing advanced in the self-help arguments so widely circulated in these years by the likes of Samuel Smiles.[53]

We can gain some view of this contention by looking to an 1872 address by Lord Shaftesbury, long a notable figure for his efforts on behalf of improved housing for the working classes.[54] One Saturday in August, even as the Claimant was stumping about the country to drum up funds for his defense at the criminal trial, Shaftesbury laid the first stone at a model village in Wandsworth called Shaftesbury Park Estate. Efforts toward improved housing for the poor were not exclusively liberal. Indeed, paternalistic Toryism legitimates itself morally by enjoining the lord to look benevolently after those below him. A sounder way to discriminate between liberal and conservative sentiment in this regard lies in spotlighting the effort in liberal policies to elevate and cultivate working men, to put them in a position of social progress. Conservative thinking improves housing to sustain a peaceful social hierarchy, with an injunction in mind such as that offered famously by Disraeli: "the palace is not safe when the cottage is not happy." Liberal thinking, by contrast, improves housing to improve the workers themselves and, in effect, to make the workers more like their citizenly middle-class brethren.[55]

The properly liberal progressive approach runs throughout much (but not all) of Lord Shaftesbury's address, which I quote selectively, but also at some length:

We have founded this day a workman's city ("hear," and applause), and we have founded it upon the very best principles. We have founded it upon the great principle of self-help, and upon the great principle of independence. . . . I like the principles you have laid down for your guidance. You have shown your wisdom in a moral point of view by excluding publichouses and the tap room. . . . There are schools for the children, and there will also be a library and reading-rooms for yourselves, and a clubroom, where you will have the advantage of indulging in beneficial amusements. I hope, however, you will not forget the women, who are by far the best part of you, let me tell you. (Laughter.) In those intellectual amusements take care that your wives and daughters are not excluded, for you will find there is no social progress without the aid of the female sex. . . . I am delighted, too, to find that you have established a recreation-ground in the centre of your city for the healthy enjoyment of your children; but I would strongly urge you not to devote this space to flower beds and gravel walks, but to leave it free for cricket, for football, and for all those manly and exhilarating games by which the healthy development of the body may be promoted and secured. The schools which will be established I hope will be turned to good account, and thus save your children from the temptation of the pothouse and the "penny gaff."[56]

Several matters are worth highlighting here. To begin, the "you" that Shaftesbury addresses does not correspond, it seems, to any actual person who would be living in Shaftesbury Park. He suggests that this "you" has wisely prescribed the banning of public houses, when in fact public houses were banned in all housing projects built by the sponsoring organization.[57] There was never any such thing as a vote taken among likely residents-to-be. Also, we can judge by other text in the *Times* story that Shaftesbury's comment about preferring playing fields for "manly" exertions[58] over flower beds and benches along gravel walks is motivated by a determination on his part to plead against the indications of a lithographed plan of Shaftesbury Park Estate, which actually stood there on that occasion and *specified* flower beds, benches, and gravel walks. To the extent that future residents might have heard this speech, they would seem to constitute a version of what Garrett Stewart, writing of second-person address in this period's fiction, has called a "conscripted audience."[59]

In these and other ways, philanthropic projects can arrive heavily loaded with lessons and morals that might initially look like generosity but that in fact underline a highly specific ethos of middle-class progressive conduct. And these values themselves begin to assume a nakedly quietistic bearing in Shaftesbury's concluding remarks. "There is nothing so economical as humanity," he later declares, meaning that the humane treatment of the poor saves wasteful expenditures later in public-support schemes. "The domiciliary condition of the people involves health, comfort, and happiness. It also involves contentment, and people who are contented always give a Government less trouble than those who are not. When men are contented, they become excessively reasonable, and employer and employed find that their interests are identical. They must hold together, and by united action give force to progress."

Shaftesbury's declaration that residents might become "excessively reasonable" under the model village's blandishments is peculiar. Does excessive reason boil down to unreason of some sort? We can wonder about possible errors in the reporter's transcription, but a vaguely thought-out desire for intensification could also explain such language. In that conveniently hazy light, excessive reasonability emerges as the fulfillment of a vision of social harmony, whereby the interests of the employer and the employed are felt to be no longer incommensurable but instead identical. Coming from the likes of Foucault, of course, the expression "excessively reasonable" could hardly be more apt, signaling, as it would, the triumph of a liberal governmentality, establishing a richly elaborated and docile subjectivity in service to the maintenance of the bourgeois state.[60]

Shaftesbury's points overlap in key respects with those that we saw earlier in Bagehot. While Bagehot's tone is grim and Shaftesbury's tone is, in contrast, loftily upbeat, both men set a renegade potential of the social spectrum over against the prospect of a reflective, learned social domestication. The demos might refuse that invitation to sober reflection (Bagehot's complaint) or embrace it (Shaftesbury's hope). From our critical perspective today, however, we are fairly well placed to suspect, even to perceive, a good deal of hegemonic content in the vision of rational citizenship that Bagehot and Shaftesbury offer. The "trained intellectual powers" that Bagehot speaks of, like the workers' "excessively reasonable" identification of their own interests with those of their masters, look very much like terms in service to an emerging middle-class and liberal progressivism.

Sympathy for the Claimant

Although middle-class and respectable society generally dismissed sympathy for the Claimant as madness or idiocy, that sympathy was indeed widespread, powerful, persistent, and deeply implicated in the social and political landscape in these years (Figure 19). What motivated masses of English sympathizers to embrace a cause so remote from their own immediate interests? The question is especially pressing, to the extent that one wishes to argue for an idea of interest along class lines. As I noted at this chapter's outset, modern historians of popular politics such as Rohan McWilliam and Michael Roe suggest that class interests account poorly for the actual contours of the Tichborne sensation.[61] To be sure, contributors to the Claimant's defense fund were not from the working classes alone but instead spanned the entire social spectrum.[62]

My own sense, however, is that the major exhibits in that line of historical argumentation do not get us far away from class as a key. Horace Pitt-Rivers, Lord Rivers, took an early interest in the cause and was responsible for calling the barrister Kenealy into the affair.[63] But it seems that Rivers's support hinged to some large degree on his initial sense that the Claimant was clearly a gentleman in manner, and doubting the Claimant later would have entailed doubting his own skills in assessing station. The MP Guildford Onslow was a tireless supporter, although his support also reflected in part a sense of duty to the deceased Lady Tichborne, to whom he had made assurances of continued support for the cause before her death. The MP George Whalley was actively involved, but an opportunism fed by his notoriously venomous anti-Catholicism has to be factored heavily into our estimation of his investment in the cause. After the criminal trial, when Kenealy traveled England giving speeches, he often held two meetings, aimed separately at middle-class and working-class audiences. These events—late in the sensation and absent the then-imprisoned Claimant—should be understood to reflect support as much for Kenealy himself, with his movement on behalf of free-born Englishness.[64]

In short, the Claimant's prominent supporters from the upper classes are each more readily graspable as special cases than as indications of the Claimant's appeal in the middle and upper ranks of society. Often, his highly placed supporters needed to defend themselves against public charges that they were fomenting class conflict, apparently understood by many observers to be of a piece with rallying support for the Claimant.[65] The *Sunday Times* offered a

19. The Claimant greets his supporters. Unknown publication data. Image taken from a period scrapbook. By permission of the London Library.

typical view of the Claimant and his support: "That he was a favorite of the masses of people was evident from first to last, and the utter failure of his case is another proof that the judgment of the masses is unworthy of reliance."[66] In a climate where class interests so palpably inform the discussion, there is no avoiding the sticky question: Why any popular zeal at all for restoring wealth and title to a prodigal son of the aristocracy?

The pro-Claimant press and rallies themselves throw one promising answer into high relief: supporters were outraged at the thought that an innocent individual was being excluded from his birthright by corrupt establishment forces. Insofar as the Claimant appeared to be a victim of unjust exclusion, then, he could be a sympathetic image in broadly popular terms, notwithstanding his ostensibly noble standing. When the Claimant's fund-raising campaign was underway between his civil and criminal trials, the Tichbornite press was strident about the failures of justice: "Lawyers may cram their clients with the stale aphorism that Law is the perfection of Reason; but there is good *reason* for fearing that the ADMINISTRATION of the law in England is gradually becoming the perfection of INIQUITY."[67] Such complaints drew their sustenance from concrete instances both within and without the Tichborne case proper. The foregoing quotation turns immediately on an episode in which the

Claimant's parliamentarian supporter George Whalley had petitioned the legislative body for funds to be put at the Claimant's disposal, so that the Claimant might stand some chance of matching the state's expenditures in gathering prosecution witnesses from Chile and Australia. The petition was rejected on ordinary procedural grounds—there was no precedent for such parliamentary funding—but the Claimant himself was derided openly in Parliament and Whalley's willingness to speak at fund-raising rallies on the Claimant's was mocked as a "mountebank performance."[68]

The Claimant's popularity appears to have depended on a widespread state of social-political contestation over the practical and theoretical administration of law. Apparently a virtuoso on the instrument of popular feeling, the Claimant hit this very note in his most memorable public declaration. Initially incarcerated after his failure in the first trial, he published his "Appeal to the British Public" in several newspapers. His bid for financial support in preparation for his criminal trial effectively conjures the image of a solitary and unjustly accused individual, about to be crushed by the iniquitous system of law and the personal venom of its insiders: "I am not surprised at six counsel being engaged at the expense of the country; my only wonder is that the Attorney-General, who will on the approaching trial have to represent the 'Crown and Justice,' did not employ the whole of the English Bar to crush me, to gratify the personal feelings he has expressed."[69] He comments further that every legal maneuver seems to have been employed to restrain him from release on bail. (Indeed it does seem that such efforts were vigorously pursued and rather smugly regarded by the middle-class and respectable press as proper.[70]) Thus the Claimant's ringing conclusion: "Cruelly persecuted as I am, there is but one course that I can see, and that is, to adopt the suggestion so many have made to me—viz., to 'appeal to the British public' for funds for my defence, and in doing so I appeal to every British soul who is inspired by a love of justice and of fair-play, and who is willing to defend the 'weak against the strong.' "[71]

That the law went easier on the rich than on the poor was a widely current and barely disputable idea. Popular in the *Tichborne News* were all manner of stories reporting inordinately harsh penalties levied against men found guilty of petty theft or even for inadvertently breaking a beer glass in a pub.[72] But the bitterness of lower-class resentment depended, of course, on serious charges of large-scale inequitable treatment. The "grievance ideas" of the working classes are sympathetically glossed by Thomas Wright in various essays from the early 1870s. Wright notes how the government instated elaborate schemes of compensation for those affluent and middle-class interests affected adversely by Liberal reforms, such as the disestablishment of the Irish Anglican Church and professional changes in entrance to the civil service and army. "But when the same kind of State policy that led to the abolition of purchase and reconstruction of the Civil Service, brought about the closing of the Government dockyards, there was no talk—except to disclaim obligation in the matter—of compensating the disbanded artisans, who in a time of almost unparalleled dulness of general trade were turned adrift in shoals, to starve if they could do no better."[73] The recent application of laws banning Sunday trading cut seriously into many working-class livelihoods, a point that Wright recalls in humorous style: costermongers who had been fined for plying their trade on Sunday turned the establishment's logic around to lodge summonses against the coachmen of the lord mayor and the Marquis of Lorne for plying their avocations on Sunday. Predictably, observed the working men, the magistrates who had earlier professed having no choice but to punish under the law found that the law did not require enforcement in this case. Wright brings his point to a head:

> The things that sting and rankle, that perpetuate and intensify class jealousy and hatred, are such as the invention of kleptomania for the benefit of the well-to-do pilferer; the manner in which "mad doctor" theories are allowed to stand between the gallows and well-to-do murderers; the abolishing imprisonment in bankruptcy cases, and not in the cases of county-court debtors; the "raiding" upon small betting-houses, while Tattersall's remains untouched; and the attempt to close public houses on Sundays, while leaving the clubs—the public houses of the rich—unmolested.[74]

Such matters of real or apparent unfairness were quite graspable and therefore widely debated.[75] And thus we need only assume two things to rationalize popular interest in the Claimant: (1) interest in greater social respect and autonomy for those so moved; and (2) an affective function that we might describe through the term *identification*, whereby these persons find in the Claimant's tale, not their own exact predicament, but instead a sufficiently recognizable image of the social predicaments that they find themselves confronting in their own concrete forms.

Such explanation, however, leaves the explanatory role of *interest* and *self-imaging* underexamined. Such explanation, that is, first casts as a problem the fact that numerous, largely working-class figures somehow came to regard the comfort of an ostensible aristocrat as a matter of personal interest. Then this explanation offers as a solution the observation that there is, after all, a way to understand the Claimant's plight as sufficiently equivalent to working-class circumstances, through the metaphor of disenfranchisement, to make sense of their interest. First the place of interest is presented as provocatively unclear, and then the place of interest is recuperated in a saving critical perception. But the Tichborne sensation gives us some cause to question what we actually must mean by ideas like interest and identification, and what the role of these terms is in determining individual and collective action. For it is not so clear what it means to "make sense" of many actual aspects of pro-Claimant feeling.

The mysteriousness of that feeling was not lost on Victorians. "Perhaps nothing has been more remarkable in this way than the sources of sympathy for the Claimant," writes a reporter for the *Saturday Review*, just after the Claimant advertised for funds to secure bail after his first trial: "His evident pluck and the romantic character of his story appealed strongly to the popular taste; but his chief attraction to the mob which used to cheer him seems to have been a kind of confused notion that somehow or other he was fighting their battle, and vindicating the rights of a butcher, or, at any rate, of a man with a butcher's manners, to a place among the aristocracy. They would probably not have insisted so strongly on his being Roger if they had not half believed him to be Orton."[76]

This idea of half-belief in the Claimant indicates a prospect that merits much more scrutiny than it commonly receives. Historians of this case often suggest this prospect only to drop it. After testifying to the sincerity of feeling in the pro-Claimant crowds, for example, Michael Roe observes in passing that it "might be even more true, although less logical, that maximum interest in the [Claimant's] case resulted from simultaneous belief in both the truth and the falsity of the claim."[77] The very idea of a "more true" although "less logical" viewpoint is deeply problematic in general, and it gains some urgency once it is admitted as a vision of social or ethical agency. The idea of half-belief presents problems, for one thing, when one wants mind-sets to be accountable, defensible, reckonable, acting according to interests, and rational. How will we construe a psychology of half-belief in the Claimant's cause? What does a state of half-belief feel like? How does one act on such a belief? And crucially, who is in a position to see half-belief as such? Is half-belief perhaps never self-consciously one's own, but always someone else's? All these questions bear on ideas of agency, and on the collective identity that we might assign to pro-Claimant crowds. I argue here that the state of half-belief presents a sort of limit-case concerning what can or should count as an agential identity at all.

In part, we can understand half-belief in terms of a psychological state— say, ambivalence—in respect to which the Claimant can be an idol of popular discontent simply on the basis of a generically human fascination with roguery. Conspicuously unencumbered by respectable values, the Claimant was not only obese but also a confessed seducer, a heavy drinker, an apparent philanderer, a bearer of venereal disease, and, to top it all off, a figure seeking to keep his fires stoked by living off the fat of ancestors—whether his own or someone else's. Freud often posited that figures of this sort can sometimes exert a very general fascination, as in the charm supposedly proper to "narcissistic" figures—Freud's examples include beautiful women, young children, humorists, criminals, cats, and large beasts of prey. His underlying logic: "It is as if we envied them for maintaining a blissful state of mind—an unassailable libidinal position which we ourselves have since abandoned."[78] But the universalizing cast of Freud's thinking comports poorly with the facts of the Tichborne sensation, because it is hardly true that everyone found the Claimant charming. His gustatory and carnal accomplishments both increased his hold on public attention and marked him as repellent to the respectable and the middle-class forces most exercised by his effrontery. All the same, Freud's image of a marvelousness attachable to an "unassailable libidinal position" indeed captures a perception that applied broadly in accounts of the Claimant, both sympathetic and unsympathetic. The *Morning Advertiser* remarks on a "fascination" that the Claimant managed quickly to win even over "men of position and character."[79] And this quite representative comment from the anti-Claimant *Sunday Times* appeared after the Claimant's criminal conviction: "Starting on a career of imposture which bristled with inherent difficulties of the most formidable nature, this coarse and unlettered butcher was able, notwithstanding, to maintain an attitude, that for a time staggered the faith of thousands, baffled the force of argument, and seemed to hold in temporary abeyance the very laws of evidence themselves."[80] Even in the anti-Claimant press, the Claimant's "career" looks like rogue heroism. Laid waste by this figure were several prime guarantors of respectable society, including "faith," "argument," and "the very laws of evidence themselves." (I will suppose in the coming pages that the word *faith* here has no substantially religious indication.) Such characterizations abounded, and understandably so: even today we have to struggle with the astonishing chutzpah of his endeavor. What emboldened a low-born individual to stride with confidence into the midst of an aristocratic family that he had never met, claiming he was a son of the family and a onetime member of Hampshire's broader community of nobles and gentlefolk? Sometimes the sheer improbability of anyone wagering such a claim was actually adduced as a reason for believing the Claimant. And very often, a review of the sensation's key points would culminate in abject amazement: "If . . . you set one improbability against the other, it was singularly difficult to strike a balance of credibility and incredibility."[81] Another report: "The very unlikeliness of the man, his vulgarity, his immorality, his personal appearance, weighed against, as much as for, the theory of fraud."[82] Like most mainstream newspapers, the *Standard* openly deplored the Claimant and his supporters, but even that newspaper had to allow, after his loss in the first trial, that he had made a name for himself as "the most audacious of adventurers."[83]

Such characterizations arose all but exclusively in the middle-class press, however, as the vantage point (even apart from the vituperative rhetoric) presumes that the Claimant is pulling something off. True, some working-class cynicism in the same vein was recorded. Upon the conclusion of the criminal trial, a reporter for the *Morning Post* visited pubs in Orton's home terrain, London's Wapping district, and gave this account of the scene: "[T]he Claimant's cleverness in 'keeping up the game' so long and in 'gittin these here Onslows and Whalleys to keep him on the fat of the land these eight years' was extolled in a way which was very significant."[84] Thus we can see that even where the idea surfaces that the Claimant might be a fake, a poser, his very audacity can resonate with some facets of the popular Victorian consciousness precisely insofar as his fakery comes to look like a sort of radical action—a scam, indeed, but an instance as well of uproarious agency.

Notwithstanding those remarks from Wapping, however, it proves very difficult to document much self-conscious popular cynicism. What is more, it seems presumptuous simply to assume that cynicism about the Claimant's identity was a governing factor in pro-Claimant feeling. To judge by the rhetoric of the pro-Claimant press, indeed, the charge of cynicism should be cast in the other direction. In effect, the pro-Claimant press offers a mirror claim to that which we saw in the *Saturday Review*. This mirror claim declares that middle-class and respectable critics of the Claimant's case would not have been so eager to disparage him if they had not in fact "half-believed" that he really was a defected aristocrat who compromised his standing by consorting with bushrangers for a time. Especially during the fund-raising campaign preceding the Claimant's criminal trial, notices in the *Tichborne News* confirm that supporters saw considerations of social hierarchy to be generating upper-class bad faith: "We firmly believe that the majority of those of the upper classes, who are either hostile to, or hold themselves aloof from, the Claimant, are not actuated by any doubt of his being who and what he states himself to be, but they are swayed by a morbid and *snobbish* conventionalism."[85]

When we characterize and weigh various perspectives on this case, all that remains clear is a powerful correlation between categories of social life at this time—especially, but not exclusively, class—and particular viewpoints on the Claimant's case. The middle classes and respectability were overwhelmingly skeptical of the Claimant, although they seemed interested nonetheless in the sensation, perhaps in part from the kind of psychic rationale suggested by Freud. Those sympathetic to the Claimant, in turn, were preponderantly of the working classes, although we still lack any empirical basis for supposing that an actual majority of working-class people favored the Claimant's cause. Significantly, the class-based correlation was apparent to both sides of this controversy, and in that perception, if nowhere else, there was a kind of common ground. But the Tichborne sensation also throws up profound obstacles to viewing this common ground in the light of a genuinely reciprocal understanding or debate. If we wish today to follow all credible historians in asserting that dispassionate assessment of the Claimant's case will identify there an imposture, how can we account for pro-Claimant feeling without regarding that feeling either as cynicism, naivete, or stupidity? Must we see pro-Claimant crowds as critical failures? In a word, yes.

Liberal and Conservative Reasons

The pro-Claimant crowds, understood as agents of half-belief, might well be seen as critical failures, but only in that provocative sense whereby people holding religious beliefs might also be seen as critical failures. This conclusion gains in strength, to the extent that the pro-Claimant movement is understood to proceed from a structure of feeling related conceptually and historically to conservative commitments in the face of a broadly modern rise of liberalism. This study's opening chapter already touched on the conservative altercation with liberal culture by treating Uday Singh Mehta's view that imperialistic liberalism properly consists in a lack of "reverent humility."[86] On the one hand, I viewed Mehta's claim as confused in implicitly invoking a liberal valuation of fairness. But Mehta's argument, I suggested, also stands importantly apart from liberalism, insofar as he deplores liberal reason's failure to credit "what the stranger is deeply and hence not provisionally *invested* in"—those investments including "religious piety" and the possibility of accepting a position in "an imperfectly mobile and traditional hierarchy."[87] Largely in keeping with Mehta's apparent view is Charles Taylor's concluding appeal to Judeo-Christian theism in his *Sources of the Self*, whereby the "promise of a divine affirmation of the human, more total than humans can ever attain unaided" stands as his hoped-for salve against psychic fissures wrought through liberal modernity.[88] Most relevant to my discussion are those conservative stances on ideas such as natural law, moral realism, and national versus cosmopolitan identity that make sense of the otherwise curious demographic fault lines making up the Tichborne sensation. Pro-Claimant feeling, I suggest, proceeded characteristically from a congeries of conservative viewpoints—ranging from popular Toryism to aspects of popular radicalism—that were commonly threatened by, and thereby unified in opposition to, the positivistic and utilitarian trends defining an ascendant mid-Victorian liberal culture.

This chapter's previous section treated such popular unrest concerning legal administration, an unrest fed by stories concerning inequities in the prosecutions respectively of lower-class and middle-class individuals even in the wake of the Liberal electoral sweep of 1868. Here I will call on another dimension of legal culture: a formal transition away from natural-law perspectives characteristic of eighteenth-century and earlier thinking and toward a positivist conception of law. While the increasingly embattled status of natural law since the early nineteenth century reflects some of modernity's broadest features, notably secularization, some quite specific features of mid-Victorian liberal culture can be brought into view by looking to these matters of legal theory and practice.[89] For only in the mid-Victorian period did legal positivism gain meaningful impact on jurisprudence and on actual policy and law, despite the fact that it had been articulated conceptually over half a century earlier by Jeremy Bentham.[90] What allowed at last the proper "uptake" of legal positivism was the increased of authority of liberal ideology in the 1860s. Thus by reading the conservative-liberal distinction in these terms, we can make better sense of a rapprochement underway from the early 1870s onward between certain facets of popular radicalism and the Tory establishment, both factions increasingly united in a common opposition to liberal culture.

Natural-law theory characteristically posits a superhuman authority for right and wrong, moral and immoral. This view was widely credited from ancient times into the early nineteenth century, and its standard reference point for modern argumentation is William Blackstone's *Commentaries on the Laws of England* (1765–69).[91] Legal positivism takes a different tack by asserting that law expresses and legitimates a more or less arbitrary system of human power relations. For legal positivists following Bentham, judgments of right and wrong proceed from the structure of sovereignty and from actually existing ("positive") law, not from any basis in an independently constituted morality. Although Bentham's view is fully formed and gave impetus to projects of rationalizing and codifying the law—processes understood to facilitate calculations of a given law's felicity—Bentham's critique was also historically premature, and his disciple John Austin would be the crucial figure in the rise of legal positivism.[92]

As a matter of jurisprudence, the most provocative aspect of Austin's thinking and of legal positivism more generally has been its replacement of moral evaluation with analytical assessment. "The existence of law is one thing; its merit or demerit another," declared Austin in a famous statement epitomizing the so-called separation of law and morality.[93] Questions concerning the possibility and the utility of such separation define modern contestation in jurisprudence and illuminate the liberal-conservative distinction that I here deploy. In general, conservatism refuses or resists the distinction of law and morality while liberalism founds itself upon that very distinction.[94] In arguing with the positivists that law, as such, is but the command of a sovereign—understood either as an individual or as a collective—one must candidly locate the force of law in human power relations rather than in divine sanction or in an otherwise transcendent authority. The view's liberal cast depends very generally on the humanism and social voluntarism taken for primary in the posture.

Even beyond the precincts of legal theory, the program of analytical jurisprudence and rational codification also influenced characteristically mid-Victorian institutional reforms. The 1873 Supreme Court of Judicature Act, for instance, produced a unified court structure in which all courts could administer previously separate systems of common law and equity law—often referred to simply as law and equity.[95] Over centuries, because the precedent system of common law did not allow for decisions on matters deemed without precedent, there grew a separate body of equity law driven not by precedent but by the creation of a code. These laws were administered largely in separate courts, and in cases of conflict over which body of law was properly at issue, no single agency had an especially compelling claim to authority in the judgment. Thus the frustration central to Dickens's *Bleak House* (1853), in which John Jarndyce, caught in a dismal circuit, says, "Equity sends questions to Law, Law sends questions back to Equity; Law finds it can't do this, Equity finds it can't do that."[96] The Judicature Act formally enacted a "fusion" of common law and equity, gathered oversight in a new high court, and specified that whenever common law and equity conflicted, the law of equity would prevail.[97]

Little mass attention accrued to such specific legal developments, of course, but the fusion movement was topical enough to inspire treatments in *Punch*.[98] And there is, in any case, an intellectual momentum here, with concrete social meaning. These rationalizing processes reflect broader claims of rationalization in the culture of the time, especially after midcentury with the slow rise of interventionist liberalism. Increasingly, it could count as virtuous progressivism to regularize, centralize, and systematize. So another Dickensian figure, the pompous Mr. Podsnap of *Our Mutual Friend* (1864–65), is speaking very topically when he inveighs against "centralization." Podsnap's immediate concern is the unwelcome idea of state-sponsored action on behalf of the starving poor. But his larger concern is the very idea of state interference in his actions—and his purse—for such interference is "Not English."[99] But Dickens's larger point, of course, is that Podsnap is a backward-looking creature: mid-Victorian England must learn to leave its Podsnaps behind—and, in so doing, redefine Englishness.

Austin's troubled career confirms the increased purchase of liberal thinking in the mid-Victorian period, as against the 1830s when his major writing appeared. His *The Province of Jurisprudence Determined* (1832) had been reviewed favorably enough, when it was reviewed at all.[100] But practicing lawyers and judges at the time deemed the very idea of jurisprudence absurd, and Austin's academic career stalled, never to recover. A young John Stuart Mill was among the few students in Austin's seminar at the newly established University of London in the 1830s, however, and in 1861, shortly after Austin's death, *The Province* was reissued. Now a flood of mid-Victorian writers debated the merits of his theory.[101] Austin's thinking in its key aspects—the separation of law and morality, the contingency rather than the natural authority of sovereign legitimacy, and the sanction for a rigorous rationalization of law—was romantic and Benthamite as to its historical inception but decisively mid-Victorian in its actual uptake. In that fact we find a usefully concrete means of highlighting conceptual and ideological developments between the early and mid-Victorian periods. The earlier period is marked out by the Great Reform Bill and the strivings of popular radicalism. The mid-Victorian period can be defined sociopolitically, not only by the relative falling away of radicalism and, especially, Chartism after 1850 or so, but equally by the way in which the touchstone figures and ideals of liberalism came to dominate the culture's rhetoric of agency from the 1850s through the 1870s.

With these more theoretical and speculative aspects of law behind us, we can return now to details of the Tichborne sensation to spot out a subtle contestation within the pro-Claimant movement itself, one that moves well past popular outrage at discrepancies in the legal treatment meted out to the poor and the rich. For the rhetoric in the Tichbornite rallies unselfconsciously deploys two apparently divergent means of legitimating support for the Claimant. The one line of argument hews principally to the truth of the Claimant's identity as Sir Roger Tichborne; the other view emphasizes how the Claimant should be treated, regardless of his actual identity.

While this divided stance is implicit in most meetings during the Claimant's stumping campaign in the summer of 1872, it is usefully explicit in one report from the *Swansea & Glamorgan Herald*. As the chairman of the Tichborne defense committee in Swansea, Mr. Cutting, offers his opening remarks to a typically large and enthusiastic crowd, he answers one of the miscellaneous charges recently levied against the pro-Claimant demonstrations by critics—namely, that the money gathered was simply lining the pockets of organizers. Mr. Cutting promises that

every farthing over and above the expenses would go to the benefit of the Claimant in the gigantic cause which he would have to defend. (A voice: "Call him Sir Roger.") He thanked them for the correction, but really his delicate nature—(laughter)—had prevented him from saying too much in favour of an opinion in which his own feelings were so strongly engaged. He need hardly tell them that after most carefully looking into the matter he was thoroughly satisfied that the Claimant was no other than Sir Roger Tichborne. (Loud cheers.) He did not, however, ask any lady or gentleman present to pin their faith to his sleeve. He simply asked, "Had the Claimant had fair play or not?" (Loud cries of "No, no.") He did not ask them to say that he was or was not Sir Roger—(cries of "He is")—all he said was that he had not yet had what every true Briton had a right to demand—fair play, and that they would agitate till he got it.[102]

This excerpt appears at first to spotlight a counterpoint of speaker and crowd. Strictly speaking, Mr. Cutting enjoins an attitude of indifference to the question of the Claimant's actual identity. For him, the motivation—the "cause" at hand—is fair play for free-born Englishmen. The parenthetic insertions from the crowd, however, are plainly at odds with the speaker's rationalization. In its rejoinders, the crowd rejects Mr. Cutting's invitation to treat the Claimant in, as it were, a sheerly procedural light. Two styles of pro-Claimant feeling seem plain here: one style focuses on the factual dimension of the claimant's case (he is or is not Roger Tichborne), and the other, on a value-principle (fair play) that must apply to him and to others equally.

Previous historical accounts of the Tichborne sensation would most likely see in this moment one more example of the confused—or, at least, the radically polyphonal—character of pro-Claimant feeling. I think it is mistaken, however, to diagnose a poor fit between the ethos of the speaker and that of the audience. Speaker and crowd here are hardly on the verge of an as-yet-unperceived falling out. Of course, there are differences within this Swansea setting. The speaker can be more readily seen as strategically reflective, employing a rhetoric of process and social order, while the audience members might seem like naïve realists, interested merely in their sense of the local facts. But these two different bases for supporting the Claimant would coexist for some years with relative ease. Only two years later, under the direct influence of Kenealy's *Englishman*, did the factions supporting the Claimant began to work at odds. It is striking, in fact, that they often divided exactly along the fault line that we see intimated in the Swansea meeting.[103]

At this juncture, however, these differences seem not to matter. And here we can put to work my earlier suggestion that a "structure of feeling" can be our guiding interpretive object in this case. For a unity in pro-Claimant feeling emerges in the movement's ideology of natural rights and natural law, an ideology apparently shared by all these Swansea demonstrators, speaker and crowd alike. And in this structure of feeling, these figures are united in a profound aversion to key trends in mid-Victorian liberalism. Here, as so often happens, commonalty is forged from the collective sense of an "other," and the other in this case is the ascendant liberal culture of these years.

This point is easier to establish in regard to the voice of crowd here than it is in regard to the speaker, Mr. Cutting. The crowd plainly tenders an assertive belief that will not brook question, holding it as self-evident truth that the Claimant is Sir Roger. Further, we may suppose that, for the crowd, their agitation on his behalf is authorized by that fact. In the absence of that fact of identity, we can predict the evaporation of the crowd's support. But the speaker's rather different stance—with his rhetoric of rights and due process—seems much akin to aspects of progressive liberal theory. Note that the speaker's appeal, however, is not to any ideal of universal rights. The speaker's appeal is to the rights of the "true Briton." In this form of nationalistic feeling, and in a related jingoism centered on the notion of the "free-born Englishman," we find the strand of radical libertarianism that Kenealy would draw on in founding his *Englishman* and also his *Magna Charta Association*, both ventures taken up after the Claimant's conviction and after Kenealy's own expulsion from the bar. This line of thinking is indeed different enough from the viewpoint apparent in the voice of the crowd at Swansea that the pro-Claimant movement would fragment seriously along these lines, especially by late in 1875.[104] But an overarching similarity persist in what a liberal perspective on this case would call a certain provincialism or nativism of viewpoint. We should consider in that light, for instance, Matthew Arnold's ironically intended observation that the English, for all their professed love of liberty, do not scruple at abridging the liberty of the non-English.[105] Pro-Claimant feeling, in speaker and crowd alike, stands opposed to the cosmopolitan pretensions that are gradually coming to define liberal-mindedness.

   This large speculation, inherently incautious, at least allows us to rationalize the puzzling multiplicity of positions and interests gathered in support of the Claimant. The movement was, as McWilliam has documented so well, a "curious pastiche" of causes and emotions.[106] The unity of this pastiche—indeed, the point of view that renders the movement a good deal less "curious"—lies in the movement's struggle to privilege "natural" over political authority in this and other matters. As we saw earlier in connection with natural law, the idea of the natural is prone to serve mundane interests that seek, usually vaguely, a kind of impunity from interrogation through the traditional authority of the natural. And it is in the probably ill-understood but nonetheless strong popular aversion to liberal morality that both conservative Toryism and popular working-class feeling could find a certain common cause in exactly these mid-Victorian years.

   In terms of the pro-Claimant movement, this point becomes plain in what otherwise might appear to be a very odd contradiction: the movement seems to have used the language of republicanism—cheering the name of Oliver Cromwell, for example—even as the crowds were also warmly responsive to popular royalism.[107] This conjunction is odd, in that the modern English state is founded in an act of regicide engineered by Cromwell. As Blair Worden has recently argued, however, the latter half of the nineteenth century broke with the nation's earlier conceptions of Cromwell as antiroyal radical, finally assimilating him into a more "politically ecumenical conspectus of the nation's past."[108] Where Cromwell was earlier regarded in "predominantly secular" terms as a dangerous rebel, he came after the mid-Victorian period to been seen less in those terms and more in terms of his religiously dissenting convictions.[109] In the later nineteenth century, the opposition of Tory and Whig that had long underwritten a conservative (Tory) hostility to Cromwell was replaced by a kind of rapprochement, made sensible in the face of increasing secularization and the interventions of liberal administration. At this historical juncture, that is, Cromwell and the monarch each stand as figures for a kind of older and naturalized authority. And in this respect, they are each fodder for conservative resistance to the most recent developments of liberal culture.

   Thus while we might see the difference between the speaker and crowd as a difference between the fact-mindedness of the crowd and the value-mindedness of the speaker, I mean to foreground their actual and substantive unity, which is premised on a broadly conservative refusal of the fact-value distinction itself. The various voices at the Tichborne rally are, in other words, of one party, precisely because they refuse the fact-value distinction that underlies, as Roberto Unger and others have usefully argued, the liberal tradition at its largest levels.

   In the political arena, this alignment of conservative and popular viewpoints brought about the fall of Gladstone's ministry in 1874. After several years of unprecedented Liberal legislative action—much of it seeming progressive-minded to this day, much else looking like the halting give-and-take of a democracy-fearing elitist liberalism—the Liberals were losing their claim on the symbolics of libertarianism and natural rights. Said one pro-Claimant voice in 1872, "Let no man or woman forget that the battle has been forced on the 'Claimant' by, we regret to say, a Liberal administration, which authorises and sanctions the perversion of national money to the iniquitous purpose of indirectly defeating and overwhelming one party in a family dispute, and that party the already wronged and injured one."[110]

It is in this context of popular disaffection that appeals to traditional images and values like that of the free-born Englishman gained in attractive power within the range of mass sensibilities. Those appeals, precisely in the vaguely gestural character that Disraeli would wield so effectively, became ever more the province of conservatism, understood as set over against a liberal vision of rational agency and voluntaristic sociality. From this point, the seeds are laid for a split within the Liberal party between its traditional libertarianism and its more recent interventionism. That split would weaken the party in consecutively greater fits until it effectively dissolved the party itself in the early twentieth century.

Part II
Aesthetic Agency

Part 1 of this study explored liberal subjectivity in selected historical and theoretical contexts, and the points argued there can now provide some basis for a closer examination, at last, of Victorian aesthetic agency. In Ruskin, of course, we already encountered a seminal figure in this period's aesthetic culture. But he came into mature authorship a quarter century before such works as Walter Pater's *Renaissance* (1873) set the terms for late Victorian aestheticism. And even in his later writings, contemporary with Pater's work, Ruskin entertained a substantially different vision of art's relation to morality from that vision to be found in aestheticism proper. Pater's call to burn always with a hard gemlike flame was rigorous in enjoining perpetual attentiveness but also provocatively languorous in its indifference to any social or conventionally moral grounding of such experience's value. Paterian drift can have the feel of an ethic, but for those such as Ruskin who fundamentally privilege the subscription of the self to a higher-order authority, such aestheticism must finally seem a mistaken hyperindividualism.

In the social contestation surrounding the Tichborne case, in turn, we find groundwork for a broader perspective on aesthetic culture's relation to liberal culture than has been common in recent years. In my view, Victorian ideas of liberal and aesthetic agency must be considered beyond this period's elite literary cases—a principle of selection driving otherwise telling critical work such as Linda Dowling's—if we are to understand how liberal culture or aestheticism contended with alternative cultural perspectives.[1] Thus only will we see, for example, how Walter Bagehot's dread of the "untrained intellects" supporting the Tichborne Claimant reflects a broader mid-Victorian liberal agony. And indeed, the mid-Victorian rhetoric of cultivation poses the deepest · challenges for us today in such cases as Bagehot's, for we seem obliged to allow that he has a credible point even as he also serves a hegemonic middle-class perspective. A kindred complexity emerged from my earlier readings in J. S. Mill and Arnold. It bears saying here, again, that my principal concern in all these cases is not so much to argue for the stability or unproblematic virtuousness of such liberal perspectives. Instead, I explicate these ambitions toward cultivated agency to suggest that we underread those ambitions, and our own contemporary share in them, when we see there simply hegemonic ruses easily disavowed or frowned upon today. This study's second part considers how such mid-Victorian debates over liberal agency came to inform late Victorian understandings of properly "aesthetic" experience.

It is a commonplace that artists and critics from the 1870s onward increasingly claimed for themselves a prerogative of aesthetic autonomy epitomized in the art-for-art's sake slogan. As Pierre Bourdieu has most definitively argued, albeit in connection with a roughly parallel French culture, the claim to autonomy at this time was not mere wishful thinking. In fact, it indicates a substantial development in what Bourdieu calls the overall field of cultural production, made possible when increasingly diversified social power formations come to operate independently from one another. This view invites us to see aesthetic culture as reaching a sort of critical mass, a footing within the larger culture that allowed artists to set up art as a form of cultural capital in competition with other forms of value, such as economic capital in business.[2] But it is also crucial to see that this phase in the modern history of art further establishes what Fredric Jameson sees as art's "political unconscious," engendering a newly complicated and consequential obfuscation of art's relation to larger social currents and material productive relations. What is repressed in this unconscious is not simply art's thralldom to the economic base. Aesthetic interpretation and creation also come to encode a utopian energy, an informing devotion to the premise that the world might be qualitatively rethought and remade.[3] Variations on the twofold characterization implied in Jameson's view dominate current work in literary and cultural history: we are routinely given to understand art as ideology, while almost as often, and for reasons that are seldom explored critically, we are also given to suppose that aesthetic creation and interpretation can vehiculate a kind of heightened perception with transformative potential.

As a result, literary scholars in recent decades have employed sometimes quite subtly aggrandized visions of aesthetic agency. Obviously, the works of avowedly politicized writers such as Émile Zola, Bertolt Brecht, and Richard Wright are commonly understood to solicit critical reflection on social realities. My special focus goes, however, to the manner in which contemporary critics characteristically propose that a socially conscious literary or aesthetic agency is best secured through a strategically deployed indirectness. Literary writers, that is, are supposed to sidestep the programs of assertion, argument, and evidence that drive more direct forms of critique such as social theory or philosophy. Writers take up the distinctive stance of literary authorship—indeed, of distinctively modern Western artistry in general—precisely by avowing an interest in social issues even while disavowing any "reduction" of their work to a declaration, claim, or message. To resist the reduction of literary labor to a "message" is to conceive of literary practice as an alternative form of critique, an aesthetic agency irreducible to description and axiom but nonetheless "critical." This prospect bespeaks a distinctively Kantian account of aesthetic judgment, understood as a feat of reflection poised between the regimes of "fact" and "value," provinces respectively of science and moral rationalism.[4]

In the last decade or so, critics such as Jonathan Freedman and Regenia Gagnier have related this broad pretension of aesthetic agency to British aestheticism in particular. In this light, aestheticist authors enact a distinctive version of commodity consciousness that is simultaneously implicated in, and critical of, the dominant culture's assumptions about human action and value.[5] Already in 1930s, of course, writers in and around the Frankfurt School urged similar claims—Walter Benjamin, for instance: "Baudelaire was, through his deep experience of the nature of the commodity, enabled, or perhaps forced, to acknowledge the market as an objective."[6] Since Althusser and the poststructuralists, however, a new urgency attaches to the questions about agency that Benjamin spells out but leaves undecided—is Baudelaire better viewed as *enabled* or *forced?* Styling such alternatives as too reductive, recent critical work typically layers passivity and activity over each other to arrive at an idea of active or productive determination. In that view, subjective agency is bodied forth precisely through subjection, understood in the sense of ideological conditioning. It follows that wise critical action will proceed, not from an assumption that writers and critics might gain a perspective outside ideology, but from an assumption that they must work cannily within it.[7] In picturing British aestheticism's oppositional character, then, Freedman styles his writers, not as active or reactive simply, but as engaged in a mode of "imaginative response" (3).

We can see how Freedman's argument valorizes a specifically indirect style of critical agency by looking to his governing characterization of aestheticism as an "embrace of contraries" (1). I fully credit his view that crucial divisions and instabilities inform the aestheticist ethos overall: on the one hand, we have aestheticism's militant frivolity, epitomized in Max Beerbohm's comic satires and Oscar Wilde's cello-shaped coat, an aspect of aestheticism eagerly lampooned by *Punch* and Gilbert and Sullivan and countenanced happily enough by many aestheticists; on the other hand, we have aestheticism's serious-minded engagement with alienated subjectivity, wrought in forms ranging from William Morris's socialism to the dark romanticism of writers such as Dante Gabriel Rossetti and Algernon Swinburne. Freedman argues that aestheticists circumvent the opposition of frivolity and earnestness by taking up instead a both/and relation to those terms. At the same time, however, Freedman emphasizes that aestheticism proposes no triumphant or complacent settling of these tensions. Instead, "irresolution and failure are written in to the program of British aestheticism," and Freedman rounds off the point by suggesting that "this very failure, paradoxically enough, may serve to define the ultimate ground of its [aestheticism's] value" (3).

Failure can become a ground of value, however, only insofar as aestheticists can be understood to embrace rather than merely to weather their contraries. My general point is that contemporary literary-critical work very ably reads such dynamics of *contradiction* while routinely failing to read the dynamics of agency, volition, and affect admitted in such terms as, in this case, *embrace*. (Other terms for self-conscious agency that are commonly invoked in this way include *engage*, *deploy*, and the ostensibly innocuous *acknowledge*.) After all, Ruskin embraces self-contradiction to valorize his vigorously mobile interpretive agency, as I argued at the close of Chapter 2. This mobility, I have argued, reflects a self-conception underlying the liberal ethos of many-sided reflective agency, understood both as a disposition and as a capacity to view things from different perspectives, to engage the idea of many forms of life. To the extent that we credit ideas of subjective contradiction or ethical impasse and then *also* credit certain agents with a capacity to deploy such contradictions to some critical purpose, we presume that what Freedman calls aestheticism's "resolutely double vision" (24) is something that agents are *in a position* to manage.

Such a view posits a heroic, if also complicated, aesthetic agency. I have been arguing in Part 1 that liberal subjectivity names that managerial position, that consciousness in a position not only to see itself within and without a given set of paradigms but also to act with a view to that complex self-conception. In Part 2 my concern is to suggest in two detailed cases how this liberal complexity was taken up as a basis for modern aesthetic agency.

Chapter 4

Replicating Agency: Dante Gabriel Rossetti and Victorian Manchester

This chapter treats an unlikely pair of Victorian focal points: the poet-painter Dante Gabriel Rossetti and the city of Manchester. My selection is not based on any obvious association between the two cases. While some of Rossetti's most significant art patrons lived in Manchester, and that point will be a factor in my discussion, my initial warrant for linking painter and city rests on the word *replica*: I examine Rossetti's practice of replicating his own paintings, and I examine the production in 1887, during Victoria's Golden Jubilee, of a large-scale replica of preindustrial Manchester. In one sense, the discussion depends on an abstract or formal observation, a point about the relations built into a definition: replicas rehearse what has already been and they are also, at the same time, new things under the sun. In this fact lies their bearing on the discourse of original agency that has been a part of each of this study's cases. But I also want to tender a more concrete point. In the cases both of Rossetti and the Manchester replica, engagements with replicas emerge as procedures of self-inspection—individual and collective, respectively. At issue in each case, furthermore, are self-reflections of agency, variously threatened, compromised, ironicized, and even aggrandized. In trying to uncover two concrete occasions of such self-inspection, I hope to go some way toward a careful and broad-minded engagement with this period's discourse of *autonomy*. For as an ideal with any bearing on issues of action or agency, autonomy implies not merely independence but also a kind of self-inspection, an idea of conduct founded in purposeful reflection.

I begin with Rossetti, offering a critical overview of his replication practices, outlining essential facts and points of material dispute in that regard, and then relating the sort of repetition at issue in the replica to Rossetti's self-image as an artist charged with performing one Victorian answer to the question of modern agency. In the following section, I turn to Manchester to look at replication in an apparently nonartistic context, where the replica of "Old Manchester and Salford" functions to solidify a desired civic self-image by offering a point of mediation for the contrasting material and aesthetic aspirations that gave Manchester its identity. The chapter closes with a brief critique of the rationale that we are likely to employ when we redeem Rossetti's replication practices finally as a kind of aesthetic agency while casting the Manchester replica as a scene of ideological mystification.

Rossetti and His Replicas

In January 1883, nine months after Rossetti's death, two exhibitions of his artwork opened in London and ran concurrently for several months. One show, numbering 82 items, was assembled by the Royal Academy as part of its annual Winter Exhibition; the other show, numbering 157 items, was put on by the Burlington Fine Arts Club as a special exhibition. Although Rossetti's work had been shown more often than commentators to this day often suggest, he had remained to the end an artist with negligible public exposure.[1] So the two exhibitions attracted much commentary, feeding a public concern to take stock at last of an enigmatic artist. Reviewers praised Rossetti's gifts as a colorist and his manner as an idealist and mystical dreamer; often they felt compelled to make allowances for his shortcomings in draftsmanship and in the rendering of action and perspective. But commentators unanimously commended Rossetti's singularity. Said the writer for *The Graphic*, "Whatever place in the hierarchy of Art may ultimately be assigned to Rossetti, there can be no question as to his originality. He obviously owed little to the example of his predecessors."[2] Writing for *The Nineteenth Century*, Rossetti's friend Theodore Watts (later, Watts-Dunton) makes the same point in arguing that Rossetti's art "simply represents himself" (as opposed to representing a "school"). Watts then tenders what comes to seem the standard observation: "The Rossetti note is the note of originality."[3]

These estimations are unsurprising to this day, for Rossetti—chiefly through his images of self-possessed women with superabundant tresses—remains the most stylistically recognizable of the Pre-Raphaelites. But if these two exhibitions were the first to bring Rossetti's "note of originality" into full public light, they did so along with that other dimension of his work, frequently forgotten today: his replication of his own paintings. In visiting both shows one revisited a great number of images. A walk through the Royal Academy exposed the aesthetic tourist to *Beata Beatrix, The Blessed Damozel, Dante's Dream at the Time of the Death of Beatrice, How They Met Themselves, The Loving Cup, Pandora, Proserpine,* and *Venus Verticordia.* But then again, so did a visit to the Burlington Club, where different examples of all those works were to be seen.[4]

To judge by the public commentary, the bounty of replicas had no bearing on Rossetti's distinction as an artist. Cosmo Monkhouse offered one of the few comments on replicated versions, then only to prefer quite casually two images at the Burlington Club to the corresponding images at the Royal Academy.[5] And Monkhouse's comment was motivated, it seems, not by an interest in replication as such but by the irony of preferring versions from the Burlington

Club, as the Royal Academy was the more prestigious venue, with the first pick of images.[6] Monkhouse's equanimity no doubt reflects the larger truth that such replication was commonplace in the centuries leading up to and including the nineteenth century. But recent art-historical scholarship indicates that late Victorians increasingly looked askance at replication, although up to that time patrons were paying the same price for replicated versions as for original ones.[7] The replica, it seems, was becoming more problematic in line with growing anxieties about originality and art's relation to material contexts, two cruxes often developed in connection with high modernism and the make-it-new aesthetic. And, indeed, private correspondence from the time can tell a more conflicted story than did the public reviewers. The artist William Bell Scott, writing of the Burlington Club display to the merchant and art patron James Leathart, offers a viewpoint more in line with our present-day assumptions: "It is an exceedingly interesting collection. Rossetti never had any scruple in making *replicas*, triplicas, quadruplicas, in fact he only attained to the command of a subject by repeating it, so in these two exhibitions one sees the same subject over and over again."[8]

While Monkhouse casts replication merely as Rossetti's occasion for greater or lesser accomplishment of an idea, Scott casts it as a sign of technical and imaginative shortfall. Rossetti himself internalized these contending views, and other views as well, involving the economic determination of aesthetic production In replication, Rossetti found at once a field of creative action and a reminder of his subscription to assorted psychological and socioeconomic determinations. While many Victorians were free to adopt either a sanguine or a condemning view of replicas, and many more could ignore the issue altogether, Rossetti's artistry obliged him to gather these conflicting views into his own self-image. In that sense, he illustrates the ambivalent self-conception characterizing Victorian bids to original agency in general.

In testing this account, we can try to proceed from the facts of his replication practices. Including finished studies, Rossetti produced approximately 450 works. If we exclude portraits, of which Rossetti made no replicas at all, his works number about 330, and of that number, about 40 to 50, or 15 percent, might well count as replicas.[9] But such numbers can provide no basis for sustained discussion, because any attempt to generalize about Rossetti's practice of replication must confront at least two substantial difficulties not to be treated by mere enumeration. One challenge is a matter of formal analysis and aesthetic theory: the issue there is how to judge whether a given work is a replica or, instead, a new "version" of a prior work. The second challenge is a historical matter, for conflicting accounts of Rossetti's working habits have come down to us from various quarters, and here the special point of controversy is the extent to which the replicas were actually done by Rossetti at all. I will look first at the matter of authenticity, as a prelude to examining some of the images themselves and engaging the question of their variation.

From Rossetti's death onward there have been arguments that his replicas were largely the work of his studio assistants, especially Henry Treffry Dunn, who worked with Rossetti from 1863 to 1881.[10] In his memoir, Dunn writes that his first assignment was to create a replica of *The Loving Cup*, and he implies that the assignment was a test of his suitability as an assistant: "Rossetti liked my replica so well, that when it was completed he set me to work upon something else."[11] But it should also be noted that this is the only reference in Dunn's memoir to the painting of replicas.[12] Other figures in Rossetti's circle speak more emphatically to the role of assistants: Charles Fairfax Murray, one-time assistant to Rossetti and later a collector of his works, observed in 1911 to the American collector Samuel Bancroft, "Much work of Rossetti's assistants (principally Dunn's) exists and as you know passed for the work of the master himself." Murray goes on to count the *Lady Lilith* currently at the Metropolitan Museum of Art in New York as one such spurious image, albeit touched up later by Rossetti.[13] But Murray's claim should not be taken to mean that Rossetti eagerly marketed any painting executed by his assistants. An 1896 letter by Murray, again to Bancroft, excoriates William Michael Rossetti for allowing questionable paintings and replicas left in Rossetti's studio after his death to be sold indiscriminately as works by the artist himself.[14]

In his correspondence Rossetti frequently addresses his production of replicas. A typical letter to Dunn clarifies the literally marginal role of the assistant in completing a version of *Proserpine*: "Do you think you could . . . copy these accessories into it from the other picture which is here? I have painted these twice—in Leyland's version and in the one remaining here with me—and don't feel up to doing them a third time."[15] And the topic was not an utterly confidential matter between Rossetti and his assistants, as one sees in an 1862 letter from Rossetti to fellow artist G. P. Boyce: "Would you mind lending me the Borgia drawing as I want to have a copy made of it—to be commenced by my pupil and finished by myself."[16] Like countless other letters, this one attests simultaneously to the involvement of Rossetti's assistants and also to the primary role of Rossetti himself. That balance seems to reflect the likely truth of the matter.

Examining the images themselves, we see that Rossetti's replicas vary in their degree of resemblance to the initial versions. A number of works are difficult to distinguish at first sight—for example, the *Proserpine* owned by Frederick Richard Leyland and that owned by William Turner.[17] Of the seven or eight known versions of *Beata Beatrix*, several are strikingly similar—the original, purchased by Lord Mount Temple (Figure 20); a version purchased by Frederick Craven (Figure 21); and another purchased by William Graham (Figure 22)—but some other versions of *Beata Beatrix* more clearly depart from the original. A strong resemblance is also apparent in Rossetti's two full-scale treatments of *The Blessed Damozel* (1875–78; 1875–79), in which several differences are clear but only after a bit of deliberate cross-comparison on our part,

20. D. G. Rossetti, *Beata Beatrix* (c. 1864–70). Oil, 34 x 26 in. Surtees item 168. Tate Gallery, London / Art Resource, N.Y.

21. D. G. Rossetti, *Beata Beatrix* (1871). Watercolor, 27¾ x 21½ in. Surtees item 168, R. 2. Fogg Art Museum, Harvard University Art Museums, Bequest of Grenville L. Winthrop.

22. D. G. Rossetti, *Beata Beatrix* (1872). Oil, 33¾ x 26½ in. Surtees item 168, R. 3.
Charles L. Hutchinson Collection, Art Institute of Chicago.

23. D. G. Rossetti, *Dante's Dream at the Time of the Death of Beatrice* (1856). Watercolor, 18½ x 25¾ in. Surtees item 81. Tate Gallery, London / Art Resource, NY.

revealing background variations above the head of each Damozel, and, in Graham's version (1875–78), the head of an additional child below the Damozel.[18]

Yet Rossetti's replicas just as often vary to the point that it becomes doubtful how pertinent the term *replica* is as opposed to *version*. Rossetti's two treatments of *Dante's Dream at the Time of the Death of Beatrice* are a dramatic case in point. The initial version, an early watercolor dating from 1856, was purchased by Miss Ellen Heaton of Leeds, and it presently hangs in the Tate Gallery (Figure 23). The subsequent version, executed fifteen years later in oil, was purchased by the Walker Gallery in Liverpool, where it remains (Figure 24). Journalistic accounts at the time of Rossetti's death routinely identified the later work as his major achievement. The two paintings evince a stylistic difference: the early Beatrice is modeled by Elizabeth Siddal, and the later, done in the image of Jane Morris, reflects the lusher type of female beauty that people still associate with Rossetti. Also, the photographic reproductions included here obscure a substantial size difference: the early version is really one and a half feet high and just over two feet wide, whereas the later one, Rossetti's largest work, is about seven feet high and ten feet wide.

24. D. G. Rossetti, *Dante's Dream at the Time of the Death of Beatrice* (1871). Oil, 83 x 125 in. Surtees item 81B, R. 1. Board of Trustees of the National Museums and Galleries on Merseyside (Walker Art Gallery, Liverpool).

So it is difficult to bring any rule to bear when assessing Rossetti's replication practices. When Sir Frederick Leighton, then president of the Royal Academy, began setting up the 1883 exhibition, he wrote to Rossetti's brother, William Michael Rossetti, that "the question of duplicates is my great practical stumbling block because all Gabriel's duplicates or many are a little varied and to admit one makes it even more difficult than it is to refuse others."[19] Leighton's concern reflected restrictions of space, as the Royal Academy devoted only two rooms to Rossetti's images, having much other ground to cover in the course of the annual Winter Exhibition.[20] But it seems that replicas were also being construed as unflattering to artist and gallery alike. In her discussion, Macleod insists on this point but she implies an officialness in the resistance to replicas that seems not actually to have been in place at this time. In the context of the 1883 Rossetti shows, Macleod writes of the replica, "A further sign of its demise was the Royal Academy's belated realization that the replica did not constitute a separate work of art."[21] The council minutes of the Royal Academy actually record no discussion or resolution to that effect, but it does seem that the delegitimation of the replica was apparently gaining force informally.[22] Francis Hueffer, critic for the *Times*, noted in his review that "replicas, . . . with very few exceptions, have been rigorously excluded from the Royal Academy."[23] William Bell Scott remarked on the show at the Burlington Fine Arts Club in a letter to James Leathart, noting that it "embraces first ideas, sketches, & c. as well as finished pictures, some of his best—only duplicates—Leighton [that is, the Royal Academy] declining to receive two of the same subject very properly."[24] Scott's word *properly* suggests that the resistance to replicas was a function of stigma rather than space.

Despite these reports, or perhaps because of them, we should note that the Royal Academy show did, in fact, include replicated examples of two paintings—*Beata Beatrix* was on hand in two versions, as was *Venus Verticordia*.[25] If one counts studies and clearly distinct versions, there were nine more "pairs" of works to be found, meaning that roughly a quarter of the Royal Academy's eighty-two Rossetti works were displayed in the company of a replica or some other, more or less similar counterpart. But as if to underline the notion that Leighton and the Royal Academy had some reservations about replicas, the map included in the exhibition catalogue reveals that Leighton separated duplicate images by placing one in each of the two rooms, and the deliberation in doing so is clear from the numbering of the works. The first room, Gallery V, would contain items 286–323, were it not for a handful of omitted numbers in between, which correspond to the replicas and the other duplicates from that series, which were sent to Gallery VI.

Such minutiae bring us to a more vivid sense of the complexity at hand just then in dealing with replicas, a complexity indicating the ambivalence that replicas must have inspired at this moment.[26] Precisely because Rossetti produced his replicas at a time when replication was becoming increasingly problematic, it becomes crucial to isolate the assorted psychological energies, especially identification, that Rossetti himself brought to their production. And while economic imperatives must inform any accurate assessment of Rossetti's creative practices—I conclude this section with a view to those imperatives— we do well to begin by noting that Rossetti's replicas served several purposes, many quite ambiguously figured.

For example, Rossetti understood his repetitions to reflect a pursuit after "the ideal," a notion that he nowhere defines for all purposes but that seems to depend on its lack of definition to enable a kind of contradictory service. This ideality ministers to a familiar aestheticist self-construction, promising release from a too-true reality, but at the same time it indicates an increasingly commodified practice of aesthetic production. Often, "the ideal" for Rossetti is tethered to monetary implications, with the degree of ideality bearing by some private logic on the price of the work. Rossetti remarked to Leyland that it would be impossible to paint so ideal a subject as *Astarte Syriaca* for less than two thousand guineas—over twice what he had charged Leyland for such works as

Proserpine and *The Blessed Damozel*.[27] But sometimes Rossetti avows a more mundane rationale of improvement in the image, as when he noted his greater satisfaction with one of his *Proserpine* replicas: "There is nothing dismal or gloomy in the colour & lighting of this picture,—a tendency to such defect in the first picture having been one of the reasons which determined me to repeat it."[28]

A sheer pleasure in repetition seems to have been another rationale for Rossetti's replicas. Freud would link the compulsion to repeat to the pleasure principle,[29] and there is no doubt that Rossetti's images of women can come to look like replicas even when they are not. This fact has to be counted, to some extent, as a signal feature of Rossetti's temperament. In 1856, some years before any practice of outright replication would figure largely in Rossetti's work, his sister Christina Rossetti begins her sonnet "In an Artist's Studio" by noting the repetitiousness in her brother's visual art: "One face looks out from all his canvasses, / One self-same figure sits or walks or leans."[30] The specific reference would be the face of Elizabeth Siddal, Rossetti's wife-to-be at that time and the model, most famously, for his *Beata Beatrix* and also for John Everett Millais's *Ophelia*. But even after his wife's apparent suicide in 1862, when Rossetti worked with several models, the similarities in his renderings of, for example, Jane Morris and Alexa Wilding were so striking that casual observers can take them to be the same person.

Rossetti's tendency to repetition was plain to observers less intimately involved with him than his sister was. In July 1882, a few months after Rossetti's death, the *Daily News* reported on the sale of items from his London home, calling the Cheyne Walk address a "melancholy place," the "walls hung with repeated pictures of the same mournful face."[31] Commenting on the retrospective exhibitions in 1883, an anonymous writer for *Blackwood's Edinburgh Magazine*, positioned unconvincingly as a "partial apologist," delivered a fairly commonplace verdict concerning Rossetti's rendering of the female ideal: "Of his latest form, oft repeated—the lips pouting, the elongated throat abnormally swelling, the hair weighted as a mane, and crowning the facial façade as a massive overhanging pediment—few could be enamoured but the painter himself."[32] Popular appropriations of Rossetti's images of women have since disproved the reviewer's notion that Rossetti's aesthetic had only private appeal, and, as recent work by J. B. Bullen has shown, the reviewer's rhetoric of bodily excess and deformity had a long-standing and widely disseminated application by conservative voices critical of Pre-Raphaelite and aestheticist artwork in general.[33] But the reviewer's characterization is nonetheless on target. The replica is not the only issue to address when gauging Rossetti's relation to originality, especially when one notes that sense in which, for example, two of Rossetti's *Pandoras* (Figures 25–26) look less alike than do the ostensibly unrelated images *Astarte Syriaca* and *Mnemosyne* (Figures 27–28).[34]

The sameness in Rossetti's efforts appears to reflect an inner compulsion,

25. D. G. Rossetti, *Pandora* (1871). Oil, 51½ x 31 in. Surtees item 224. In a private collection. Reproduced here from H. C. Marillier, *Dante Gabriel Rossetti: An Illustrated Memorial of His Art and Life* (London: G. Bell, 1899), between 162 and 163. Courtesy of Special Collections, University of Michigan Libraries.

but one channeled and cultivated by external factors. This claim simply confirms a truism that internal and external motivations tend to blur deeply, and especially, perhaps, in the question of agency in aesthetic creation. As Pierre Bourdieu notes, "[T]he artist who makes the work is himself made."[35] And if the self or ego provides a central image to which we can anchor a conception of inner compulsion, it would be money, or more generally the relations of cultural production, that provide the immediate image of external determination at this historical juncture. Nowhere in Rossetti's art was money more the issue than in the production of replicas.

The determining effect of buyer demand figures centrally in what might well have been Rossetti's last letter of consequence, a reply to the French art critic Ernest Chesneau. While preparing his book *La Peinture anglais* (1882),

26. D. G. Rossetti, *Pandora* (1879). Colored crayons, 38 x 24½ in. Surtees item 224D,
R. 1. Fogg Art Museum, Harvard University Art Museums.

27. D. G. Rossetti, *Astarte Syriaca* (1877); also called *Venus Astarte*. Oil, 72 x 42 in. Surtees item 249. Courtesy of the Manchester Art Gallery.

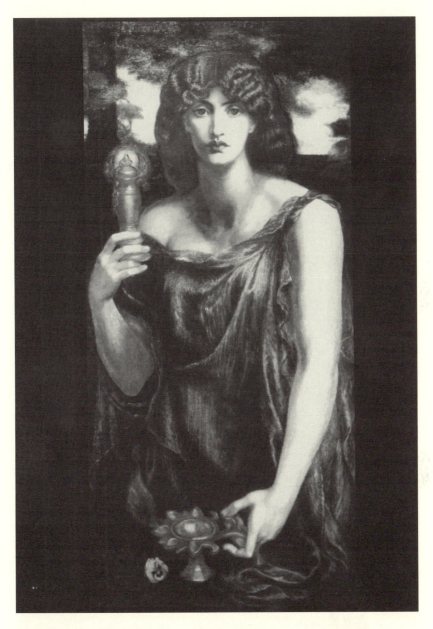

28. D. G. Rossetti, *Mnemosyne* (1881); also called *The Lamp of Memory* and *Ricordanza*. Oil, 47½ x 23 in. Surtees item 261. Courtesy of the Bancroft Collection, Deleware Art Museum.

Chesneau wrote to Rossetti to ask about the character of his work, and Rossetti replied, "I will now give you such answer as I can about my paintings. I have had few opportunities of producing important compositions as I have always lived in a very retired way and such works are not easily disposed of to advantage. This has led to my producing a number of life-sized figures or half-figures of a poetical character, for which I found the demand much greater."[36] The logic of market expediency that Rossetti announces here drove his lucrative practice of replication as well. It was an inviting path, as several of Rossetti's patrons exhibited a good deal of equanimity about replication. Graham, one of Rossetti's chief patrons, declared to Rossetti that there could be no question of identity among two replicas.[37] So Graham avowed a "more-is-more" attitude that is also voiced, rather surprisingly, in an 1893 issue of a serial called *The Collector*, where the editor cheerfully asserts that the distribution of reproduced images "rather augments than diminishes the value of a good picture."[38] In our time, scholars sometimes downplay Rossetti's trade in replicas, emphasizing that he was satisfying patrons who urged him to reproduce for them something already done for another buyer.[39] (Notable in this respect is a fervent request from William Graham for a replica of *Beata Beatrix* [Figure 22].[40]) But sanguine approaches toward replication seem to have been losing ground at this time to more worried viewpoints. Many significant players in Rossetti's circle of patrons expressed increasingly vocal opposition—especially Leyland and James Leathart, each of whom supposed that replication might reduce the monetary value of their originals.[41]

That such northern industrial businessmen were the dominant force in Rossetti's patronage is little surprise, for their geographical and social circumstances align their interests with those of an artist like Rossetti. Unfortunately, numerous omissions in the long-standard edition of Rossetti's letters struck especially hard on the matter of his correspondence with patrons, a resource that can provide much clarification and that is only now coming into clearer view with a new edition of the letters.[42] Key patrons include James Leathart, a Newcastle lead merchant; Frederick Richard Leyland, a Liverpool shipper; William Graham, a cotton and wine merchant based in Glasgow and Liverpool; William Turner, a Manchester manufacturer; George Rae, a Birkenhead banker; William Coltart, a Liverpool iron merchant; Frederick Craven, a Manchester printer; Thomas Plint, a stockbroker from Leeds—and then intermediary figures such as the Liverpool merchant and art world operator John Miller, who originally directed Leyland to Rossetti. Few major collectors of Rossetti's work were Londoners or belonged to aristocratic or professional classes. And to judge by the list of works completed by William Sharp at the time of Rossetti's death, the Londoners who owned works by Rossetti tended to be fellow artists or art dealers, such as the photographer Clarence Fry and fellow painter George Price Boyce.[43]

These facts suggest a British parallel to a phenomenon noted by Pierre

Bourdieu in his sociological analyses of aesthetic production in nineteenth-century France. Artists began at this time to internalize values of progressiveness and generational supercession, thus installing into cultural practice what many people today regard as an obvious feature of all new art, namely, its affinity with youth and novelty and its hostility to the establishment. At the point when new art becomes aligned against the establishment, suggests Bourdieu, it begins to mirror a kindred alignment, against the aristocracy, that virtually defines the affluent middle class.[44] In a British Victorian context, too, we can propose a homology of interests between new-wave artists and new money. In the case of England's northern industrial art patrons, solidifying and identifying with a standing conception of aristocracy was hardly their goal: "Not content to imitate the aristocracy, these energetic businessmen recast the cultural system in their own image in an attempt to create a stable social category for their class."[45] So the affinity might be schematized this way: new money tends to construe itself as the originating point of its accumulated wealth, its own "onlie begetter." This self-reflection puts new money into a welcoming frame of mind when it comes to what modernists were to call avant-gardism, insofar as avant-gardism also constitutes itself in a refusal of prior forms, a striking out into new aesthetic ground. But like adolescent rebellion, which expresses still another bid for autonomy, claims to aesthetic and economic autonomy also take shape through an anxious self-awareness of precursors and other aspects of derivation.

So the increasing disrepute of the replica was not necessarily the result of a face-off between artists and patrons in which the unproblematically avowed monetary interests of patrons happened to win out. It doesn't seem to be the case that prosperous collectors, objecting to a dilution of value that would supposedly follow from rampant replication, battled a cadre of artists committed to churning out replicas and profits as they did of old. To polarize the interests of artists and patrons in this way, one must turn a blind eye to the peculiar closeness and reciprocity of the patrons and artists in the high-aesthetic line. Leyland's relations to Rossetti and to James McNeill Whistler provide cases in point. The correspondence between Leyland and Rossetti evinces a remarkable degree of interaction in the production of paintings. Leyland was especially concerned about plain matters of size and orientation (upright or horizontally oblong), but he also would specify the number of heads or the accessories, and he coveted especially images of women playing musical instruments. According to Francis Fennell, Leyland was the one to suggest to Whistler that paintings might be titled after musical styles, like "symphony" and "nocturne." For his London house at Prince's Gate, Leyland commissioned the famous Peacock Room of Whistler, and the artist occupied the residence throughout the project. Whistler also lived for several weeks at Speke Hall, Leyland's address in Liverpool, while making portraits of Leyland's family members.[46]

If we can credit this concept of a homology of interests between new art and new money, we can comprehend how both parties could go hand in hand into a future in which the replica has no place. For the replica can only be a reminder that one does not so much make it new as make it anew. Any high-modern aesthetic that sustains its self-image in a disavowal of antecedence and derivation can only see in the replica a failure of individual accomplishment, a failure of originality. Resistance to the replica is therefore built into the self-image of artist and collector alike when art's bid for autonomy has finally taken hold in the culture at large. Notwithstanding Lady Eastlake's famous verdict that nouveau-riche collectors preferred new art simply because they lacked the educational background to discriminate in matters of historical connoisseurship,[47] it seems important to see that new art was itself a reassuring scene of identification for the evolving middle classes. And as for artists: at a time when the larger modern process of casting aesthetic interest as disinterest was reaching its high point, the replica became a scene of identification as well, but an anxious one, for under the new aesthetic regime the replica was a disconcerting index of art's relation to money.

So while Rossetti's replication practices can be said to have served his desires in certain respects, we should remain mindful that he seldom displayed any relish in creating a replica. Indeed, his sense of demoralization in their production is often visible, as, for example, in a letter to William Michael Rossetti: "I have been doing a replica here (of that Beatrice)—a beastly job, but lucre was the lure."[48] Writing in 1873 to Ford Madox Brown, Rossetti reflects bluntly on his economic compulsion—implicitly registering the eclipse of use values by exchange values—when affiliating his artistic activity with that of the prostitute and her sobering reduction of love to the rule of exchange: "I have often said that to be an artist is just the same thing as to be a whore, as far as dependence on the whims and fancies of individuals is concerned. . . . The natural impulse is to say simply—Leyland be d———d!—and so no doubt the whore feels but too often inclined to say and cannot."[49]

This jarring affiliation of artist and prostitute suggests that the modern artist is a fallen figure. Artist and prostitute share a circumstance whereby "natural" impulses and inclinations are not only forced into submission but redirected into unwelcome acts, compelled by economic exigencies. At this time Rossetti was working up one of his *Proserpine* images to pay off a debt to Leyland—Rossetti frequently took partial payments before completing paintings—and he resented Leyland's attempts to influence the final form of the promised work.[50] But the particular instance should not obscure a more general point: Rossetti identifies with this fallenness. And fallenness, in turn, is increasingly the verdict to be passed on the painted replica at this time. So there is in the replica, as with the prostitute, something for Rossetti to identify with.[51]

The idea of fallenness, like one prevalent idea of original agency, has an imposing theological pedigree: the fall from grace and the concept of creation ex nihilo both underlie Judeo-Christian narrative. But Amanda Anderson has examined the Victorian rhetoric of fallenness to find there a specifically modern negotiation with the issue of agency. In her account, "the fallen woman is less a predictable character than a figure who displaces multiple anxieties about the predictability of character itself."[52] That is, the fallen woman is regarded at once as a figure determined by social injustices and as a figure who must be held accountable for her actions. This divided treatment is no mere happenstance, for the collision of viewpoints stakes out the terrain of a conceptual aporia internalized by the culture at large, which comes to act out its informing ambivalences about the nature of human responsibility through the idea of fallenness. The division, in other words, creates—indeed, constitutes—the culture's interest in the fallen figure. To cast Anderson's point even more fully into this chapter's terms—even if also to elide her concern for a gendering that typically informs this discourse—I offer the following hypothesis: that which is fallen interests a figure like Rossetti not by virtue of what it is in itself, but rather by virtue of his sense of identification with it as a complex and ambiguous emblem of originality.

Replicating History in the 1887 Manchester Exhibition

At this point, I turn from the 1883 Rossetti retrospectives to another scene of exhibition and replication, four years later. As in the previous section, my purpose is to show how replication serves as a staging term for a kind agential self-reflection in a specific Victorian milieu. The Golden Jubilee in 1887 marked Victoria's fiftieth year as monarch, and exhibitions and celebrations were executed throughout Britain.[53] Prominent among these events, the Manchester Exhibition was an immense affair featuring eight themed areas: Industrial Design, Machinery in Motion, Chemical and Allied Industries, Handicrafts, Fine Art of the United Kingdom During Her Majesty's Reign, Irish Industries, Old Manchester and Salford, and Fairy Fountains.[54] The exhibition's goal was "to illustrate, as fully as possible, the progress made in the development of Arts and Manufactures during the Victorian era."[55] By all accounts the effect was impressive. Indeed, notices about the exhibition are hyperbolic—"It is as splendid a display as any the world has yet seen" (Figure 29).[56] Such reports might provoke incredulity today, as the Manchester Exhibition is less widely known than exhibitions with international pretensions, on which scholars have typically focused.[57] By the end of the exhibition's six-month run, however, the visitor count totaled almost 5 million, thus bearing comparison to other major exhibitions in this age of exhibitions.[58] (The Great Exhibition in 1851 had 6.5 million visitors.)

Following recent precedents in London and Edinburgh, Manchester fashioned, with "Old Manchester and Salford," a full-scale replica of a preindustrial town atmosphere.[59] The replica featured interconnected avenues and

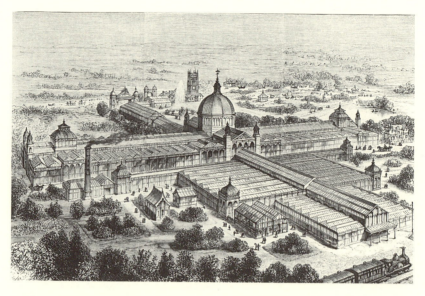

29. Overview of the Manchester Exhibition, with "Old Manchester and Salford" behind the main building. In Walter Tomlinson et al., *The Pictorial Record of the Royal Jubilee Exhibition, Manchester, 1887*, ed. John H. Nodal (Manchester: J. E. Cornish, 1888), 4. By permission of the British Library. BL shelfmark 7957.g.8.

smaller streets lined with two dozen buildings and assorted other structures recalling periods from the Roman occupation to the eighteenth century in Manchester (Figures 30–31). The replica therefore departs from the exhibition's overall charge of celebrating Manchester's accomplishments during the reign of Victoria, for in the replica we have a self-conscious effort "to represent each phase of [Manchester] society; Roman remains to Chartist pikes."[60] Opening his latter-day discussion of the Manchester example, Alan Kidd finds at this period the roots of present-day historical theme parks, associated with the international exhibition movement.[61]

I look here to the Manchester replica, rather than to the earlier replicas at London or Edinburgh, for two reasons. In the first place, Manchester had, by a large measure, the most elaborate display of this sort—"truth to say," said the fulsome review in *Punch*, "more substantial than 'Old London.' "[62] Where London and Edinburgh had recreated single streets, Old Manchester and Salford amounted to a veritable district. According to the *Observer*: "Old Manchester, through a development of the South Kensington idea of Old London, is carried out upon so large a scale and to such perfection that when passing through it is difficult to believe we are living in the nineteenth century. The Manchester people are evidently apt pupils, and in this case have far surpassed

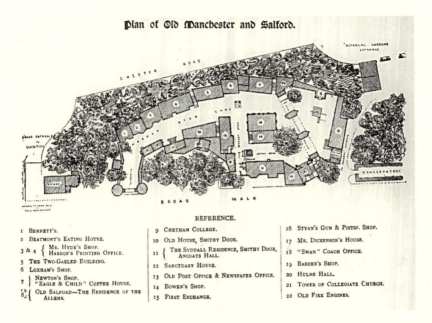

Plan of Old Manchester and Salford.

REFERENCE.

1 BENNETT'S.	9 CHETHAM COLLEGE.	16 STYAN'S GUN & PISTOL SHOP.
2 BEAUMONT'S EATING HOUSE.	10 OLD HOUSE, SMITHY DOOR.	17 MR. DICKENSON'S HOUSE.
3 & 4 { MR. HYDE'S SHOP. / HARROP'S PRINTING OFFICE.	11 { THE SYDDALL RESIDENCE, SMITHY DOOR, ANCOATS HALL.	18 "SWAN" COACH OFFICE.
5 THE TWO-GABLED BUILDING.	12 SANCTUARY HOUSE.	19 BARBER'S SHOP.
6 LOXHAM'S SHOP.	13 OLD POST OFFICE & NEWSPAPER OFFICE.	20 HULME HALL.
7 { NEWTON'S SHOP. / "EAGLE & CHILD" COFFEE HOUSE.	14 BOWEN'S SHOP.	21 TOWER OF COLLEGIATE CHURCH.
8 { OLD SALFORD—THE RESIDENCE OF THE ALLENS.	15 FIRST EXCHANGE.	22 OLD FIRE ENGINES.

30. A plan of the city replica from Alfred Darbyshire, *A Booke of Olde Manchester and Salford* (Manchester: John Heywood, 1887), 48.

their masters."[63] But the greater size of the Manchester example is only one reason, and finally a rather inconclusive one, for looking there. More important is how it ministered to the self-image of its host city. Meeting and surpassing their masters was no mere happenstance in this case, as one sees in an account of local pride in the exhibition generally: the exhibition, writes a reporter for the *Manchester City News*, "bears the impress of the character of our people. No city in the empire excels Manchester, and few equal it, in the power of its citizens to concentrate their energies to practical ends."[64] Manchester's unprecedented degree of involvement in the creation of a historical civic replica likewise reflected the city's concern to assert a place for itself, playing out a dynamic of self-interest and identity that animates the modern concern for originality.

In Manchester, modernity was an inevitable and complex issue.[65] In 1819, the Peterloo Massacre, turning on the deaths of eleven Radicals in a field outside Manchester, solidified the city's association with bloody political strife. Its cotton industry led the way to a sixfold population increase in the decades leading to 1831, with almost half of that increase dating to the last ten years of the period.[66] The "Social Problem" novels of such writers as Benjamin Disraeli (*Coningsby*) and Elizabeth Gaskell (*Mary Barton, North and South*) evoked

31. A multipoint view of "Old Manchester and Salford" from *The Graphic* (7 May 1887), 495.

Manchester as a flashpoint of labor conflict and industrial progress's mixed blessings. Friedrich Engels focused on Manchester in his portrait of modern class division, shocked at the squalor to be found in "the second city in England, the most important factory town in the world."[67] The Manchester school and the Anti-Corn-Law League, both midcentury movements advocating laissez-faire economic measures, were born in the city. In 1877 John Ruskin vilified the city as a cultural wasteland, where capitalism had produced the unwisest and least sustainable form of political economy.[68] So Manchester's local history was an index of progressive modernity's often harsh essentials—industry, machinery, riot, urban starvation, and the rule of money.

On the other hand, and in step with its development in industrial prominence, Manchester was a formidable purveyor of culture. The Manchester Literary and Philosophical Society was founded in 1781 and stood at the head

of what Michael Rose has called an "almost endless stream of societies cater-
ing to an ever-widening range of cultural and intellectual interests."[69] The city
hosted the epochal Art Treasures Exhibition of 1857, motivated in part by a
concern to popularize art among the less advantaged people of the Manchester area.[70] To this day, the display of Pre-Raphaelite images at the Art Treasures Exhibition has served as a reference point to establish Manchester's role
in the promotion of progressive art.[71] Thirty years later, the Golden Jubilee
would feature Fine Art of the United Kingdom During Her Majesty's Reign,
an exhibition that rivaled the 1857 exhibition and underlined, once more,
Manchester's prowess in marshaling resources to the public dissemination of
culture. A month after the opening, a *Guardian* essayist unselfconsciously noted
the city's divided emphasis on industry and culture in terms of Golden Jubilee
Exhibition: "The general verdict about the Exhibition appears to be that the
pictures and the machinery are the finest parts of the show."[72] While the city's
reputation rested on its industrial prominence, that accomplishment needed
both to be affirmed and also, as it were, civilized by a palpable interest in the
fine arts.

In the light of these emphases, Old Manchester and Salford might seem pe-
ripheral to the main work of the exhibition. And, indeed, the replica sat literally on the periphery of the exhibition grounds. But insofar as Manchester's
identity was a compound of its prowess in machinery and picture showing, the
determination of people in and around Manchester to hold together those two
agendas proceeded from a larger psychosocial dynamic. Pierre Bourdieu's
concept of a "field of cultural production" shows how separate fields (materi-
alizing in, for example, art and machinery) reflect an interconnected system of
social relations, played out as a series of choices by the agents who occupy positions made possible within the overall field of cultural production.[73] Manchester's identity turned on its sense that it could proffer both machinery and
art, containing contraries, as it were. In this sense, Old Manchester and Salford, by giving forth a replica of a mythologized past and presenting it in present experience, embodies contraries as well. The replica's uncertain relation to
a project of historical acknowledgment mirrors the city's uncertain relation to
the competing value spheres of industry and art. The fabrication of a preindustrial Manchester district within modern-day Manchester pressed, much
more vividly than the similar examples in Edinburgh and London, the question of what this place was *before* it was industrial. For Manchester's civic identity, and its national and international reputations, turned all but entirely on
recent and sobering events of the sort itemized above. This replica had special
work to do. Old Manchester and Salford was not merely a scene of innocently
nostalgic recuperation but an attempt actively to define for the city a sense, in
the here and now, of its authentic character as a place to be from.[74]

The special role of Old Manchester and Salford in the exhibition is addressed indirectly in the report of the exhibition's executive committee. The

subcommittee report treating "Handicrafts and 'Old Manchester and Salford'"—the two areas were administered together—begins dryly, "It may be observed that the commercial prosperity of Manchester is practically founded on the extinction of handicrafts."[75] In this sense, the replication of a preindustrial Manchester district is at once the evocation of a remote origin and an indication of a break from that origin. A writer for one Lancashire newspaper also characterizes the replica in such terms, insisting on the replica as a scene of identification but culminating in a poetically charged reminder of the pastness of these matters: "The facsimiles of old historic buildings in Manchester and Salford present to the nineteenth century a living and faithful picture of the streets through which our forefathers walked, of the houses in which they dwelt, of the shops and market-places in which they transacted business, and of the churches in which they worshipped, and beneath the shadows of which many of them now sleep."[76] The people of Manchester found something to identify with in a replica that was at the same time an embattled gesture of historical recovery.

Old Manchester and Salford was unique among the exhibition's various scenes of identification by emphasizing a view of deep history. George Milner, president of the Manchester Literary Club, opened on such a note in his introduction to Alfred Darbyshire's *A Booke of Olde Manchester and Salford*, which was printed during the Golden Jubilee as a guide to the replicated city district:

The idea of such a re-production is not an original one. "Old London" and "Old Edinburgh" have set the fashion, and their success fully warranted the experiment of "Old Manchester and Salford." It is no wonder that scenic presentations of this character should be attractive. The piquancy of life depends on its contrasts, and when people visit a great Exhibition, where modern ingenuity is at its highest level, and where the last triumphs of culture and civilization are put on record, they are naturally pleased to see the quaint surroundings of an older life side by side with that which is familiar and new.[77] (14)

While Milner's opening declaration about originality might seem to be most pertinent to the present discussion, his concluding affiliation of the familiar and the new is actually the more telling point. When the *familiar* is associated not with the *old* but rather with the *new*, we have a brief but workable definition of modernity. Indeed, as Richard Altick has shown, a fixation on novelty is a signal feature of Victorian popular culture generally.[78] Milner continues in his next paragraph to solidify this modernity's pertinence in the project of historical self-construction that was Old Manchester and Salford:

It might have been said that it was dangerous to enter into competition with either the Southern or the Northern Metropolis. We have neither London's enormous wealth or historic association nor Edinburgh's unrivalled natural position. In the general estimation we are regarded as prosaic, if not debased; our history is believed to be without distinction; our immediate locality and even our near surroundings have been "soiled by all ignoble use;" we are regarded as reprobate and past redemption, and such a phrase as "Picturesque Manchester," applied either to the past or the present would with most Englishmen only excite a smile."[79]

Milner offers this withering ventriloquy as a prelude to contesting its terms, for he goes on to itemize Manchester's ennobling associations with Arthurian romance and fifteenth-century college life. These antidotes to a modern sense of Mancunian inadequacy are less crucial to my argument than the nature of that sense of inadequacy. And while I will defer for a moment longer any return to the larger issues of replication and agency, it is well to note the identity between Milner's charged reflections on Manchester's public image and the evolving characterization of the artistic replica: both, that is, are prosaic, debased, without distinction, reprobate, and past redemption.

Darbyshire's own discussion in *A Booke of Olde Manchester and Salford* offers similarly tangled accounts of the replica's intended effects and its supposed warrants. Most of its short chapters concern individual buildings, noting the building being replicated; its original location in Manchester; the historical interest of the original building; and the sources, usually preserved artistic renderings, that permitted a high degree of accuracy in the replica. Commending the organizers' efforts at "adding realism to the scene," Darbyshire declares that "Manchester of the *past* has been reproduced anterior to its spoliation by the officious and ignorant 'improver' of modern generations." But Darbyshire also displays total equanimity about the fact that this recovery project offers "many aspects of the town from the time of the Roman occupation to about the middle of the Georgian era, or just before that modern period which marked the commencement of the total annihilation of the fine old architecture of the past."[80] The polytemporal replication is accomplished not merely in the architecture but also in the players: "The various buildings are occupied by persons carrying on old-fashioned handicrafts, habited in costumes peculiar to the styles and periods of the architecture; and the custodians of the Old Town are dressed in costumes of the Roman, Edwardian, Elizabethan, and Georgian periods."[81]

In keeping with the tangled facts of Old Manchester and Salford, Darbyshire's rhetoric oscillates between an earnest devotion to historical verisimilitude and a pleasure in having history all ways at once. And in his case, at least, both tendencies are driven by a self-conscious relation to a disconcerting modernity. In the account of agency that informs my discussion, there is cause to suppose that Darbyshire's oscillation of terms is not merely an incidental but a functional response to that anxious interest in the modern. The historical complexity of this civic representation, its incoherence even, is not merely a compromise allowed by the creators of the exhibition and tolerated by the visitors. Instead, it is a positive point of attraction. Therein lies, in effect, the appealing character of the replica. This speculation seem warranted by the regularity with which reports about the replica link its appeal and its tangled character as a representation of history. The effect is noted from afar in the *Times*, which cast the whole of Old Manchester and Salford as "a charming medley, anachronisms in one respect being balanced by a most scrupulous regard for appropriateness in the details of each period."[82] A passage from the *Manchester City News* makes a similar point, and more concretely:

The stalwart Roman soldiers in tin-plate armour, knee-breeches, cotton stockings, and sandals, who keep watch and ward from early morn to dewy eve over the principal entrance to Mancunium, are typical of the pleasant incongruities which go to the making of that wonderfully delightful jumble known as Old Manchester and Salford. This quarter of the exhibition is—or would be if it were not always so crowded—the most charming lounge in all our big show. It is a sort of dreamland, where nothing happens but the unexpected. The Roman gateway leads to Tudor houses. You have stocks and pillory, and hideous ancient crosses, and Chetham College, and the first Exchange, all in a heap; a fine old bridge spanning a river of cobblestones; a cathedral tower ninety-three feet high without any cathedral attached. Edward the Third's cross-bowmen wander about the streets, looking very shame-faced concerning their resurrection; and whilst you are trying to evade the glittering eyes of these very ancient mariners, and endeavouring to dodge the terribly fierce and warlike body-guard of the Young Pretender, you come full tilt upon the ghost of a Georgian watchman, billhook and all, looking as dreadfully charged with impotent thunder as was the wont of those guardians of the peace when in the flesh. There is a post office from which you don't post; a coach-office from which no coaches start. Pretty and pert Elizabethan shopwomen wait in the shops next door to Master Caxton, the printer; and fascinating Marie Stuart—like the Mormon's wife, there are several of her—flashes along the street and is jostled by Chowbent. You go to a crockery shop for some jewelry, to the blacksmith's to see Queen Elizabeth's maids of honour use the knitting machine, to a bookseller's for watches, and to a barber shop to see fustian-cutting.[83]

The reporter initially emphasizes anachronism: Romans in cotton socks (recall that the modern manufacture of cotton was Manchester's key claim to industrial fame); the heap of historically incommensurate structures and individuals; and so forth. But the reporter soon shifts into another order of incongruity, more properly dreamlike: the multiple Marie Stuarts, the river of cobblestones, the cathedral tower without a cathedral, Queen Elizabeth's maids of honor improbably occupied with knitting, and in a blacksmith's shop, no less. In one sense we have here only an enriched variation on that theme reiterated continually in reporting on the replica, namely, that the replica was an unabashedly tangled account of Mancunian history. But the language also underscores the sense of pleasure generated in local visitors to the replica. We are to understand the replicated city as soliciting a particular kind of interest by virtue of its tangled form, its "delightful jumble." My key suggestion is that the incoherence on display in the replica constitutes the very formal trait that qualifies Old Manchester and Salford as an object with which to identify.

But why should a historical jumble be delightful? The replica's dream-logic in itself is but partial explanation. We can recall Freud's strikingly similar account of dreaming as that state in which temporal constraints are erased and our waking either-or logic gives way to a potentially contradictory both-and logic. But as we do so, we should recall that he was also presupposing an elaborate theory of psychological identity—repression and castration anxieties—that give such precipitates of the unconscious their critical and emotional specificity. To what psychic organization, then, is the Manchester replica's historical jumble a matter for delight?

We can pursue that question through another Freudian moment. In *Civilization and its Discontents*, Freud proposes an analogy between the buried ruins under Rome and the human psyche. A city's accumulation of structures, like a mind, harbors specters, ghosts, traces of past events, all superimposed on one another or interleaved into one another. Decisive in this matter, for Freud, is the fact that these elements need not cohere rigorously, nor need they even be consistent with one another. Only an extended quotation will let us retrace Freud's progress in treating a city as if it were a "psychical entity,"

an entity, that is to say, in which nothing that has once come into existence will have passed away and all the earlier phases of development continue to exist alongside the latest one. This would mean that in Rome the palaces of the Caesars and the Septizonium of Septimius Severus would still be rising to their old height on the Palatine and that the castle of S. Angelo would still be carrying on its battlements the beautiful statues which graced it until the siege by the Goths, and so on. But more than this. In the place occupied by the Palazzo Caffarelli would once more stand—without the Palazzo having to be removed—the Temple of Jupiter Capitolinus; and this not only in its latest shape, as the Romans of the Empire saw it, but also in its earliest one, when it still showed Etruscan forms and was ornamented with terra-cotta antefixes. Where the Coliseum now stands we could at the same time admire Nero's vanished Golden House. On the Piazza of the Pantheon we should find not only the Pantheon of to-day, as it was bequeathed to us by Hadrian, but, on the same site, the original edifice erected by Agrippa; indeed, the same piece of ground would be supporting the church of Santa Maria sopra Minerva and the ancient temple over which it was built. And the observer would perhaps only have to change the direction of his glance or his position in order to call up the one view or the other.[84]

The passage's structure reflects a twofold intellectual conceit. Freud posits the simple revival of lost civic presences: palaces of the Caesars, the Septizonium of Septimius Severus, the castle of S. Angelo. Then he notes that, "more than this" recuperation of structures, there would be also the manifold impositions into one space of all the structures and influences in evidence at any given point in the history of that space—mixing dynasty with dynasty, creed with creed, until a dizzying spectacle results, suggesting the prodigious and even contradictory sedimentations that make up the human psyche and all its embedded memory traces. This accumulation of detail culminates in a sharpened sense of subjective vision and the *position* of the reckoning consciousness: "And the observer," Freud remarks, "would perhaps only have to change the direction of his glance or his position [*Standpunkt*] in order to call up the one view or the other."

The idea of reflective agency that I mean to highlight in this study and link to liberal aspiration is embedded in Freud's notion that one might deliberately change the direction of one's glance or one's position in respect to this welter of images. If Freud is saying, in effect, that one might be "in a position to change one's position," the term *position* is doing double and contradictory service, and in a way that bears directly on the contradictory tendencies played out still today in the theorization of critical agency. For in one sense, *position* indicates a situation of enabling constraint, whereby perspective discloses one view as it forecloses on others; in another sense, *position* indicates a circumstance of conceptual mobility, of freedom from the very constraint announced in that first sense of the term *position*. For in this second sense, changing one's position would seem to reflect a deliberation between alternative views of which one is aware and among which one is "in a position" to choose. Freud's overall image relies on a divided conception of positionality

After Freud offers his image, he goes on to revoke it in frustration, disparaging the integrity of the image: "There is clearly no point in spinning out our phantasy any further, for it leads to things that are unimaginable and even absurd. If we want to represent historical sequence in spatial terms we can only do it by juxtaposition in space: the same space cannot have two different contents. Our attempt seems to be an idle game. It has only one justification. It shows us how far we are from mastering the characteristics of mental life by representing them in pictorial terms" (70–71). Freud abandons his image of the psychic city, because it involves a logical impossibility: "the same space cannot have two different contents." But there is something disingenuous in that belated scrupulousness, notwithstanding its logical justification, insofar as Freud has clearly taken a kind of luxuriating pleasure in his construction of this impossible space. That impossible space has done its service already. As a mastering writer on the origins and structure of human experience, Freud will go to such spaces, regardless of their strict impossibility, because they give a kind of pleasure to behold conceptually, and because the failure of such images to cohere is in any case made good in the sense that such images exercise the critical agent's capacity to posit and briefly to identify with that very incoherence. Freud does not so much realize an error as disavow a mode of thinking that perpetually attracts and repels him.[85]

Such moments suggest that for some kinds of interpreting agents at least, there is a pleasure in representing and identifying with an "unimaginable and even absurd" space. My larger argument tells that an aspiration of liberal aesthetic agency is at issue here, insofar as the discourses of liberalism and aestheticism alike take shape as oscillations between an ideal of strong self-reflection and an alternative sense that such idealization cannot actually be embodied.

While no adequate treatment of these questions can take shape at this juncture of my argument, a journalistic image from the Manchester exhibition can make plain that sense in which Old Manchester and Salford's task was precisely to conjure a "space" with "two different contents." A *Guardian* writer narrates a walking tour of the replicated town, coming to this spot: "Over the front of the reproduction of Harrop's printing office now hangs the picturesque signboard of 'Master John Heywood, printer,' the official printer for the Executive Committee of the Royal Jubilee Exhibition. The interior represents an old bookbinding shop, and practical demonstration of the manner of binding in the olden time is given by one or two young women, who are engaged in binding Mr. Darbyshire's 'Booke of Olde Manchester and Salford.' "[86]

The reporter's account crystallizes, albeit unselfconsciously, the loopy logic of Old Manchester and Salford. The replica of the printing office is a properly identifiable, specific point of historical recuperation, and therein lies, supposedly, its claim on the visitor's interest, for people in the present might walk back to the past and witness a facet of their own heritage as people from Lancashire. But what the printing office feigns to produce is not an artifact of the past but rather an utterly current document—Mr. Darbyshire's *Booke of Olde Manchester and Salford*—about the exhibition's own act of historical fabrication. In the form of a joke, one could say, the replica of the printing shop enacts in small the self-reflexive contortion that defines the entire design of Old Manchester and Salford. And the pleasure engendered in viewers by that irony maps onto the pleasure that drove Freud in his image of the psychic city, although Freud's special concern for a consequential and logical methodology impelled him to discount his image in a way that the denizens of Manchester probably did not. In a limited but genuine sense, the Manchester replica performs exactly the service that Freud's image was to offer—allowing a spectatorial and mobile relation to diverse, competing, and even mutually exclusive elements of a specific identity.

Reading Replicas

Cultural historians today are likely to view this Manchester instance of mobile self-inspection with some skepticism, seeing there a mass-cultural vacuity respecting ideas of history, knowledge, and the standpoint that passes for "reflection." The city replica generally, and that jocular printing-office reflection especially, will seem most readable as anticipations of Disney World, late-capitalist demonstrations of a cultivated consumerist taste for absolute fakery or hyperreality.[87] I want to conclude by thinking a bit more about what actually distinguishes the Mancunian experience with the city replica from Rossetti's experiences with his replicas. For in that distinction lies waiting whatever story we will be able to tell about Rossetti's aesthetic agency—affirmative, critical, or otherwise. The story, in turn, will tell as much about us as about these objects of inquiry.

Concerning these two contexts of replication, one difference stands out:

Rossetti's frequent sense of chagrin—visible in his sense of self-prostitution—contrasts plainly with the sense of entertainment presumably experienced by most Mancunians in the face of their replica. But an ambivalent logic also underlies both contexts and makes them look rather alike. Rossetti's replicas indicated to him both his constraint and his creative free agency; the Manchester replica intimated both an authenticating deep history and a thoroughgoing, even absolute, currency. In each case, the interested individuals had before them not merely images of themselves but images of their agency as a tangled and even contradictory construct. By admitting this similarity, perhaps we can begin to think critically about the investments that lead most current scholars to read two such contexts in different terms, subsuming the pleasures of the Mancunians into a story about their subjection to bourgeois consumerist ideology, but, at the same time, styling Rossetti's aesthetic practices as a kind of engagement to be read in terms of his aesthetic agency. How does it happen that we are unlikely to see the "joke" of the Manchester replica's printing office, for instance, as camp critique?

At issue, I contend, is our recourse to a vision of redemptive self-consciousness, often understood to be possessed by an artist such as Rossetti but generally supposed to be lacking in the larger population visiting the Manchester exhibition. For the most influential postmodern-era critics, however, ideas of redemptive self-consciousness seem compromised as artifacts of Enlightenment rationalism. For this reason, literary-critical accounts of aesthetic agency since at least the poststructuralist moment have not offered much that will let us rationalize granting an affirmative and critical character to Rossetti's replication practices while continuing to interpret the 1880s city replicas as scenes of bourgeois bad faith. I suggest that we can meaningfully distinguish between the cultural work of the Manchester replica and that of Rossetti's aesthetic practices. But doing so will require us to credit what this study has been calling an idea of liberal agency, understood as a partial but nonetheless meaningful feat of critical reflection and action. In arguing this point, then, I am not so much proposing a new way of proceeding as I am urging a greater awareness of how most literary-critical scholarship in fact already proceeds.

According to Jerome McGann, for example, Rossetti wields an "art of the inner standpoint" (the phrase is Rossetti's own) and thus finds a discipline allowing him, in McGann's words, to "dismantle the subject's presumptive privilege of self-identity."[88] Even as McGann displays a deep awareness of this period's imbrication of aesthetic and market cultures, his argument also takes it as a given that Rossetti, by virtue of creative and critical accomplishment, is in charge of something, albeit a "game that must be lost." My own point is quite simple: McGann's Rossetti suffers a loss that is not one. A generously disposed critic can indeed style Rossettian ambiguities and failures as strategically deployed, in which light they secure nothing less than a heroic aesthetic agency. For many literary scholars, surely, the most compelling feature of McGann's work on Rossetti is likely to be this poignantly affirmative rereading of the artist-painter's supposed failings. Rossetti's lack of technical skill as a painter, then, or the flagging of his poetic inspiration in his later years, can now emerge as strengths in the light of a postmodernist worldview that would have to style any more straightforward narrative of mastery as some kind of deception. What we are left with is, however, a valorization of specifically aesthetic agency. Even if this aesthetic agency does not correspond to most conventional images of mastery, might we nonetheless call it a very fine imitation of mastery, thus echoing Eliot's characterization of Camden Farebrother and his imitation of heroism? Is it not, in fact, an imitation that we literary critics are often poised to offer as a truer mastery?

These points can move my discussion on to Oscar Wilde, who more than any other figure of the Victorian period has come in for this very sort of postmodernist recuperation. In his very refusal to add up neatly and make an earnest effort at final truths, Wilde looks as wise and as much in control as one can finally be. My concern is to suggest that current critical tastes, when celebrating Wilde's work in these terms, unwittingly construe aesthetic agency in terms deeply indebted to the modern liberal conception of self-reflecting agency.

Chapter 5

Against Originality: Oscar Wilde's Aesthetic Agency

There's a pert poetaster named Wild
Who the name of a bard has defiled
  For a bloodier big
  Young plagiary wig
Was nor Turpin nor Sheppard than Wild.[1]

This rabid limerick, which I take to be about Oscar Wilde, is scrawled in pencil on the back of an 1881 letter to Dante Gabriel Rossetti. The letter is an otherwise humdrum missive from one of Rossetti's Cheyne Walk neighbors, and the handwriting that records the limerick is not the neighbor's but Hall Caine's, Rossetti's houseguest at the time and his future biographer. We know that Rossetti often extemporized little bits of verse, and that Caine wrote down these efforts when he could, so we might have here a previously undiscovered Rossetti poem in Caine's hand.[2] And perhaps just as well left undiscovered, except that the nonce character of this expression—the ephemeral letter treated as ready paper on which to record a moment's thought—confirms that Wilde's public notoriety took shape with his originality as a special crux. This plagiary Wilde was a robber poet, not merely kin to the real-life robbers Turpin, Sheppard, and Wild—each of whom had been romanticized in assorted nineteenth-century adventure novels[3]—but grosser still than they, for the plagiarist does not merely take what is not his but offers it to others as his own creation, as a monument to his particular identity. In Wilde's early writings, the thefts from Pater and Ruskin are daring and unmistakable.[4] Most of Wilde's public parrying with James McNeill Whistler turned on Whistler's allegations of Wilde's plagiarism and phrase stealing.[5] At the same time, we must also note that Wilde was unusually generous in his turn. Richard Ellmann points out more than once the curiously unproprietary interest that Wilde maintained in respect to most of his ideas.[6] And, for a final twist in this matter, we should recall that Wilde routinely stole material from himself as well, lifting phrases and even paragraphs from one work and putting them to renewed service in another. So he discounted any notion that phrasings or ideas bear an auratic character to be hallowed in the terms we commonly apply to property rights (where theft is condemned) or individual identity (where repeating oneself signals a lack of ongoing generative spontaneity).[7]

The cultural stakes of this posture are apparent already in an incident that was probably the immediate inspiration for the above limerick: a fracas surrounding the publication of Wilde's first book, the volume *Poems* (1881). Just graduated from Oxford, Wilde had already set himself up in London as a self-styled "professor of aesthetics," and his reputation for dandiacal excess was gaining momentum. *Punch* was satirizing him under assorted ridiculous names as a precious aesthete, and soon he would be refracted into two characters for Gilbert and Sullivan's operetta *Patience* (1881). His popular notoriety probably strengthened the animus toward Wilde at Oxford, where he had been, as a student, simply too eccentric for words but also too proficient and clever to dismiss. But the Oxford establishment found an occasion to vent belatedly in July 1881, six weeks or so before the date of the letter on which the limerick would be written. Wilde had sent a presentation copy of his *Poems* to the library of the Oxford Union, and a debate ensued there over whether his book should be accepted into the library. The transcribed speech of Oliver Elton provides an amusing document of the case against Wilde's volume, a case that turned on an imperative to originality:

It is not that the poems are thin—and they *are* thin: it is not that they are immoral—and they *are* immoral: it is not that they are this or that—and they *are* all this and all that: it is that they are for the most part not by their putative author at all, but by a number of better-known and more deservedly reputed authors. They are in fact by William Shakespeare, by Philip Sidney, by John Donne, by Lord Byron, by William Morris, by Algernon Swinburne, and by sixty more, whose works have furnished the list of passages which I hold in my hand at this moment. The Union Library already contains better and fuller editions of all these poets: the volume which we are offered is theirs, not Mr. Wilde's: and I move that it not be accepted.[8]

The objection carried the day, and Wilde's book was sent back to him. Thus it seems that Elton was victorious in his concern to call Wilde to account.

This chapter's discussion presumes, however, that Wilde's final intractability to such accounting is a large part of his claim on our interest. That is, we can allow that Elton has his finger on something approaching a fact when he claims that Wilde's verse is derivative. Even today, in this most affirmative of Wildean moments, few scholars or readers find anything there but an example of belated late Victorian poetic dabbling. But neither will most people today see Wilde as the fool of this Oxford incident. Rather it is Elton who comes off as a figure with no especially compelling destination in sight: Elton appears petulantly absorbed in the very earnestness and respectability that Wilde would make a career of discounting. In this respect, Elton's assessment of the young writer's failed originality seems not so much mistaken as beside the point.

And precisely there—where we take a conventional vision of originality either to matter or not to matter—we have the fault line that continues to set some of the tone in Wilde's reception. Because originality has never been a well-defined concept, the modern versions of Oliver Elton do not always speak in terms of originality exactly, but they exhibit a related sense of Wilde's failings, not to mention much the same venom and simmering outrage one sees in Elton's remarks. In our time, such voices were apparent as they contended against Ellmann's implication, in his 1988 biography, that Wilde was someone to regard as truly substantial rather than merely amusing. For those who see in Wilde a fool who persisted in his follies, never to become wise, it was hard to credit Ellmann's effort to place him alongside the likes of Nietzsche or Kierkegaard in philosophy, Freud in psychology, or even Pater, Ruskin, and Arnold in his immediate Victorian critical context. Such estimations rankled exactly those critics who find in Wilde a final lack of seriousness and a paltry secondariness.[9]

Whether as a gleeful plagiarist, echoer of others' verses, or incorrigible rehearser of his own quips, Wilde seems consistently disdainful of commonplace imperatives to originality, and his apparent self-consciousness in this posture only makes his disdain all the more provocative. It seems that those who might deprecate his importance as an author on grounds of his limited or compromised originality—say, Wilde as a weak or trivial follower of Pater; or Wilde as a figure of mere pastiche and mechanical fancy as opposed to one of synthetic imagination—must overlook exactly the challenge that he poses to the very categories of authorship and authority invoked in such deprecation. Wilde arises in this light as an instructively difficult character to assess, a figure whose very disdain of originality as a value suggests some odd sort of metaoriginality, constituted in a refusal of originality as it is more traditionally figured. What should one make of this originality that refuses originality?

My own answer will appear largely to confirm a perception of Wilde favored by poststructuralist-era critics who see in him a presciently antiessentialist sensibility. For what seems to be at issue is whether and how Wilde is a figure of *substance*. In this study's opening chapter, I allowed for the problematic character of an unduly substantialized liberal agency, with its hard-to-credit image of the agent's essential being as something above and beyond the world of phenomenal experience. At the same time, I argued that a distinctively liberal agency can be rationalized along more practical lines by allowing for a regulative liberal subjectivity, a reflective locus of purposeful self-understanding and action that takes shape and can be read simply in its manifestations. This view tells of a kind of liberal doing rather than liberal being, even as that liberal doing seems to be marked by an aspiration to this impossible liberal being. In some respects, then, my view is compatible with viewpoints commonly called antifoundationalist or even pragmatist.

My account differs in explicating a residually metaphysical ambition both in

Wilde's practice and in the practice of those who seek to enlist his supposed antiessentialism in service to variously progressive or radical values. My initial chapter's theoretical argument also contends, that is, that the supposedly profound distinction between antifoundationalist pragmatism and deontological liberalism evaporates once we see humans as essentially disposed to thoughtful reflections *about* practice as such. And the blurriness of antiessentialism's difference from regulative liberal agency becomes especially apparent when we go on to attach interest or value to such aspiration. Thus my topic in this chapter is not simply Wilde but our commonplace estimations of Wilde as an aesthetic agent. My point is therefore not so much that we underread Wilde by seeing in his work an antiessentialist or antifoundational ethos. Better to say that such readings mistake the distinctively liberal vision of critical agency that gives to antiessentialist or antifoundational practices their ethical and political content.

My reading might be viewed as an elaboration of Ellmann's claim that "Wilde is one of us."[10] That case for Wilde's modernity emphasizes his self-conscious placement in a profoundly chastened Enlightenment. Like Nietzsche and Freud, this Wilde sees that rationalism and empiricism alike provide no conclusive authority for conduct. But Ellmann's remark, to the extent that it seems true and celebratory, also implies that we find in Wilde a *welcome* image of ourselves. This Wilde is a congenial figure, not exactly because he stood for the all the right views—that is, "our" views. Instead, his most decisive attraction proceeds from his final irreducibility to any concrete scheme of value or viewpoint. That irreducibility leaves him available, and also always slightly unavailable, to a broad range of identifications. His ostentatious aloofness from Victorian marital pieties, in this light, was never simply covert boosterism for alternative domestic relations, not a veiled invitation to others of his mind to join a cause. Instead, as aloofness, his attitude conjures a probationary freedom from social determinations of any sort. I contend that Wilde's principal force of authorial seduction proceeds from a tendency, characteristic in modern liberal agents, to be interested in a profoundly radical bracketing of the predicaments of individuality and sociality.

I begin by looking to Wilde's rather little-known short story "The Portrait of Mr. W.H.," one of those works in which Wilde most elaborately thematized originality. My concern is to unpack a difficult but distinctively Wildean way of being that looks provocatively indifferent to conventional groundings in objective truth or ethical rationalization. I then turn to a broader view of Wilde's traffic in ideas of agency, drawing especially on his play *Salome* and his novel *The Picture of Dorian Gray*. By way of an excursus through Louis Althusser's classic postmodern-era statement of subjection and interpellation, I set up the chapter's conclusion, and the study's with it, in a view to Pierre Bourdieu's influential work on modern aesthetic culture. What emerges here is a revisionary account of Wilde's interest for both historical materialist and broadly post-

structuralist theories—an account that reveals a logic of liberal agency sub-
tending those views at crucial junctures.

Forging Evidence: "The Portrait of Mr. W.H."

Wilde's short story "The Portrait of Mr. W.H" takes an apparently objective
question of originality—a forged painting and the uses to which it is put—and
transforms that question of fact into a vertiginous perspective on literary-
critical agency. The story's three main characters at turns assert, disavow, and
reappropriate a literary theory for which a forged painting is the lone material
evidence. The literary theory proposes that Mr. W.H.—the mysterious dedicatee of Shakespeare's *Sonnets*—can be identified as Willie Hughes, a boy actor
in Shakespeare's theater company. The eponymous portrait within the story, in
turn, depicts a young man in Elizabethan-era costume resting his hand on the
dedication page of a copy of the *Sonnets*. With his story's sudden twists and
swapping of roles, Wilde gives us a lighthearted farce of criticism, on the one
hand; an earnest diagnosis of criticism as farce, on the other. In either case, the
image of critical procedure is quite removed from the mainstream patrician atmosphere prevalent in journals such as *Blackwood's* and *The Nineteenth Century*, in
which Wilde published his early work.[11] Wilde's gambit is to confront his readers with a vision of criticism's propensity to proactive inauthenticity. The tale
is a serious comment on criticism's final lack of seriousness, a cheerfully embraced performative contradiction.

The theme of originality finds here a specifically Wildean treatment in that
the portrait's status as an original or a forgery comes to matter less than the
concerns of these critical subjects with thinking and acting. The tale foregrounds a sense in which originality—understood in terms of the authenticity
of objects—is in no position to regulate value or action. Seen in this very general sense, Wilde's story can recall for us some aspects of the popular interest
in the Tichborne Claimant. For in that case, too, the issue at one point was
how to construe the circumstance whereby one could regard the Claimant as
a likely impostor but nonetheless speak in favor of his cause, with a sense that
to do so was to serve the aspirations proper to popular social action. At any
rate, the issue to be isolated here is what it means to disdain the authenticity of
evidence when reckoning our criteria of critical belief.

"Mr. W.H." begins with the narrator, who is never named, recalling a conversation with his friend Erskine. Their topic is literary forgeries:

I cannot at present remember how it was that we struck upon this somewhat curious
topic, as it was at that time, but I know that we had a long discussion about Macpher-
son, Ireland and Chatterton, and that with regard to the last I insisted that his so-called
forgeries were merely the result of an artistic desire for perfect representation; that we
had no right to quarrel with an artist for the conditions under which he chooses to present his work; and that all Art being to a certain degree a mode of acting, an attempt to

realise one's own personality on some imaginative plane out of reach of the trammel-
ing accidents and limitations of real life, to censure an artist for a forgery was to confuse an ethical with an aesthetical problem.

Erskine, who was a good deal older than I was, and had been listening to me with
the amused deference of a man of forty, suddenly put his hand upon my shoulder and
said to me, "What would you say about a young man who had a strange theory about
a certain work of art, believed in his theory, and committed a forgery to prove it?"

"Ah! that is quite a different matter," I answered.

Erskine remained silent for a few moments, looking at the thin grey threads of smoke
that were rising from his cigarette. "Yes," he said, after a pause, "quite different."[12]

Erskine's pause underlines the story's guiding problem: the performatively odd
circumstance of believing in a theory and deliberately forging evidence for it.
The young man in question here, at once faithful and falsifying, is Cyril Graham. Erskine goes on to recall to the narrator how Cyril had tried to advocate
the Willie Hughes theory, which indicates that the dedicatee to Shakespeare's
Sonnets, Mr. W.H., is identical to a "Will Hews" within the sonnet story, a male
figure adored by the poetic speaker and identical to one Willie Hughes, a boy
actor in Shakespeare's company. Erskine had listened with interest but without
assent to Cyril's points in favor of the theory, points based chiefly on close
reading of Shakespeare's sonnets, with puns and other points of language in
the sonnets adduced as encoded revelation of this secret passion. But no
amount of close reading was adequate to convince Erskine, who remained a
skeptic until the discovery of the portrait. Converted in his views for a time,
Erskine soon discovered the fraud and jettisoned the theory, whereupon a distraught Cyril ran away and blew his brains out, leaving behind him a letter declaring his intention to "offer his life as a sacrifice to the secret of the *Sonnets*"
(152). Years later, as Erskine recalls this tale, our narrator is immediately en-
chanted by Cyril's theory. The body of Wilde's story relates the narrator's successive attempts to persuade Erskine, by dint of renewed close reading of the
poems, that the Willie Hughes theory is sound.

As before, Erskine remains skeptical, and in this he seems to exemplify the
intractability of a jaded everydayness. In a final desperate effort of interpretive
intensity, the narrator drafts a letter to Erskine laying out the entire reading.
But no sooner does the narrator mail off his impassioned argument to Erskine
than he finds himself instantly and absolutely bereft of faith in it. Says the narrator, in lines that I believe are key, "I put into the letter all my enthusiasm. I
put into the letter all my faith" (164). Even as writing out the letter to Erskine
leaves the narrator suddenly unconvinced by the theory, Erskine meanwhile
reads the letter and finds a renewed faith in the theory. The two men, who have
now exchanged their opinions, soon quarrel: Erskine protests the narrator's
lack of faith and shallowness—says Erskine: "You have proved the thing to me.
Do you think I cannot estimate the value of evidence?" The narrator bemoans
Erskine's credulousness: "There is no evidence at all. . . . The only evidence for
the existence of Willie Hughes is that picture in front of you, and that picture

is a forgery. . . . The one flaw in the theory is that it presupposes the existence of the person whose existence is the subject of dispute" (165–66). This drama of evidence and faith comes to a head in an episode some years later, when Erskine declares in a letter to our narrator that he means to follow in Cyril's steps by committing suicide as a martyr to the theory. Rushing to stop this action, the narrator discovers that Erskine is dead. The narrator discovers as well, however, that a case of consumption was the real cause of Erskine's death, so his "suicide" was yet another falsehood perpetrated in service to the Willie Hughes theory of Shakespeare's *Sonnets*.

At least one point seems plain now: Wilde's apparent concern is to portray literary-critical interpretation as a form of reflection and commitment potentially indifferent to claims of objective evidence. In effect, the portrait's inauthenticity is rendered moot at key junctures, and these occasions are styled as moments that enable renewed interpretation. It is in this sense that the narrator's comments about his letter to Erskine—"I put into the letter all my enthusiasm. I put into the letter all my faith" (164)—can be understood as Wilde's deft but penetrating engagement with the larger Victorian crisis of literalism and faith, energized in that broader context through concern for religious authority. The narrator loses his faith precisely when his credo is literalized. But even as his own faith is evacuated into the letter, the spirit of the theory appears to gain its hold on Erskine. In this light, the objective falseness of the painting takes shape as a matter of literal falsehood, but insofar as the very authority of literalism is itself questioned in Wilde's story, the objective falseness of the painting cannot be said to settle in any simple way what interest or meaning is proper to the painting.

The story's concluding sentences underline the uncertain bases of any interest in the painting and the theory. Reflecting on the portrait and attempting to sum up the tale he has just told, the narrator concludes with an image of the interpreter that I mean to consider as a problematic image of interpretation generally: "The picture hangs now in my library, where it is very much admired by my artistic friends, one of whom has etched it for me. They have decided that it is not a Clouet, but an Ouvry. I have never cared to tell them its true history, but sometimes, when I look at it, I think there is really a great deal to be said for the Willie Hughes theory of Shakespeare's Sonnets" (168–69). The narrator is fully aware of the facts surrounding this bogus portrait, so his closing assertion that "there is really a great deal to be said" for the Willie Hughes theory appears to end the tale on a note of rather weak irony. In this respect, we see in the narrator an image of the more critical modern accounts of Wilde himself, understood as a figure whose concern for literal truth is shallow, vague, indifferent, or inconsequential. Indeed, a plausible if rather flat-footed assumption would be that Wilde lacked any better inspiration for his closing line and simply threw in something to bring affairs to a cheap kind of closure, compromising a clever and engaging story by dissipating it in a lackadaisical gesture toward consummation. For are we not left to feel that this story—a story that can fairly be said to be about the falseness and the unverifiability of everything that has been done in the name of that portrait—ends with what can only be taken as a listless and rather happenstance affirmation of the Willie Hughes theory? If there is "really a great deal to be said for the Willie Hughes theory of Shakespeare's *Sonnets*," whatever there is to be said is left not only vague but also contingent on the narrator's happenstance glimpses of the portrait: the strengths of the theory appear to the narrator only "sometimes" and only "when I look at" the portrait. A less vigorous and focused image of interpretive consciousness could hardly be urged. Indeed, as work by James Eli Adams on masculinity in Victorian critical discourse suggests, the lack of consequential vigor in this critical intelligence is a key element in the aversion that some Victorians would experience in respect to the vaguely effeminate posturings of the aestheticist and decadent ethos.

A sharper reading might reason that Wilde intended the rather flaccid character of the narrator's final appeal, in which light the foregoing criticism comes to look as wide of the mark as Oliver Elton's points about Wilde's derivativeness, and for much the same reason. For "Mr. W.H."'s strangely listless image of the interpreter has its point to make: it signals the narrator's residual susceptibility to a thoroughly impeached viewpoint—impeached, at least, insofar as the portrait had been thought to provide objective evidence for the theory in question. In that susceptibility, the narrator embodies an idea regarding the condition of critical "saying" and critical agency. The impertinence of this critical saying in respect to the authority of fact and evidence is not simply an aestheticized refusal of materiality and social facts but a figure for a more general threat, a threat that pertains to subjectivity whether narrowly "aesthetic" or not: namely, the threat that a feeling of interpretive pleasure might overwrite any sheerly empirical or rationalist procedure of knowledge.

At stake here is the status and the character of literary-critical evidence. Of course, a theory and its evidence are not the same thing in any case: the falseness of this portrait cannot establish any conclusion about the truth of the theory. But it is not Wilde's concern to underline that particular bit of interpretive caution. Quite the contrary, in fact. For if it were Wilde's concern to remind us not to commit that fallacy of association—that is, not to take the faked image as a signal of a false theory—there would be no reason to set up the portrait as the impetus for a renewed sense of credence in the Willie Hughes theory. We need still to account for the narrator's deliberate parenthesis in the closing lines—his remark that "sometimes, *when I look at it* [the portrait], I think there is really a great deal to be said for the Willie Hughes theory"—for that parenthesis makes plain that a view to the portrait is precisely that which resuscitates the theory in the mind of the narrator. And therein lies the story's crucial affront to more than one prevailing practice of interpretation in Wilde's time. It is an affront to literalism. Like a specter bedeviling a sober scholarly point of view, the Willie Hughes theory actually arises *out of the imposture* of the portrait. That is to say, the critical truth declared in the Willie Hughes theory arises out of a falsehood, a lie. But that lie is, in this instance, nothing other than a subject's capacity to disdain objectivity as an authority. At issue in such a vision are the claims of personal authenticity and critical objectivity that Wilde consistently cast into question.

So "Mr. W.H." is characteristically Wildean in several senses. One commonly hears of Wilde as an apostle of artificiality, and putting a faked portrait in an affirmative light—or, to be more exact, putting the implication of that portrait in an affirmative light, notwithstanding the actual falseness of the portrait's representation—seems congruent with this view of Wildean procedure. Wilde is also known for espousing an impressionistic critical ethos, whereby the object of criticism is not so much that Arnoldian destination of a "thing as in itself it really is" but instead a more subjectively determined concern, notoriously suggested by Wilde's inversion of the Arnoldian formula in "The Critic as Artist": "the primary aim of the critic is to see the object as in itself it really is not."[13] Wilde's bid to cast a "false" painting in the light of an affirmative inauthenticity—and, in an extension I propose here, his bid to cast literary-critical interpretation in a similar light—reflects a Victorian consciousness struck with a sense that the truths of critical procedure might actually conform as closely to terms of inauthenticity as to authenticity.[14]

Walter Benjamin suggested once that the power of story lies in the perpetually undetermined character of its indication: a great story invites interpretation but also refuses the definitive resolution that we might, in a moment of forgetting, suppose ourselves to be seeking there.[15] From the vantage point of the interpreter, the story is an image of ongoing fruitfulness, of endless renewal and possibility. In "Mr. W.H.," the painting seems to serve much the same function as a focusing point for interpretive continuation. If it is true, however, that we turn to stories because of their propensity to outstrip any final account of their meaning, we do so not simply because we enjoy interpreting in general but because we see in the perpetual fertility of the story a very specific indication after all, an indication that *we can always interpret*. I am suggesting that this consoling affirmation of interpreting agency is the basis for that interest, spotlighted by Benjamin, in the ever-pregnant character of story. And in this light, the ongoing significance of the faked portrait in "Mr. W.H." is not so much a trivial twist added by Wilde to the end of his story; instead, it is Wilde's most decided image of the condition of critical saying, of a saying that subsists (or persists) wholly apart from the fakeness of the portrait that prompts that saying. In adumbrating an interpretive practice built upon fakeness, then, Wilde is offering yet another variant on George Eliot's affirmative "imitation of mastery," which my opening chapter read in the light of liberal heroics.

It seems clear, here as elsewhere, that Wilde aims to call into question the authoritative bases of critical thinking. One of his paths to that questioning lies in rendering problematic the regulative claim that originality—here chiefly a matter of authenticity versus fakery—has on our estimation of ideas, persons, or things. But if it is clear that Wilde refuses a set of conventional pieties about originality and critical authority, it is less clear what vision of consciousness Wilde is actually trying to embrace, and why. Indeed, most deprecations of Wilde as a literary thinker proceed from a sense that no consequential idea of critical saying can be drawn from such moments as that which concludes "Mr. W.H." To specify what vision of subjective agency might there be at hand, we must come to terms with Wilde's conception of agency more generally.

Imagining Agency

> *To be entirely free, and at the same time, entirely dominated by law, is the eternal paradox of human life that we realise at every moment.*
>
> —*Oscar Wilde in his prison letter* De Profundis[16]

Wilde's thinking about agency finds its most condensed form in the remark I take here as an epigraph. Much like Wilde himself, the utterance is at once hard to make much out of and hard also to discount. It is well to note that the remark is tendered by a literally imprisoned subject, as Wilde is at this moment approaching the end of his two years at hard labor for "acts of gross indecency"; what is more, Wilde's discussion at this point in the letter bears, in keeping with the letter as a whole, on his relationship to Lord Alfred Douglas, a relationship marked by mutual thralldom to an ill-fated passion. In those two respects, Wilde's concern with agency in chains might be said to hinge largely on some local aspects of the moment in which he is writing. But I wrest this remark out as an epigraph with the thought that it can be instructive in itself, both as a focusing point in reading Wilde more generally and as a comment worth engaging to clarify the terms in which the modern liberal vision of agency can be understood and practiced. Indeed, the key question for us to consider is if, and how, such an utterance marks any consequential "thinking" about agency at all. For here, human agency has a paradoxical form—thus a familiarly Wildean form—wherein "we realise" ourselves at once as absolutely free and as absolutely determined. Can one actually inhabit, rather than merely gesture at, such a paradoxical positionality?

My suggestion here is that we can and do inhabit paradox in some meaningful sense. Indeed, the aspiration to originality is tantamount to a self-location in paradox. To construe oneself as at once inhabiting a role and maintaining a measure of independence from the prescriptive dimensions of that role is to suggest as much. And to see in that equivocal understanding a central and defining feature of one's potency as an agent is to enter fully into the characteristic complexity of the liberal self-conception, understood as an ongoing effort to reconcile or balance opposing claims about the sources of agency—often cast in binaries like freedom and determinism, voluntarism and culturalism, the ethical self and the sociological self, and more.

Thus it can seem that Wilde's famous will to paradox might have much to do with the historical irony that he is today perhaps the most respectable of Victorian authors. In any case, the following argument explores three related claims premised on this sense of Wilde's unusual congeniality to much contemporary thinking: first, that a process of identification on our part with such a paradoxical construct is crucial to contemporary interest in Wilde; second, that such identification has everything to do with our sense of his power or, in the term I privilege here, his *agency*; and third, that asking about Wilde's agency as a literary creator is closely bound up with contemporary ideals of agency in literary-critical thinking. In short, Wilde's greatness and even his general interest as an author lie in his status as an appealing figure of generalized agency or force.

Most critics think of Wildean agency in terms of social subversion. Sos Eltis looks to the plays to see Wilde as a broad-spectrum activist for socialism and feminism, and recent scholarship by Terry Eagleton, Vicki Mahaffey, and others has presented Wilde in postcolonialist terms by looking to his Irishness.[17] But sexual politics is surely the lens through which most critics have read Wilde's subversive agency. In such accounts Wilde is, to use Jonathan Dollimore's memorable phrase, a "sexual dissident," a guerrilla tactician who baffles heterosexualist conservatism by fashioning, as Ed Cohen has it, "new discursive strategies to express concerns unvoiced within the dominant culture."[18] Finding much to sympathize with in such characterizations, I suggest as well that the most compelling dramas of agency in Wilde's writings actually emerge in the formal character of his works, and that any privileged placement of sexual "content" in reading his works bears critical examination. I particularly balk at any claim that Wilde's subversiveness consists in his effort to encode illicit subtexts into his works to say something forbidden. I cannot be sidetracked here into an engagement with that prevalent view, except to insist that encoding and decoding are alike forms of simple literalism that will never get us to the substance of Wilde's aesthetic provocations.

What might get us to the substance of Wilde's thought is a closer view to some formal aspects of his writing that have found little attention in Wilde scholarship. Let me begin by trying to specify my distinction between a literalist style of reading and a more sheerly formal reading that foregrounds the limitations of the literalist approach.

It is one thing, for instance, to regard Wilde's character Dorian Gray as a figure, to literalize him, as it were, and to meditate on how preternatural beauty and exemption from the effects of time might well open certain forbidden doors to anyone like him in the real world. Identifying with Dorian Gray himself would mean, it seems, identifying with a welcome or unwelcome idea of a position from which to act. But most canny readers of Wilde's novel allow that the deeper provocations of that text—its real interest for most of us—concern the triangulated relation of three different figures—the beautiful Dorian Gray, the insouciant and witty spectator Lord Henry Wotton, and the earnest painter Basil Hallward. Together these figures constitute a sort of exploded view of a single, complex, and rather commonplace constitution, defined by the fusion of contending schemes of value and viewpoint. Lord Henry's experimental and sheerly observational ethos aligns him with a set of empiricist and positivist values; Basil Hallward, despite his skill as an artist, is functionally an ambassador for ethical precepts emerging from a mixture of Christian self-abasement and Enlightenment universalist ethics; and Dorian Gray expresses the uncertain and contested relation of aesthetic pleasure to the prior two domains. In any case, it seems that the whole point of Dorian Gray as an individual is that his consciousness depends on his contact with two other forces: the image provided by the earnest painter Hallward and the verbal seductions of the ironical Wotton. To see in all these characters a refraction of Wilde's view of character as such is to focus on the work's formal arrangement, and it is, too, to come close to a sense of Wilde's own thinking, implicit in the narrative's form. And to find one's interest not in a specific identification but in a sense of that larger constellation of figures is to posit an alignment of one's own consciousness with the authorial effort on Wilde's part, an effort also marked as a construction of, and meditation on, this triangular relation of characters. In this style of reading, the reading itself is a species of identification—not, however, with a character but with an account of character.

Promising Subjects

In his ideas about character, as in several other respects, Wilde anticipates problems that have preoccupied critics since the 1960s, when it became increasingly common to insist that serious critical thinking needs to engage, in some way, the internal contradictions supposed to lurk within any categories invoked as authoritative or value-generating.[19] The term *character* emphasizes and indeed insists on the specification of an individual even though it is not clear whether or how individuals can be specified apart from roles and types that define and constrain them. So the key uncertainty is whether character specifies radically individual agency or a proper subjection within the terms of an outlying set of relations. Deidre Lynch's recent work in eighteenth-century topics brings renewed clarity to the point that such contradictory valences considerably predate the Victorian period.[20] Catherine Gallagher and Amanda Anderson have both offered keen arguments concerning the divided nature of character in the Victorian period especially.[21] Wilde's engagement with character therefore shows his supple treatment of agency, and nowhere more so than in the moment of promising, which plays an important but hitherto undiscussed role in Wilde's key works.

Diverse critical contexts have taken up the promise's special feature of highlighting both a radically individual act and an obligation to relate to others in an exemplary fashion.[22] A moment in *The Importance of Being Earnest* shows how deftly Wilde insinuated this aspect of agency into his works. Here Cecily and Gwendolyn are supposing that one man has proposed marriage to both of them. The absent Mr. Ernest Worthing of whom they speak is in fact not one person but two, Jack and Algy, traveling under that one name, and the young women will discover this fact soon enough. But because they do not know it just now, they proceed into a testy exchange that actually amounts to a debate about obligation and agency:

CECILY: [*Rather shy and confidingly.*] Dearest Gwendolyn, there is no reason why I should make a secret of it to you. Our little county newspaper is sure to chronicle the fact next week. Mr. Ernest Worthing and I are engaged to be married.

GWENDOLYN: [*Quite politely, rising.*] My darling Cecily, I think there must be some slight error. Mr. Ernest Worthing is engaged to me. The announcement will appear in the "*Morning Post*" on Saturday at the latest.

CECILY: [*Very politely.*] I am afraid you must be under some misconception. Ernest proposed to me exactly ten minutes ago. [*Shows diary.*]

GWENDOLYN: [*Examines diary through her lorgnette carefully.*] It is certainly very curious, for he asked me to be his wife yesterday afternoon at 5:30. If you would care to verify the incident, pray do so. [*Produces diary of her own.*] I never travel without my diary. One should always have something sensational to read in the train. I am so sorry, dear Cecily, if it is any disappointment to you, but I am afraid I have a prior claim.

CECILY: It would distress me more than I can tell you, dear Gwendolyn, if it caused you any mental or physical anguish, but I feel bound to point out that since Ernest proposed to you he has clearly changed his mind.[23]

In this exchange, two figures of Mr. Ernest Worthing are invoked: the one, a figure bound to his initial promise to Gwendolyn; the other, a figure who "has clearly changed his mind." These competing portraits of bachelor agency imply two distinct tales of subjection: the Mr. Worthing that Cecily and Gwendolyn here briefly envision is a creature uncertainly positioned in respect to his monumentalizing promises, on the one hand, and to the ongoing activity of a mind that might "change," on the other. This contest of obligation and "free" agency is, in fact, the key point of contention in the Wildean—and more generally modern—accounting of agency. The opposition of obligation and free agency, to be more precise, is not a choice but a constitutive antagonism.

A historically suggestive aspect of this problem emerges in developments of English contract law during the nineteenth century. Contractual liability reflects not only a given society's conception of promising but also that society's conception of the role of the state in enforcing the fulfillment of promises. Today we can mistakenly assume that the state always had some such role. But P. S. Atiyah has observed that eighteenth-century and early Victorian laissez-faire saw the task of law in respect to contracts chiefly as a problem of how best to permit contracts. With the mid-Victorian period, however, the issue came increasingly to be the extent to which the law should engage in enforcing contracts. When a person contracts for services with another person who proves unable to make good on the agreement, for example, classical economic thinking saw a private action on the first person's part gone bad. The prospect that the state had a role in seizing the person in default or that person's property was understood to be another question entirely. The state interventionism that was to transform liberalism so profoundly in the mid-Victorian period finds one of its earliest expression in judicial and legislative decisions that increasingly found in the enforcement of contracts a legitimate state interest.[24]

But a philosophical conception of this terrain can throw better light on the actual terms of Wilde's writings. Insisting on the high stakes of promising is part of Nietzsche's project in *On the Genealogy of Morals* (1887).[25] For Nietzsche, the promise is the key moment in a kind of self-enslavement that defines sovereignty. For in the promise we have an act that one enters into as an authoritative voice, creating social and subjective being. The second essay in Nietzsche's work begins with the question of what it means to breed an animal in a position to make promises—a vow to marry and be faithful to another person, for example. Nietzsche's answer is that breeding an animal in a position to make promises means breeding a man who is, in effect, *not* in a position to change his mind, or not, at least, in any position to do so without running afoul of the societal prohibitions against doing so.

Societal prohibitions have their outward mechanisms of enforcement, of course—epitomized in imprisonment, ostracism, excommunication, impeachment, and so forth—but much contemporary theory turns on a supposition that social prohibition is experienced more crucially in an inward respect, through a *conscience* that subsists as the internalization of an outlying social norm. Freud argues this case in *Civilization and Its Discontents* when he describes conscience as the internalization of parental authority; Foucault's concern in *Discipline and Punish* lay in detailing how the "soul" assumes its modern function as an internalization of society's disciplinary structures; and Judith Butler has more recently voiced such views as well.[26] But I take the substance of the issue to be at hand already in Nietzsche. With the promise, according to Nietzsche, we make free to subject ourselves to a logic extending beyond the present moment; with the promise, our "will" becomes an inflexible and enduring master rather than the ongoing and changing emanation of a presubjected, undomesticated agency. In order for promise-making to take shape as an activity, says Nietzsche, "Man himself must first of all have become *calculable, regular, necessary*, even in his own image of himself, if he is able to stand security for *his own future*, which is what one who promises does!" (58).

Nietzsche's implied alternative—a vision of faithless unsubjected agency—circulates as a kind of phantasmic prospect rather than as a role that one might or might not adopt, and perhaps some shying from the enormity of such a selfhood was especially the rule in the English population to which Wilde addressed himself. Nietzsche's specter of radical free agency, let us not forget, arises in a work that began as a rejoinder to English moralists and what he saw as their absurd attempts to reduce human values to rules. And to the extent that one of these moralists would have offered a Nietzschean idea of agency for consideration, the offering would probably arrive defanged in advance, just as J. S. Mill could note, in a somewhat different context, "that very frequent infirmity of English minds, which makes them take a preposterous pleasure in the assertion of a bad principle, when they are no longer bad enough to desire to carry it really into practice."[27] It is in this sense that Wilde's literary persona and his works were both well positioned to pose ideas without realizing them to an especially threatening degree, so that while some persons, no doubt, were indeed threatened by Wilde's implied sexuality and the affront to masculinity and high seriousness that he figured, most people knew that this figure could be regarded in fun.

While the collision of perspectives on agency envisioned by Cecily and Gwendolyn actually evaporates in the sequel—they are discussing not one man but two—it remains broadly true that Wilde's central literary efforts continually conjure versions of this subject in subjection. The one-act drama *Salome* (1893; 1894) is an especially concerted instance. The story is drawn from a biblical episode in which the ruler Herod strikes a bargain with his stepdaughter, the princess Salome: if Salome will dance for him, Herod will give her anything she asks, up to half his kingdom. She dances, and then she requests the head of John the Baptist as her prize. Herod grants her request, and such is the Salome legend in its traditional form. Wilde's additions to this traditional narrative clarify his concern to portray Herod's fulfillment of his promise as a moment certifying the ruler's subjection to sociality. Even before Salome's dance, we find Herod reveling in the obligation that will soon prove so repellent to him. Herod's suspiciously urgent protestations that he is happy lead him to gloat in anticipation of seeing Salome dance, and he recalls his promise to Salome, as if to urge her haste in performing before him:

HEROD: I have sworn an oath, have I not?

SALOME: Thou hast sworn it, Tetrarch.

HEROD: And I have never failed of my word. I am not one of those break
          their oaths. I know not how to lie. I am the slave of my word, and
          my word is the word of a king.[28]

Wilde here makes explicit how we are to understand Herod's agreement to go through with killing the prophet: Herod's word binds him to the exchange. The word here, in the figure of his kingly promise, initiates a mechanism linking the dance and the dancer's reward, so that once inaugurated, the linkage assumes a life of its own. That is, his edict acquires an autonomy that turns back upon the very authorizing agent that brought the matter into play: Wilde's Herod pleads with Salome to alter her request; she refuses repeatedly, and Herod must finally follow through. After this exchange, Herod recognizes himself anew, realizing himself as a figure in a predicament of power.

But Wilde's most singular addition to the massively popular Salome theme is his drama's final moment, when Salome is killed by Herod's order. In a brilliantly condensed image of the ruler's subjected sovereignty, Wilde indicates how Herod's progress lies in seeing that he is caught in a web of determinations and constraints that stretches beyond his sight for its footings. At the drama's end, Wilde's formal spatial arrangements intimate the ruler's realization of this circumstance: Herod resolves to leave this scene, where the exercise of his rule and the pursuit of his desire have together bound him to an act that he regrets deeply, for in consenting to kill the prophet Iokanaan he fears divine retribution. Thus chastened in his sense of mastery, Herod remarks in his penultimate line, "I begin to be afraid" (328). He then attempts to ascend a staircase to exit, but he turns about, sees Salome taking her pleasures with the head of Iokanaan, and delivers his fatal order: "Kill that woman!" (329). The play ends, however, not with Herod exiting the scene but rather frozen midway on the ascending flight of stairs. Again, in a formal specification within the literary work—the ruler Herod fixed midway on the very stairway that he has proposed to use as a means of egress—Wilde suggests a richly complex image of a figure's subjection. Herod's power and his capitulation are of a piece, and he cannot simply walk away from this scene.

Wilde's novel *The Picture of Dorian Gray* is likewise the story of an aftermath to a promise. Upon "recognizing himself" in his painted image, Dorian Gray vows to trade his soul so that he may remain ageless like an artwork, leaving the portrait to age in his stead. And more so than in *Salome*, where a minimalism inherited from the symbolist idiom keeps the ideas rather cryptic, *Dorian Gray* offers layers of characterization and narratorial positioning that conjure a more ramified image of agency. As with Herod, Dorian's process of self-recognition and promising is at once a birth of empowered self-consciousness and an enslavement to a logic that defines his life from that point onward. In this sense, the portrait plays an interpellative role, as in the Althusserian fable of subjection that I will turn to in a moment. In both Herod and in Dorian Gray, a "paradox" unfolds in that the characters are born into states of sovereign self-awareness precisely as their states come to exert on them orders of power and obligation to which they are definitively "subjected."

When Dorian sees his image he is caught in stunned self-recognition. Looking on his portrait for the first time, the narrative shows off the moment as a sort of birth: "The sense of his own beauty came on him like a revelation"[29] (66–67). What follows is a fateful decision that Dorian effects in the form of a vow. The fin-de-siècle Faust inaugurates his progress through a commitment:

> "How sad it is," murmured Dorian Gray, with his eyes still fixed upon his own portrait. "How sad it is! I shall grow old, and horrible, and dreadful. But this picture will remain always young. It will never be older than this particular day of June. . . . If it were only the other way! If it were I who was to be always young, and the picture that was to grow old! For that—for that—I would give everything! Yes, there is nothing in the whole world I would not give! I would give my soul for that!"(67)

To locate a commitment in these words is, of course, to allow for an order of magical efficacy that Dorian seems unaware of having at his command. His astonishment later, as he sees the portrait begin to deform and degenerate, shows that he is oblivious to this exclamation's power to effect any change. But Wilde's magical premise is not merely a expedient narrative trick—a deus ex machina plot convenience that might license some trivialization of Dorian's fate on realistic grounds, as if to say, "Well, whatever else one sees in Dorian Gray's story, one sees something that in fact cannot happen *really*." Far from it. For Dorian here does as we all do in entering our fundamental commitments: the moment of decision takes place in the context of unknowing. One does not consciously decide—one does not decide to decide—to denominate one's language as one's own, to see one's name as one's own, to call one's culture one's own. Like the portrait on its way to Dorian, these things come to us from without, but we take them as our own, even as ourselves. An identification is forged with these unwitting commitments, and a fate is given by the nature of the ensuing determinants.[30]

This moment of recognition and commitment is then a moment—both within this novel and in terms more generally of the ideological problematic I am exploring here—when that which can be called one's "own" actually comes to issue. And it is in this fundamental sense that one's relation to originality can seem so pertinent to one's sense of agency and identity more generally. In the novel, right before Dorian makes his fatal wish, Basil and Lord Henry are debating the matter of the portrait's ownership. Lord Henry covets the portrait and declares immediately to Basil, "I will give you anything you like to ask for it. I must have it." Basil replies that it is not his property, but rather Dorian's. Later, in fact, Basil will note, "You know the picture is yours, Dorian. I gave it to you before it existed." Given the transformative effect of the portrait on Dorian, we see that Basil might have just as well have said he gave the portrait to Dorian before Dorian existed. Or that he gave Dorian to the portrait. Basil would not say such a thing, as it is very much a part of Basil's character not to see his model in such a way. Basil's oblivion to this problematic is an aspect of his characterization: like any good artist in Wilde's scheme of thinking, Basil knows not what he does. But the structure of this scene implies a mindfulness on Wilde's part of a problem concerning the meaning of Dorian's self-consciousness.[31] In traversing the path from unselfconsciousness to self-consciousness, Dorian figures the emergence of his reflective agency. There is in this agency both a promise of fulfillment and also, as the subsequent story makes plain, a move beyond any certainties about the purview or the prospects of such agency.

THE INTERPELLATIVE AESTHETIC

In a classic statement of modern theory, "Ideology and Ideological State Apparatuses" (1970), Louis Althusser proposes to outline a mechanism through which individuals are incorporated into the material practices that constitute and perpetuate reigning ideologies. As regards the prospects of critical agency, Althusser's account is notable for its pessimism. He describes the process of ideological "interpellation" or "hailing," whereby the individual is not properly a "subject" until he or she is named into being as such, addressed or interpellated into subjectivity.[32] This process of *assujetissement*—variously rendered in English as *subjectivation, subjectification, subjection*—names a process that enforces constraint and conformism and simultaneously allows a liberating sense of being born into a role, of being brought into a state of almost theatrical being that regards itself to be "obviously" free and not, in a negative sense, "subject" to coercion. In a gesture hardly less comprehensive than Plato's suggestion that we regard our common sense of reality as mere appearance, Althusser proposes that we regard common ideas of free agency as mere illusion. In the following pages I want to show how Althusser's points bear on Wilde's thinking, and vice versa, respecting the agent's role in determining his or her own fate and intellectual purview.

A moment in *Dorian Gray* brings me to examine Althusser's argument in this light. As I have already intimated by spotlighting Dorian's Gray's quasi-Faustian act of bargaining away his soul, questions of personal action and responsibility are subtly but invariably at issue in the critical moments of Dorian's progress. At that moment he is not clearly a willing agent, we should recall, but instead a figure whose predicament suggests that his agency has taken him, ironically, unawares. Thus we confront in Wilde's characterization of Dorian a curious prospect that what one does is at once proper to oneself but somehow still not a simple refection of radically autonomous, self-conscious deliberation and will. A passage later in the novel helps us ask about the sense in which Dorian—or anyone, more generally—might come to be aware of himself in this peculiarly mixed state of willing agency and unwilled determination. After hearing of the apparent suicide of Sibyl Vane, Basil goes to Dorian with the thought of consoling him. Basil assumes, mistakenly, that Dorian is distraught, and he assumes as well, again mistakenly, the falsity of reports placing Dorian at the opera shortly after the fatal news was out. Basil is therefore perplexed to encounter Dorian's steely composure in the face of Sibyl's death. This newly indifferent, decadent young man chills Basil with the following account of his own development:

To become the spectator of one's own life, as Harry says, is to escape the suffering of life. I know you are surprised at my talking at you like this. You have not realized how I have developed. I was a schoolboy when you knew me. I am a man now. I have new passions, new thoughts, new ideas. I am different, but you must not like me less. I am changed, but you must always be my friend. Of course, I am very fond of Harry. But I know that you are better than he is. You are not stronger—you are much too afraid of life—but you are better. And how happy we used to be together! Don't leave me, Basil, and don't quarrel with me. I am what I am. There is nothing else to be said. (130)

The passage provides a telling constellation of those terms and issues that inform this novel and most of Wilde's works fundamentally—spectatorship, escapism, the courage and the delusion underlying programmatic passions, the personality that compels assent, the distinction of strength from goodness, and the nostalgia for an original unity now fallen away: "And how happy we used to be together!" Culminating this dense sequence comes the most illuminating locution: Dorian's "I am what I am." The remark leaves, as Dorian points out immediately, "nothing more to be said," thus effecting a closure on the matter.[33] Reminiscent also of the "art for art's sake" locution, Dorian's remark seems a declaration of "Dorian for Dorian's sake." Dorian, it seems, has not only aspired to, but attained, the condition of autonomy increasingly arrogated by art.

Dorian's circular self-definition echoes that utterance of the God of Moses: "I am that I am." Recall the biblical situation: a bush engulfed in a hard, gemlike flame, but somehow not consumed in the burning. The voice of God calls to Moses, who trembles. But like the bush that burns without burning up, Moses endures the confrontation with terrible divine beauty. Having been given his mandate from God, Moses asks, "Who am I that I should go unto Pharaoh, and that I should bring forth the children of Israel out of Egypt?" God responds that His presence will attend Moses, and, so it seems, the divine presence will overcome any questionings regarding *who* Moses is to undertake this task. Moses is then a representative of/for God, a representation, now called on to deliver or translate the Word of God to the children of Israel. But the legitimacy of such representation troubles Moses; the question that he has asked of God is none other than a question of entitlement. And so, too, is his next question. Anticipating that he will have to name the origin of this call to lead, Moses asks what name should be given to this God. Here, where a title is once again at issue, come the words that Dorian Gray echoes: "I AM THAT I AM. Thus shalt thou say unto the children of Israel, I AM hath sent me unto you."[34]

I conjoin the Old Testament passage and Wilde's novel not to nail down influences on Wilde's text but to map out certain structural similarities in the two texts. For doing so can show how fully figured both texts are in terms of certain elementary moments in divine-mortal relations, in the giving of purpose, and in the transference of authority. "To name is to define," notes Lord Henry, just as God here "identifies" Moses in calling out the name, which is to say, bestows an identity and a capacity of expression on him. (Moses will soon caution that he is not "eloquent," but God assures him that "I will be with thy mouth."[35]) The notion of entitlement, in various senses that we seldom interconnect, seems to inform each moment of the Old Testament passage: God identifies Moses by name or "title," Moses is entitled by God's decree to carry out the rescue of the children of Israel in Egypt, Moses queries God as to the proper title by which to name Him to others, and there, at the point of designating the name of the divinity, appears the recursion, the answer that is also not an answer: "I am that I am." It is, on Dorian Gray's lips too, an answer after which there is nothing else to be said. In a later scene from the novel, Dorian speaks of entitlement as he ascends with Basil to show the portrait at last, and this is the moment that leads to Basil's death at Dorian's hand; says Dorian, "You are the one man in the world who is entitled to know everything about me" (162).

Althusser's own "central thesis"—given in a section heading: "Ideology Interpellates Individuals as Subjects" (170)—finds its most concrete articulation as he reads this same moment with Moses on the mountaintop. The Althusserian notion of interpellation names a moment of ideological address that calls into being the subject as such; as soon as the subject responds to the hailing, that is, the subject is constituted as an addressable and responsive/responsible entity who feels in some position to attend to the hailing or even—as Althusser briefly allows—to disregard it. Calling out to someone presupposes, in other words, that the addressee is some *one*, a subject. Whatever the addressee's resulting action—obedience or defiance—that subject acts thereby as a subject, exercising the subject's native sense of freedom and self-awareness, even while that sense of freedom and self-awareness are, for Althusser, confirmations of the ideological interpellation.

Here is the full paragraph with which Althusser paints this scene; I highlight the final lines, which contain what I take to be the three steps crucial to Althusser's point:

It then emerges that the interpellation of individuals as subjects presupposes the 'existence' of a Unique and central Other Subject, in whose Name the religious ideology interpellates all individuals as subjects. All this is clearly written in what is rightly called the Scriptures. "And it came to pass at that time that God the Lord (Yahweh) spoke to

Moses in the cloud. *And the Lord cried to Moses, 'Moses!' And Moses replied, 'It is (really) I! I am Moses thy servant, speak and I shall listen!' And the Lord spoke to Moses and said to him, "I am that I am."* (178–79)

Althusser explicates the episode in terms of three moments: (1) God's inter-pellative address or hailing, (2) Moses' subjective/subjected response—"It is I!"—and (3) God's proclamation, "I am that I am," a proposition through which "God defines himself as the Subject *par excellence*" (179). That is all.

What Althusser represents as Moses' reply to God's hailing is not, however, in the biblical text at all; rather, the words are God's own. "It is I" seems ac-tually to be God's declaration to Moses, not Moses' reply to God. And God's self-sufficient "I am that I am" is not, in turn, a counterpart to Moses' own declaration of dependence, that (nonexistent) "I am Moses thy servant"; in-stead, "I am that I am" is God's response to Moses' query as to how Moses ought to name God to the children of Israel. Althusser obliquely indicates that he has made adjustments to this scene by offering a footnote after the word *clearly* in his introductory remark—"All this is *clearly* written in what is rightly called the Scriptures." The note offers the following caveat: "I am quoting in a combined way, not to the letter but 'in spirit and truth.' " This appeal to spirit and truth appears as a way of dispensing with "the letter," which in this in-stance evidently stands apart from the truth. So his appeal to scripture exhibits at the same time a pointed disregard for mere values of accuracy or correct representation of the letter, replacing that notion—strategically, one assumes; perhaps jokingly?—with an idealized conception of his representation. Dis-dainful of the plodding materiality of biblical scripture, Althusser installs him-self and his own text as emissaries of spirit and truth, navigating above the fray of the facts.

It is hardly my concern to discredit Althusser's argument with a pedantic plea for perfect truth and accuracy in citation. The more provocative point here is that we are left to ask what sort of truth, if not a "literal" truth, might be at hand at such moments? (This point mirrors richly the conclusion of Wilde's "Mr. W.H.," which, likewise, asks us to believe that much remains to be said for a theory that has, to the story's end, merely showcased its own dis-regard for actual fact.) What species of truth inheres in a critical subjectivity that sees fit at times to disdain or depart at will from a regime of truth-telling, understood as relation to literal factuality. What authority does this superfac-tual truth-telling carry with it?

For an answer to such questions to preserve the value of Althusser's enter-prise—or enterprises that, like it, seek to describe agency—the answer must try to name a species of knowledge that is scientific but also reflexive and, in some respects, transcendental. We can spotlight Althusser's situation in a passage fol-lowing his outline of interpellation as an episode in a street. In that episode, remember, a call or hailing results in someone turning to hear that call and thereby entering subjecthood. After delivering this image, Althusser seeks to disentangle his theoretical point from the sequentiality of the image, calling this "little theoretical theatre" a mere device for "convenience and clarity" (174). For "in reality these things happen without any succession. The existence of ideology and the hailing or interpellation of individuals as subjects are one and the same thing" (175). He then offers the following paragraph, which I adduce as an instance of the peculiar contortions ensuent upon reflexive knowledge claims concerning agency:

I might add: what thus seems to take place outside ideology (to be precise, in the street), in reality takes place in ideology. What really takes place in ideology seems therefore to take place outside it. That is why those who are in ideology believe themselves by definition outside ideology: one of the effects of ideology is the practical *denegation* of the ideological character of ideology by ideology: ideology never says, "I am ideological." It is necessary to be outside ideology, i.e., in scientific knowledge, to be able to say: I am in ideology (a quite exceptional case) or (the general case), I was in ideology. As is well known, the accusation of being in ideology only applies to others, never to oneself (unless one is really a Spinozist or a Marxist, which, in this matter, is to be exactly the same thing). Which amounts to saying that ideology *has no outside* (for itself), but at the same time *that it is nothing but outside* (for science and reality). (175)

Two apparently contradictory tendencies inhabit this passage and vie for primacy. To begin, it is clear that ideology is being granted a surpassingly pervasive character, such that conventional speaking involves both embroilment within ideology and a spurious disavowal of that embroilment. But it is also clear that an idea of scientific positionality is allowed here to be outside ideology, constituting, in effect, a true rather than deluded exemption from ideology. Althusser assimilates Marx and Spinoza in this regard, and it would seem that he has in mind that idea, most clearly associated with Spinoza, whereby one cannot be meaningfully free except in that one can richly understand one's final lack of freedom.[36] (Earlier in the essay, Althusser draws his distinction between mere "consciousness" or "recognition" of our status as ideological subjects and a specifically scientific "knowledge of the mechanism of this recognition," which knowledge alone can allow us to "break with ideology" [173].) Perhaps it is rash to call Althusser's passage contradictory, but one might just as well do so because Althusser refuses the crucial step of explaining how these two claims are complementary rather than opposed.

The problem that looms here—a problem that Althusser himself calls "heavy with consequences" even as he announces his resolution to leave it aside (175)—is how to construe a situation in which a subject reflects on subjection, or an agent on agency. For generally the accounts of agential freedom in the vein of a modern individualism have celebrated individual action as a procedure of reflection by agents on their purposes and their surroundings in order to "choose" what they mean to do and then to do it. But the line of thought from which Althusser emerges sees in such ideas of agency the quintessential illusion of ideological blindness, whereby individuals mistake routines and choices enjoined by the material relations of production for their

own willing, desiring, and acting. But even while that skeptical line of ideological analysis seeks to discount this notion of reflection on action, it nonetheless
remains invested, implicitly or (as in Althusser) explicitly, in a notion of knowledge that transcends or otherwise escapes the bad knowledge of individualistic decision. This question of agency's reflection on agency is indeed heavy
with consequences, at least for anyone concerned to understand one's thinking
as any kind of progressive action. The challenge: to locate a form of action not
fully compromised by its collusion with existing structures of value and practice, understood to be, among other things, worth fighting against for their tendency to solidify existing inequalities and injustices.[37]

To bring this excursus back to Wilde, we have only to indicate the deep
affinity between Althusser and Wilde in what I can only call their positions on
positionality. The affinity is chiefly marked by their common self-location in
paradox. Consider this passage from the middle of *Dorian Gray*, coming after
we have been given details of Dorian's definitive immersion into matters decadent. In this chapter, quite the longest and most tedious chapter of the book,
with its protracted detailing of Dorian's short-lived but intense fascinations
with tapestries and books and scents, it comes to seem that the tedium is instructive in rendering palpable an ennui that indolent connoisseurship is heir
to. This ennui, in turn, is aligned with conventional social being rather than,
as one might want to suppose, with an isolation from society in private pleasures. For through all these delectations, Dorian remains a social magnet.
Wilde's narratorial voice observes:

> Society, civilized society at least, is never very ready to believe anything to the detriment
> of those who are both rich and fascinating. It feels instinctively that manners are of
> more importance than morals. . . . For the canons of good society are, or should be, the
> same as the canons of art. Form is absolutely essential to it. It should have the dignity
> of a ceremony, as well as its unreality, and should combine the insincere character of a
> romantic play with the wit and beauty that make such plays delightful to us. Is insin-
> cerity such a terrible thing? I think not. It is merely a method by which we can multi-
> ply our personalities.
>
> Such, at any rate, was Dorian Gray's opinion. He used to wonder at the shallow psy-
> chology of those who conceive the Ego in man as a thing simple, permanent, reliable,
> and of one essence. (153–54)

In the course of this passage, the narrator appears to disparage what critics of
our own time will call, often with a similar will to disparagement, *essentialist*
thinking.[38] Indicated thereby is the notion that an ego might be reckoned as
"simple, permanent, reliable and of one essence." Several critics use this passage to argue for Wilde's prescient wariness regarding the authority of psychological essentialism, and, indeed, Wilde seems here to prefigure central
remarks by Freud or, later, any number of postmodern-era theorists advocating notions that the play of surfaces is, in the final instance, the "real thing" of
human psychological being.[39] In this latter-day context, Jonathan Dollimore
has been most conspicuous among Wilde scholars, arguing that Wilde's advo-

cacy of insincerity and a host of other antivirtues puts him on the subversive side of a litany of cultural binarisms, elevating artifice over authenticity, surface over depth, facetiousness over seriousness, and so forth.[40] But even if the passage from Wilde's novel appears to celebrate a decentered subject and to debunk bourgeois fancies of authentic individualism, we need still to ask what to make of the "I think not" at the transition of these paragraphs.

That "I think not" constitutes the only clear appearance of a narratorial "I" in the entire novel. So the novel's authoritative narratorial persona appears at the very point, and only at the point, where the text most directly destabilizes the idea of a monological, essential subjectivity. In Wilde's novel, the "I" becomes formulated into textual presence only at that moment where the point of the "I" is its own fictiveness, its ceremonial inauthenticity. Who or what wields this "I," and to what effect, and under what authority? What role does this "I" have within the antiessentialist scheme supposedly marshaled through Dorian's wonderings? Much like the "I" in Althusser's essay, we seem here to have a presence that outstrips the declarative content of the text it supposedly serves. What is there to say about the conditions of possibility for such a position?

Contemporary critical reluctance to press this question in the ways that I intend here seems motivated by an awareness that one cannot press it without, at the least, rendering our most common critical projects these days rather unstable in their pretensions to unmasking. I suggest, that is, that something meaningful lies behind facts such as this: in his study of Wilde's antiessentialism, Dollimore actually uses an ellipsis to eradicate that "I think not" from a quotation of this very passage. And this, in a study that begins by quoting Wilde's remark to André Gide: "Never say I."[41] As with my point about Althusser's adjustments to the moment from Exodus, however, it is not my concern to expose Dollimore's argument as fatuous, as his study has a specific political work to do, and, what is more, it is little trouble to imagine his elision as a mere decision of expositional economy. But I do suggest that such elision reflects a habit among Wilde scholars of underreading Wilde's engagement with issues of subjective agency and selfhood. I am happy to grant that Wilde is, in effect, *essentially antiessential*, but I also think that we should reflect on the performative contradiction that comes to light when we present him in those terms.

It is all the more important that we reflect on these terms, to the extent that we now style Wilde as "deploying" such performative contradiction. We can order that inquiry by noting that the passage's "I think not" appears to indicate one of three possible voices: perhaps it is a narratorial assertion, or it is a momentary bit of indirect narration of Dorian Gray's own thinking, or it is an authorial intrusion. In this sense, the question of who wields this "I" takes a potentially richer form than the similarly paradoxical "I" of the Althusser essay, a richness won through the literary character of the text. But once we have specified the assorted reference points that might be indicated here, we should also ask what is at stake in the answer lying one way or another. And with that question in mind, it is well to recall Wilde's own comments regarding his sense of placement in this text.

Identifying Wilde

In 1894, replying to a reader of *Dorian Gray*, Wilde suggests with a measure of flippancy, one suspects, a neatly ramified self-presentation in his novel: "it contains much of me in it. Basil Hallward is what I think I am: Lord Henry Wotton what the world thinks me: Dorian what I would like to be—in other ages, perhaps."[42] Wilde means to generate a few surprises in this comment. That Wilde would deem himself "really" like the fundamentally earnest and pious artist Basil Hallward is a bit surprising. Also, there is considerable oddity in anyone wishing to be so puerile and ill-fated a figure as Dorian Gray. Further, in noting that Lord Henry is "what the world thinks me," Wilde suggests that the world is not quite right, as his comment implies a separation between the epigrammatic insouciance of Lord Henry and Wilde as he in himself really is. My concern with this tripartite self-characterization turns, not on any one of its valences, but instead on Wilde's project of understanding himself as refracted in several directions. Such refraction was cultivated by Wilde and noted by his contemporaries.[43] In our own time, a kindred conception of refracted selfhood has figured prominently in gay/lesbian studies.[44] The issue I mean to isolate is how to conceive Wilde's reflected self-consciousness, especially understood as indicating a resource for critical thinking.

A start here is to consider the critical status of Lord Henry, an inverter of language who knows, as well, that inversion as such provides a mere farce of progression. While he appears to know this, serious consequences ensue for Dorian Gray, who does not read Lord Henry unseriously but rather quite literally, with a will to enact the theories of Lord Henry. It is well to note, in this connection, the insistence with which Basil Hallward reiterates to Lord Henry that "I know you do not mean what you are saying." Dorian Gray never makes any such remark. But even while Lord Henry is more spectator than actor, his vision of the world has a sort of cogency, a style of truth-telling from which Wilde would never fully distance himself. (Hence the soundness of Wilde's suggestion that the world thinks Wilde actually is Wotton.) Indeed, Lord Henry offers the cogency of an insight about human perspectivism, and he dilates on it perhaps most clearly after Dorian asks why the death of Sibyl has left Dorian less troubled than he had supposed it ought to have left him. Says Dorian, "It seems to me to be simply like a wonderful ending to a wonderful play." In what the narrator tells us is Lord Henry's pleasure in "playing on the lad's unconscious egotism," Lord Henry responds:

I fancy that the true explanation is this. It often happens that the real tragedies of life occur in such an inartistic manner that they hurt us by their crude violence, their absolute incoherence, their absurd want of meaning, their entire lack of style. They give us an impression of sheer brute force, and we revolt against that. Sometimes, however, a tragedy that has artistic elements of beauty crosses our lives. If these elements of beauty are real, the whole thing simply appeals to our sense of dramatic effect. Suddenly we find that we are no longer the actors, but the spectators of the play. Or rather, we are both. We watch ourselves, and the mere wonder of the spectacle enthralls us. (123)

Lord Henry is unconcerned by, or oblivious to, the prospect that interested self-spectatorship might itself constitute a species of acting. This notion is, of course, theorized powerfully by cinematic theorists of our own time, who see in spectatorship an especially developed construction point of subjective consciousness as an ideological moment.[45] In this study's introduction, I tried to suggest the larger interest that we might bring to such self-inspection, casting as one facet of modern liberal culture this concern to observe oneself in a significantly bracketed way, as Lord Henry here suggests we might do. The liberal ideological program lays great store in the prospect, and in the name of political and ethical progressiveness rather than against it. What is most crucial in Wilde's remark does not lie in any of its particular identifications—whether with Basil Hallward, Lord Henry, or Dorian Gray—but instead in the very project of mobile identifications that Wilde here showcases. Although the remark might be construed to say that Wilde really sees himself only in one figure—Basil Hallward—it seems sounder to suppose that Wilde's sense of self is more properly to be understood as refracted into all three figures.

Support for that last view emerges later in a poignant revision of the high-spirited reply that Wilde gave to his reader. Two or three years later, during his time in prison, Wilde was approached by a man who called him "Dorian Gray." Wilde replied, "No. Lord Henry Wotton."[46] Wilde's answer to his fellow prisoner—"I am Wotton"—might be thought to reflect a change of mind, to the extent that he could seem here to be owning up to the truthfulness of his long-standing public image as a prince of paradox and epigram. But the remark seems more likely to reflect the fact of Wilde's literal imprisonment at that moment. Wotton, too, is a character both alive and in chains, tempted and piqued—quite a sad figure, finally. That Wilde always saw part of himself in Wotton seems beyond question, but this episode in prison marks, one might suppose, an ironic high point in that identification. Wilde's concern with the metaphoric potential of the prison later became explicit in a 1898 letter that refers to "the many prisons of life—prisons of stone, prisons of passion, prisons of intellect, prisons of morality, and the rest. All limitations, external or internal, are prison-walls, and life is a limitation."[47] Wilde's comment that he is Wotton comes at a moment when Wilde was unprecedentedly constrained to live out the divorce from "practice" that so deeply characterizes Lord Henry, who, when queried as to the condition of England, replies, "I don't desire to change anything in England except the weather. . . . I am quite content with philosophic contemplation" (78).

Lord Henry carries prison around with him, and in this respect, he figures an idea that has had a lively career in contemporary critical thinking—an idea, namely, that individual character is deeply informed by material and cultural constraint. Where Lord Henry can say to Dorian, perhaps with some good reason, that "I represent to you all the sins you have never had the courage to commit," it remains nonetheless true, as Dorian would later remark to Lord Henry, that Dorian is the one to "put into practice" the theories of the spectator Lord Henry. Almost as if Lord Henry were of a mind to exploit the ambiguities of representation so sharply examined in our own time, Lord Henry's claim to "represent" Dorian's wishes is far from being a claim actually to enact or make "real" that which he represents. But in his very distance from a model of action as immediate expression of will or desire, Lord Henry figures a different aspect of action realized in reflection, strategizing, experimenting, and mere knowing.

So for Lord Henry, too—like Herod and Dorian Gray—a paradox emerges in that the characters have their sovereign self-awareness only as their states come to exert orders of power and obligation on them that "subject" them fundamentally and wreak on their lives dismaying and tragic finales. In such literary conflations of sovereignty and subjection, Wilde intimates that paradoxical vision of subjective agency that he would condense several years later into the prison declaration quoted earlier: "To be entirely free, and at the same time, entirely dominated by law, is the eternal paradox of human life that we realise at every moment."

But even allowing that such readings of Wilde's literary texts are on target, it remains to be said whether any kind of "critique" that way lies. Can we construe Wilde's literary practice as a scene of critical agency? Indeed, do not his literary images of agency themselves seem to emphasize the constraints and pressures that inform his characters and rein in their freedoms and choices? How can we construe Wilde's practice as a service to any progressive conception of subjectivity? As I noted earlier, we are now on the point of asking a very general question about what at least one literary practice might be said to *do*, if anything. In particular, we are landed on the difficult question of literature's status as a tool for or against ideology.

Interpreting Liberal Agency

Questions about aesthetic agency go to the heart of this study's concerns with liberal culture. A difficulty that has hardly been settled in my discussion is whether and how one can reconcile the individualist element of liberal culture with the picture of aesthetic resistance favored by many writers in the historical materialist tradition. Many critics in and around the Frankfurt School—for example, Benjamin and Adorno—sought explicitly to theorize the redemptive or emancipatory potential of aesthetic practices. Their concern, however, was to redeem contemporary life from ills generated by capitalism, itself linked to liberal culture in its possessive-individualistic extrapolation. In their view, liberal individuality's pretensions to autonomy and rationalization reflect a pseudoindividuality, a false valuation of particularity that finally enforces a standardization of mind-sets in keeping with the capitalist imperative to recast the world under the sign of exchangeable commodities.[48] Adorno therefore prized certain high-cultural forms of aesthetic difficulty for their promise in wrenching audiences out of their categorial grooves, and Fredric Jameson later saw such a critical function as a potentiality even in mass-cultural art forms.

The Critical-Theory appropriations of the aesthetic, despite their diverse approaches and object domains, deploy a common assumption that actually throws us back to Kant. The assumption is that aesthetic experience in some way mediates between scientific knowledge and practical morality—or between fact and value—and, in so doing, disturbs the pretension of either of those spheres to define human life entirely. Anthony Cascardi has recently argued this point by rereading Kant's aesthetic philosophy in a way that mirrors the distinction I introduced in the opening chapter between substantive and regulative aspects of liberal agency. Like other critics, Cascardi notes the importance in Kant's aesthetic theory of the *sensus communis*, the stipulation of common humanity that grounds aesthetic judgment in something broader than private experience. Hannah Arendt and Jürgen Habermas, notes Cascardi, have also invoked Kant's stipulation in order to link art and politics, giving aesthetic agency some purchase on political and moral agency. But he contends that such critics tend to underread the importance in Kant's scheme of the indeterminate character of aesthetic judgment, which has the effect, for Cascardi, of rendering chimerical the search for a substantive grounding of judgment. Kant's aesthetic theory, argues Cascardi, is actually better suited to the theorization of how agents manage in their contingent and unfolding circumstances to organize their judgments and other actions with a regulative ideal of *sensus communis*. Although that ideal rationalizes art and politics, it is a mistake, implies Cascardi, to posit a free-standing fact of *sensus communis* that makes assertions about art and politics determinable as true or false.[49]

In the sort of view offered by Cascardi, things aesthetic suggest release from an ossification and rigidity to which regimes of fact and value seem prey. I have been suggesting that Oscar Wilde mirrors this positioning of the aesthetic. Wilde's appeal as a figure of agency, in this account, lies in the sense that he inhabits a domain of individual assertion where both factual refutation and rational value formations seem unsuited to the judgments he invites. If one asks whether Wilde is right or wrong, either factually or morally, it quickly comes to seem that one has somehow missed his game. But what does it mean for one to occupy such a stance, and in what does the appeal to us of such a stance consist? If Wilde is somehow about elusiveness, then what is it about elusiveness that appeals? And to whom? My suggestion has been that this Wildean elusiveness appeals to those who can find their sense of ideal agency formally echoed in the paradoxical positionality that they see in him. Wilde's antioriginality serves just as well as any idea of Wildean originality ever could to underline his interest for modern agents. For Wildean antioriginality actually promises a kind of metapositional potential, a capacity to stand outside of, and to play with, that image of an original agency that, one might say, colors within the lines.

I can broaden this discussion now by asking what it means that Wilde looks very much like the field of aesthetic production and reception more generally, as it was taking shape at this time and sped along in Britain, to some degree, by Wilde himself. Pierre Bourdieu provides our most provocative and persuasive justification for such a historical conclusion—although he would balk at granting Wilde agency in this process. In *Rules of Art*, Bourdieu shows how the literary order—indeed, the entire scene of aesthetic cultural production—comes in the later nineteenth and early twentieth centuries to pose a "real challenge to all forms of economism," by which he means not only that artists relate differently to everyday projects like paying the rent and obtaining food but also that artists inhabit and seek to promulgate a wholly new scheme of value and self-construction. The literary field acquires its autonomy from other schemes of valuation—such as those in charge of the bureaucratic or entrepreneurial fields—and "presents itself as an inverted economic world: those who enter it have an interest in disinterestedness."[50]

In most of his discussion, Bourdieu emphasizes that the "challenge" posed by the literary field's "autonomy" is impressive only within that field. That is, a kind of power or "cultural capital" accrues within the field to those who play the game correctly, who know the rules of art. But the aesthetic domain as such remains toothless outside its own inverted corner of the larger social field: "The cult of disinterestedness is the principle of a prodigious reversal, which turns poverty into rejected riches, hence spiritual riches."[51] Modern artists who dispute the role of money as the arbiter of value in aesthetic creation tend as well to think of the aesthetic life as a saving renunciation of earthly value forms and a deliverance into a new, more spiritual order of value. This is the reversal of which Bourdieu writes.

Wilde's engagement with the romantic cult of creative agency is clearly also a prodigious reversal of that cult's agential values, which are aligned with a bourgeois revolutionary ethos. But my reading insists on a further point that Bourdieu tries but fails ultimately to dismiss—namely, that something might in fact be bought by the inverted riches proper to this new aesthetic field. I say that Bourdieu fails to dismiss the point, because numerous passages in his study, notably those concentrated on the privileged figure of Flaubert, seem so clearly to mimic the ideology of charismatic creation that Bourdieu is supposedly discounting as chimerical.[52] Indeed, he does so most powerfully in those moments when he seeks to specify the "radical originality" of Flaubert.[53] Bourdieu justifiably shies from locating that originality in some narrow characterization of Flaubert's personality or even of his works, as understood in isolation. Instead, Bourdieu extols two points: the all-encompassing character of Flaubert's social portraiture, which represents, Bourdieu argues, the entire range of social classes and viewpoints; and also Flaubert's renegade determination to write artfully about the artless everyday.[54] While neither of these qualities calls Wilde's methods quickly to mind, the fit between my treatment of Wilde and Bourdieu's treatment, despite himself, of Flaubert lies elsewhere in any case. At issue in each of our readings is an ascription of critical viewpoint, and a construction of authors as "interesting" by virtue of the multiplicity of viewpoints that we see these figures as tactically managing.

Here is Bourdieu on Flaubert's *Sentimental Education*, and notice the dimensions of affective sympathy and, one can hardly doubt, identification on Bourdieu's part; the emphasis in what follows is mine:

> *One feels* that Flaubert is wholly there, in this universe of relationships that would have to be explored one by one, in their double dimension, both artistic and social, and that he nevertheless remains irreducibly beyond it: is this not because the active integration he effects implies an overcoming? In situating himself, as it were, at the geometric intersection of all perspectives, which is also *the point of greatest tension*, he forces himself in some fashion to raise to their highest intensity the set of questions posed in the field, to play out all the resources inscribed in the space of possibles that, in the manner of language or a musical instrument, is offered to each writer, like an infinite universe of possible combinations locked in a potential state within the finite system of constraints.[55]

Flaubert here is not only prodigiously reversing; he is prodigious. He *overcomes*, he *situates himself*, he *plays out all the resources*, and he *links* the finite and the infinite. Indeed, Flaubert's autonomy here is strikingly akin to that freedom from absolute causality that underwrites transcendental consciousness in the Kantian model, whereby there is also a "system of finite constraints" (categories, conditions of intuition) and an innumerable series of possible "combinations" of perception that take shape at the "intersection" point of this system— namely, in the consciousness that serves as the privileged locus of these elements.

My point is considerably less ambitious than an attempt at the wholesale recuperation of Kantian transcendental agency. For as I allowed in the opening chapter, some essential obstacles lie in the way of establishing this liberal agency's truth by demonstrating its positive existence as liberal agency. Instead, we can only assume vantage points on our own practices and critical tactics that bring out that sense in which those practices and tactics can be understood as already implicated in that liberal self-conception. In this passage from Bourdieu, therefore, I underscore not the substantive claims for Flaubert's position but instead Bourdieu's clearly celebratory assertion that "one feels" Flaubert's special placement in this scheme, and, more subtly, that the point of social intersection occupied by Flaubert is "the point of greatest tension." One might construe this tension as an objective function of Flaubert's placement within history—for example, because writing very well about the commonplace seemed incongruous at that time, engendering resistance among publishers and audiences—and this point is probably part of Bourdieu's claim. But this tension extends beyond Flaubert's time and into the fact of Bourdieu's own processes of reading and critical identification. In this light, the tension belongs not properly to Flaubert, nor to his time period, but to Bourdieu and his own project of reflexive sociological critique. In the idea that Flaubert manages a tactical mastery of such matters as the relation of the finite and the infinite we have the principal force of seduction that he exercises on readers who are disposed to thrill at the idea of aesthetic or, more broadly, critical agency—at once "wholly there" and "irreducibly beyond" the universe of relationships.

It is in exactly this light that I have tried to diagnose the seductiveness of Wilde, whose appeal seems likewise to emerge from his availability to the identificatory yearnings of a profoundly modern and self-divided *ambition* of critical agency. And once we have linked that ambition to a broadly modern liberal aspiration—an aspiration to a kind of agency endorsed through acts of reflection and judgment—it seems clear that an operative assumption of such agency underlies even the historical materialist argumentation that has dismissed liberal agency, rightly, as a *substantive* claim. While there remain powerful points to be wagered against the idea of liberal agency as a *regulative* ideal, it nonetheless seems that efforts to make such points generally proceed according to the very light they dispute.

Notes

Preface

1. Elaine Scarry, *On Beauty and Being Just* (Princeton, N.J.: Princeton University Press, 1999); George Levine, ed., *Aesthetics and Ideology* (New Brunswick, N.J.: Rutgers University Press, 1994). See also Susan Wolfson, *Formal Charges: The Shaping of Poetry in British Romaniticism* (Stanford: Stanford University Press, 1997). At least three essay collections proceed from conferences that related aesthetic and formal issues to prevailing concerns with cultural studies. See Emory Elliott, Louis Freitas Caton, and Jeffrey Rhyne, eds., *Aesthetics in a Multicultural Age* (Oxford: Oxford University Press, 2002); Pamela Andrews and David McWhirter, eds., *Aesthetic Subjects* (Minneapolis: University of Minnesota Press, 2003); and James Soderholm, ed., *Beauty and the Critic: Aesthetics in an Age of Cultural Studies* (Tuscaloosa and London: University of Alabama Press, 1997). Special issues of journals include *MLQ: Modern Language Quarterly* 61 no.1 (March 2000); *New Literary History 31* (2000). For a journalistic account, including references to changes in teaching and to conference meetings, see Scott Heller, "Wearying of Cultural Studies, Some Scholars Rediscover Beauty," *Chronicle of Higher Education* 45, no. 15 (4 December 1998), A15–A16.

2. Stefan Collini, *Public Moralists: Political Thought and Intellectual Life in Britain, 1850-1930* (Oxford: Oxford University Press, 1991), 305.

3. Immanuel Kant, *Critique of Judgment*, trans Werner S. Pluhar (Indianapolis: Hackett, 1987), 175.

4. Variously poststructuralist works up to the late 1980s, with the waning of deconstruction, make up the bulk of post-1960s scholarship on originality. See Rosalind Krauss, *Originality of the Avant Garde and Other Modernist Myths* (Cambridge, Mass.: MIT Press, 1985); Jean Baudrillard, "The Precession of Simulacra," in *Art After Modernism: Rethinking Representation*, ed. Brian Wallis (New York: New Museum of Contemporary Art, 1984), 253–81. Behind such argumentation looms Jacques Derrida's *Of Grammatology*, trans. Gayatri Chakravorty Spivak (Baltimore: Johns Hopkins University Press, 1974, 1976). A *marxisant* tradition of commentary, in turn, has fundamental reference to Walter Benjamin, "The Work of Art in the Age of Mechanical Reproduction," *Illuminations: Essays and Reflections*, trans. Harry Zohn, ed. Hannah Arendt (New York: Schocken, 1969). See also Peter Bürger, *Theory of the Avant-Garde*, trans. Michael Shaw (Minneapolis: University of Minnesota Press, 1984), esp. 59–63.

5. For a compact account of the 1848 events, see John Belchem, *Popular Radicalism in*

Nineteenth-Century Britain (Houndsmills, U.K.: Macmillan, 1996), 90–94. This work is a good introduction to the radicalist context more generally.

6. On O'Connor's romantic rhetoric, see James Epstein, *The Lion of Freedom: Feargus O'Connor and the Chartist Movement, 1832–1842* (London: Croom Helm, 1982), 253. On the waning power of that rhetoric by 1848, see John Belchem, "1848: Feargus O'Connor and the Collapse of the Mass Platform," in *The Chartist Experience: Studies in Working Class Radicalism and Culture, 1830–60* (London: Macmillan, 1982), 269–310.

7. For the mid-Victorian transition from Chartist to Liberalist terms, see Margot C. Finn, *After Chartism: Class and Nation in English Radical Politics, 1848–1874* (Cambridge: Cambridge University Press, 1993).

8. See, for example, the characterization of the Brontë sisters in Sandra M. Gilbert and Susan Gubar, *The Madwoman in the Attic: The Woman Writer and the Nineteenth-Century Literary Imagination*, 2d ed. (New Haven, Conn.: Yale University Press, 2000).

Chapter 1. Cultivating Victorians

1. Samuel Smiles, *Self-Help* (London: John Murray, 1958), 36. Originally published 1859.

2. John Stuart Mill, *On Liberty*, in *Collected* Works *of John Stuart Mill*, ed. J. M. Robson, vol. 19 (Toronto: University of Toronto Press, 1963–91), 310. Further citations to Mill's *On Liberty* are given parenthetically in the text.

3. For a comparative analysis of individualism's varieties, see Steven Lukes, *Individualism* (Oxford: Blackwell, 1973); Lukes treats methodological individualism at 110–22. For a recent essay with bearing on the Victorian culture of individualism, see Regenia Gagnier, "The Law of Progress and the Ironies of Individualism in the Nineteenth Century," *New Literary History* 31 (2000), 315–36.

4. For an incisive reading of this latter-day Victorianism, see Elaine Hadley, "The Past Is a Foreign Country: The Neo-Conservative Romance with Victorian Liberalism," *Yale Journal of Criticism* 10, no.1 (1997): 1–26. See also the discussion by Alison Booth, who addresses the point through reference to Samuel Smiles, "Neo-Victorian Self-Help, or Cider House Rules," *American Literary History* 14, no. 2 (2002), 284–310.

5. Locke's key account of property is in chapter 5 of *The Second Treatise of Government*. See John Locke, *Two Treatises of Government*, ed. Peter Laslett (New York: New American Library, 1960, 1963), 327–44. For a critique of Locke's theory, see Matthew H. Kramer, *John Locke and the Origins of Private Property: Philosophical Explorations of Individualism, Community, and Equality* (Cambridge: Cambride University Press, 1997). Kramer deems Locke's theory incoherent but, in keeping with a trend in recent arguments against liberalism Kramer, also seeks to redeem Locke's thinking by connecting it with a communitarianism presumed to offer a more wholesome picture of individuality. I critique that general trend later in the present chapter (pp. 14–25).

6. This feminist indictment of liberal agency is usefully glossed and contested by Gal Gerson, "Liberal Feminism: Individuality and Oppositions in Wollstonecraft and Mill," *Political Studies* 54.4 (September 2002): 794–810.

7. *The Graphic* 2 (6 August 1870): 136–36.

8. Pierre Bourdieu, *Distinction: A Social Critique of the Judgement of Taste*, trans. Richard Nice (Cambridge: Harvard University Press, 1984); Regina Gagnier, *The Insatiability of Human Wants: Economics and Aesthetics in Market Society* (Chicago: University of Chicago Press, 2000).

9. The terms *surveillance* and *discipline* find their key contemporary reference point in the works of Michel Foucault. See, to begin, *Discipline and Punish: The Birth of the Prison*, trans. Alan Sheridan (New York: Vintage, 1977, 1979). For an influential literary-critical study along these lines, see D. A. Miller, *The Novel and the Police* (Berkeley: University of California Press, 1988). Lauren M. E. Goodlad has recently argued that Foucault's ideas of discipline and surveillance are less suited to the analysis of British nineteenth-century contexts than are his reflections on "governmentality," which have been less widely debated. Goodlad sees Foucault himself confronted by a liberal paradox that turns on how to comprehend the relations of rationalizing social administration, on the one hand, alongside concerns for individual liberty, on the other. See "Beyond the Panopticon: Victorian Britain and the Critical Imagination," forthcoming in *PMLA* 118, no. 3 (May 2003). See also Michel Foucault, "Governmentality," in *The Foucault Effect: Studies in Governmentality, with Two Lectures and an Interview with Michel Foucault*, ed. Graham Burchell, Colin Gordon, and Peter Miller (Chicago: University of Chicago Press, 1991), 87-118. In the present study, I second Goodlad's observation in chapter 3, on the Tichborne case, especially in the section headed "Opposing the Claimant."

10. Amanda Anderson, *Powers of Distance: Cosmopolitanism and the Cultivation of Detachment* (Princeton, N.J.: Princeton University Press, 2001), 8.

11. Charles Altieri, *Subjective Agency: A Theory of First-Person Expressivity and its Social Implications* (Oxford: Blackwell, 1994), 5.

12. Many readers would follow Raymond Williams in privileging Will Ladislaw over Farebrother: Ladislaw's lack of definition within any one of the novel's carefully crafted web of social determinations, says Williams, implies an effort on Eliot's part at "thinking beyond, feeling beyond" such existing determinations for a "thread to the future." Raymond Williams, *The English Novel from Dickens to Lawrence* (New York: Oxford University Press, 1970), 93. Such an account styles Ladislaw in keeping with a number of characters from socially self-conscious literature of this era, including Stendahl's Julian Sorel and Flaubert's Frédéric Moreau. In the Coda to the present study, I clarify my perspective on this sort of literary characterization by looking to Pierre Bourdieu's account of Flaubert's *Sentimental Education*. Entering those issues here would involve moving prematurely—before my account of liberal culture is in place—to the relations of aesthetic agency and historical materialism.

13. George Eliot, *Middlemarch* (Harmondsworth: Penguin, 1994), 187. Subsequent references are given parenthetically in the text.

14. In this gloss on Farebrother's moral rationalism, I paraphrase a key feature of Kant's categorical imperative. For this point of Kantian ethics, one does well to begin with Immanuel Kant, *Groundwork of the Metaphysic of Morals*, trans. H. J. Paton (New York: Harper & Row, 1964), 88 and passim.

15. See also the reading of this Homeric episode in Max Horkheimer and Theodor W. Adorno, *Dialectic of Enlightenment*, trans. John Cumming (New York: Continuum, 1994), 32ff. There the general issue is the nature of a privileged Enlightenment self-subjection.

16. Hadley, "The Past Is a Foreign Country," 15.

17. Maria H. Morales, *Perfect Equality: John Stuart Mill on Well-Constituted Communities* (Lanham, Md.: Rowman & Littlefield, 1996), 63–64.

18. This claim about the agent's "being" as distinct from its actions epitomizes an essentialist model of subjectivity that has seemed problematic in recent decades. For a survey of the issues here, see Diana Fuss, *Essentially Speaking* (New York: Routledge, 1989). A powerful philosophical precedent to the antiessentialist argumentation so prevalent today is in Nietzsche, notably in his *Genealogy of Morals*, where he asserts that

"there is no being behind doing, effecting, becoming—the 'doer' is merely a fiction added to the deed—the deed is everything." Friedrich Nietzsche, *On the Genealogy of Morals*, trans. Walter Kaufmann and R. J. Hollingdale [with *Ecce Homo*] (New York: Vintage, 1989), 45. For a recent and searching account of the Nietzschean topos in the light of contemporary critical accounts of agency, see James I. Porter, "Unconscious Agency in Nietzsche," *Nietzsche-Studien* 27 (1998), 153–95.

19. Thomas Nagel, *The View from Nowhere* (New York: Oxford University Press, 1986).

20. For treatments of projective rationality, see Donald Davidson, *Inquiries into Truth and Interpretation* (Oxford: Oxford University Press, 1984); and Daniel Dennett, *Brainstorms* (Cambridge: Bradford, 1978).

21. Martha C. Nussbaum, *Poetic Justice: The Literary Imagination and Public Life* (Boston: Beacon, 1995).

22. "Intellectual Vigour," *Saturday Review* 21 (19 May 1866), 584.

23. Ibid., 584–85.

24. James Eli Adams, *Dandies and Desert Saints: Styles of Victorian Manhood* (Ithaca, N.Y.: Cornell University Press, 1995).

25. Michael J. Sandel, *Liberalism and the Limits of Justice* (Cambridge: Cambridge University Press), 1982.

26. Immanuel Kant, *Critique of Pure Reason*, trans. Norman Kemp Smith (Houndsmills, U.K.: Macmillan, 1929, 1933), 210–11 and passim.

27. The earlier argumentation is in John Rawls, *A Theory of Justice* (Cambridge, Mass.: Harvard University Press, 1971); the later, in Rawls, *Political Liberalism* (New York: Columbia University Press, 1993, 1996).

28. This concession would probably not apply very powerfully to someone like Alasdair MacIntyre and some other proponents of virtue ethics, a line of thinking that I underplay here on grounds of economy. For MacIntyre, "the essence of moral agency" in modern moral philosophy consists in the regrettable ability "to stand back from any and every situation in which one is involved, from any and every characteristic that one may possess, and to pass judgment on it from a purely universal and abstract point of view that is totally detached from all social particularity." *After Virtue: A Study in Moral Theory*, 2d ed. (South Bend, Ind.: University of Notre Dame Press, 1984), 31–32. In my view, the claims of virtue ethicists—featuring substantive commitments to traditions and ideas of the good—simply represent more embedded versions of the communitarian difference from liberalism, which I treat in what follows.

29. Note, however, that she takes this point to license not legislative action but simply a theoretical assessment. Seyla Benhabib, *Situating the Self: Gender, Community, and Postmodernism in Contemporary Ethics* (New York: Routledge, 1992), 35, 59–60 n. 34.

30. Uday Singh Mehta, *Liberalism and Empire: A Study in Nineteenth-Century British Thought* (Chicago: University of Chicago Press, 1999). Subsequent references to this text are given parenthetically in the text.

31. Compare recent discussions that critique liberalism's imperiousness in respect to race and globalism, respectively: David Theo Goldberg, "Liberalism's Limits: Carlyle and Mill on 'The Negro Question,'" *Nineteenth-Century Contexts* 22 (2000): 203–16; Timothy J. Reiss, *Against Autonomy: Global Dialectics of Cultural Exchange* (Stanford: Stanford University Press, 2002).

32. See Horkheimer and Adorno, *Dialectic of Enlightenment*.

33. J. L. Austin, *How to Do Things with Words* (Oxford: Clarendon, 1962).

34. Ludwig Wittgenstein, *Philosophical Investigations*, trans. G. E. M. Anscombe, 2d ed. (Oxford: Blackwell, 1953, 1958), 139.

35. Benhabib's *Situating the Self* is a keen effort in this direction. Here I will add that Anglo-American historians have been seeking amendment of Habermas by way of de-

termining the usefulness of his early argumentation about the bourgeois public sphere. See especially Geoff Eley, "Nations, Publics, and Political Cultures: Placing Habermas in the Nineteenth Century," *Habermas and the Public Sphere*, ed. Craig Calhoun (Cambridge, Mass.: MIT Press, 1992), 289–339.

36. Alice Crary, "Wittgenstein's Philosophy in Relation to Political Thought," in *The New Wittgenstein*, ed. Alice Crary and Rupert Read (London: Routledge, 2000), 118–45.

37. Richard Rorty, "Hilary Putnam and the Relativist Menace," *Truth and Progress: Philosophical Papers 3* (Cambridge: Cambridge University Press, 1998), 45, 43–62.

38. Charles Taylor, "The Politics of Recognition," in *Multiculturalism: Examining the Politics of Recognition*, ed. Amy Gutmann, 2d ed. (Princeton, N.J.: Princeton University Press, 1994), 52–60, 25–73.

39. K. Anthony Appiah, "Identity, Authenticity, Survival: Multicultural Societies and Social Reproduction," in Gutmann, ed., *Multiculturalism*, 163, 149–63.

40. Ludwig Wittgenstein, "A Lecture on Ethics" [1929], *Philosophical Occasions, 1912–51*, ed. James C. Klagge and Alfred Nordmann (Indianapolis: Hackett, 1993), 44, 37–44.

41. In *Powers of Distance*, 33, which dovetails very much with this aspect of my argument, Amanda Anderson spots out a similar moment in respect to the latter-day pragmatist theorist Stanley Fish.

42. For his basic argument in this vein, see Jürgen Habermas, *Theory of Communicative Action. Vol. 1. Reason and the Rationalization of Society*, trans. Thomas McCarthy (Boston: Beacon, 1984), and *Theory of Communicative Action. Vol. 2. Life-World and System: A Critique of Functionalist Reason*, trans. Thomas McCarthy (Boston: Beacon, 1987).

43. For "cryptonormativism," see Jürgen Habermas's indictment of Michel Foucault's thematization of power: *The Philosophical Discourse of Modernity: Twelve Lectures*, trans. Frederick G. Lawrence (Cambridge, Mass.: MIT Press, 1987), 294. For this term's pertinence to poststructuralist argumentation more generally, see Amanda Anderson, "Cryptonormativism and Double Gestures: The Politics of Post-Structuralism, *Cultural Critique* 21 (1992), 63–95.

44. Christine M. Korsgaard, with G. A. Cohen, Raymond Geuss, Thomas Nagel, and Bernard Williams, *The Sources of Normativity*, ed. Onora O'Neill (Cambridge: Cambridge University Press, 1996), 92.

45. Stanley Fish, *The Trouble with Principle* (Cambridge, Mass.: Harvard University Press, 1999), esp. 309–12.

46. In addition to Samuel Smiles, *Self-Help* (1859), see also his *Character* (1871); Herbert Spencer, *Principles of Ethics*, 2 vols. (1893), 2:251; T. H. Green, *Lectures on the Principles of Political Obligation* (1895), §21; John Stuart Mill, *On Liberty*, passim, but esp. 264. Useful, sociologically ordered discussions of character in Victorian discourse include Stefan Collini, "The Idea of 'Character' in Victorian Political Thought," *Transactions of the Royal Historical Society* 35, 5th ser. (1985): 29–50; and, newly, Lauren M. E. Goodlad, "Character and Pastorship in Two British 'Sociological' Traditions: Organized Charity, Fabian Socialism, and the Invention of New Liberalism," in *Disciplinarity at the Fin de Siècle*, ed. Amanda Anderson and Joseph Valente (Princeton, N.J.: Princeton University Press, 2002), 235–60.

47. William Ewart Gladstone, *Juventus Mundi: The Gods and Men of the Heroic Age* (Boston: Little, Brown, 1869), 405.

48. For Homer's usage, see the first line of the *Odyssey*. According to the Liddell and Scott *Greek-English Lexicon*, Plato's *Lesser Hippias* (364e) is the source for the interpretation of *polutropos* along the lines of *wiliness*.

49. "Intellectual Vigour," 584.

50. In *Utilitarianism*. John Stuart Mill, *Collected Works of John Stuart Mill*, 10:213. For

Mill's work on ethology, understood as a rigorous science of character formation, see his *System of Logic*, book 6, esp. chap. 5: *Collected Works of John Stuart Mill*, 8:861–74.

51. I. M. Greengarten, *Thomas Hill Green and the Development of Liberal-Democratic Thought* (Toronto: University of Toronto Press, 1981). Green was an Oxford student, and then a teacher there, who promulgated a version of liberal theory through sources in German idealism. See also Melvin Richter, *The Politics of Conscience: T. H. Green and His Age* (Cambridge, Mass. Harvard University Press, 1964). For an account of Herbert Spencer, another figure with bearing on mid-Victorian intellectual liberalism, see Tim S. Gray, *The Political Philosophy of Herbert Spencer: Individualism and Organicism* (Aldershot, U.K.: Avebury, 1996).

52. John Stuart Mill, *Considerations on Representative Government*, in *Collected Works of John Stuart Mill*, 19:371–577. See esp. chap. 8, pp. 467–81. Regarding what turn out to be Mill's strongly divided feelings about straight representation, see Catherine Gallagher's argument, much in line with my own, that political liberalism of the 1860s was torn between a generalized impulse to represent diversity and a more specific impulse to protect and cultivate liberal values. *The Industrial Reformation of English Fiction: Social Discourse and Narrative Form, 1832–76* (Chicago: University of Chicago Press, 1985), 229–33.

53. Much to the point here is the recent scholarly discourse surrounding American writers like Emerson and Whitman, with their aspirations toward an ongoing project of human perfectionism. See Stanley Cavell, *Conditions Handsome and Unhandsome: The Constitution of Emersonian Perfectionism* (Chicago: University of Chicago Press, 1990).

54. For an affirmative account of Mill's developmental ideas, see Wendy Donner, *The Liberal Self: John Stuart Mill's Moral and Political Philosophy* (Ithaca, N.Y.: Cornell University Press, 1991).

55. I have in mind especially Stanley Fish in various works; see also Steven Knapp and Walter Benn Michaels for a trenchant argument in this vein, figured as an account of how we cannot "entertain" beliefs that we do not in fact have. Steven Knapp and Walter Benn Michaels, "Against Theory," *Critical Inquiry* 8 (1982), 723–42.

56. Nietzsche, *On the Genealogy of Morals*, 119

57. Steven Knapp, *Personification and the Sublime: Milton to Coleridge* (Cambridge, Mass.: Harvard University Press, 1985), 28. For Coleridge on genius, see the second chapter of *Biographia Literaria*, ed. James Engell and W. Jackson Bate, 2 vols. in 1, Bollingen Series 75 (Princeton, N.J.: Princeton University Press, 1983), 1:30–47. For Coleridge's idea of genius contrasted with Mill's, see the extensive note in Donner, *The Liberal Self*, 101–2 n. 5.

58. Matthew Arnold, *Culture and Anarchy*, in Matthew Arnold, *The Complete Prose Works of Matthew Arnold*, ed. R. H. Super, vol. 5 (Ann Arbor: University of Michigan Press, 1965), 85–256. Arnold's reference to Bright's genius is at p. 130. Further citations to *Culture and Anarchy* are given parenthetically in the text

59. Anderson, *Powers of Distance*, 91–118.

60. Ibid., 92.

61. John Locke, *Essay Concerning Human Understanding*, book 2, chap. 21, §48.

62. Pierre Bourdieu, *Distinction: A Social Critique of the Judgement of Taste*, trans. Richard Nice (Cambridge, Mass.: Harvard University Press, 1984); and *The Rules of Art: Genesis and Structure of the Literary Field*, trans. Susan Emanuel (Stanford, Calif.: Stanford University Press, 1995); Terry Eagleton, *Ideology of the Aesthetic* (Oxford: Blackwell, 1990); several works by Fredric Jameson, notably *Marxism and Form: Twentieth-Century Dialectical Theories of Literature* (Princeton, N.J.: Princeton University Press, 1971).

63. A chronological ordering of touchstone arguments: Theodor Adorno, *Aesthetic Theory* [1970], trans. Robert Hullot-Kentor, ed. Gretel Adorno and Rolf Tiedermann (Minneapolis: University of Minnesota Press, 1997); Peter Bürger, *Theory of the Avant-*

Garde, trans. Michael Shaw (Minneapolis: University of Minnesota Press, 1984); Jonathan Freedman, *Professions of Taste: Henry James, British Aestheticism, and Commodity Culture* (Stanford, Calif.: Stanford University Press, 1990); Regenia Gagnier, *The Insatiability of Human Wants: Economics and Aesthetics in Market Society* (Chicago: University of Chicago Press, 2000). For a recent argument detailing the Kantian aesthetic remainders in the argumentation of Adorno and his heirs, see Robert Kaufman, "Red Kant, or The Persistence of the Third Critique in Adorno and Jameson," *Critical Inquiry* 26, no.4 (summer 2000): 682–724.

64. W. J. Courthope, "Modern Culture," *Quarterly Review* 137 (October 1874), 409. Subsequent references appear parenthetically in the text.

65. This point is, of course, hardly novel: much of what I have to say has been elegantly argued in David DeLaura, *Hebrew and Hellene in Victorian England: Newman, Arnold, and Pater* (Austin: University of Texas Press, 1969). I write from a sense that much current scholarly work neglects to relate humanism carefully and candidly to varieties of metaphysical realism, including religion as Victorians like Courthope construe it. Also relevant as forms of metaphysical realism are moral realism and ideas of natural law. I examine the Victorian engagement with these latter ideas in the course of Chapter 3 below, on the Tichborne sensation.

66. Thomas Carlyle, [*Characteristics*,] *The Centenary Edition of the Works of Thomas Carlyle*, ed. H. D. Traill, vol. 4 (London: Chapman and Hall, 1896–99), 20.

67. Linda Dowling, *The Vulgarization of Art: The Victorians and Aesthetic Democracy* (Charlottesville: University Press of Virginia, 1996).

68. Qtd. in Courthope, "Modern Culture," 411. I have corrected some incorrect punctuation in the quotation. See Walter Pater, *The Renaissance: Studies in Art and Poetry*, ed. Donald L. Hill (Berkeley: University of California Press, 1980), 98.

69. In a review dated one year prior to Courthope's, William Dean Howells quotes the same passage by way of diagnosing a "vice" of projective feeling in modern art criticism, "invented" by Ruskin. William Dean Howells, *Atlantic Monthly* 32 (October 1873): 497–98.

70. Kant's edict that we should treat persons as ends and never as means is foundational in his moral philosophy; Pater's reference is more obviously a biblical allusion, of course: 1 Corinthians 10:11.

71. Altieri, *Subjective Agency*. My references will appear parenthetically in the text.

72. Henry James, *Selected Letters of Henry James to Edmund Gosse, 1882–1915: A Literary Friendship*, ed. Rayburn S. Moore (Baton Rouge: Louisiana State University Press, 1988), 152.

73. Pater, *Renaissance*, 188.

74. The distinction of transcendental and empirical agency has great consequence for Kant's moral philosophy, as it is by this route that he theorizes humanity's share of freedom from natural causality, which allows Kant in turn to rationalize freedom of will. For his actual epistemological argument, however, see Kant, *Critique of Pure Reason*, esp. 151–65.

75. See Talia Schaffer, *The Forgotten Female Aesthetes: Literary Culture in Late Victorian England* (Charlottesville: University Press of Virginia, 2000); Talia Schaffer and Kathy Alexis Psomiades, eds., *Women and British Aestheticism* (Charlottesville: University Press of Virginia, 1999).

76. George Eliot, *The George Eliot Letters*, ed. Gordon S. Haight, vol. 7 (New Haven, Conn.: Yale University Press, 1955), 455.

Chapter 2. Reflections of Agency in Ruskin's Venice

1. John Ruskin, *The Works of John Ruskin*, ed. E. T. Cook and Alexander Wedderburn, vol. 10 (London: George Allen, 1904), 191–92, 196. The full library edition runs to 39 vols., published from 1903 to 1912. I quote from this edition unless otherwise specified, using parenthetical citations, e.g. (10:191–92, 196).

2. For Morris's reprint, see John Ruskin, *The Nature of Gothic; A Chapter of "The Stones of Venice"* (Hammersmith, U.K.: Kelmscott, 1892).

3. On Ruskin's relation to liberalism, especially in his later career, see Judith Stoddart, *Ruskin's Culture Wars: "Fors Clavigera" and the Crisis of Victorian Liberalism* (Charlottesville: University Press of Virginia, 1998).

4. Robert Hewison, "Notes on the Construction of *The Stones of Venice*," *Studies in Ruskin: Essays in Honor of Van Akin Burd*, ed. Robert Rhodes and Del Ivan Janik (Athens: Ohio University Press, 1982), 131–52. The conclusion of this essay references the earlier work: Robert Hewison, *The Argument of the Eye* (Princeton, N.J.: Princeton University Press, 1976).

5. On Ruskin's engagement with modernity, see especially Jonah Siegel, *Desire and Excess: The Nineteenth-Century Culture of Art* (Princeton, N.J.: Princeton University Press, 2000), xvii–xxiv; 183–84. See also the essay collection *Ruskin and the Dawn of the Modern*, ed. Dinah Birch (Oxford: Oxford University Press, 1999).

6. See, for example, Leslie Stephen's charge, in an 1874 review of *Fors Clavigera*, that Ruskin was hoping vainly to "meet corruption by returning to a simpler order of society": "Mr. Ruskin's Recent Writings," *Fraser's Magazine* new series 9 (1874): 691.

7. In Ruskin's diary for 6 May 1841, quoted in Joan Evans and John Howard Whitehouse, eds., *The Diaries of John Ruskin*, vol. 1 (Oxford: Clarendon, 1956): 183. Ruskin later quotes it himself in *Praeterita* (35:296).

8. Dinah Birch, "Fathers and Sons: Ruskin, John James Ruskin, and Turner," *Nineteenth-Century Contexts: An Interdisciplinary Journal* 18, no. 2 (1994): 156, 161.

9. The speaker of these lines in Wordsworth's poem is actually a Wanderer encountered by the framing speaker, but it seems warranted not to stall on that distinction here, especially as Ruskin himself does not do so. For an acute treatment of Ruskin's changing response to Wordsworth, a response that generally tended over the years from early adulation to later concern that Wordsworth's idiom was excessively egoistic, see Elizabeth Helsinger, *Ruskin and the Art of the Beholder* (Cambridge, Mass.: Harvard University Press, 1982), 41–110); see also John Beer, *Providence and Love: Studies in Wordsworth, Channing, Myers, George Eliot, and Ruskin* (Oxford: Clarendon, 1998), 233–312; John Beer, "Ruskin and Wordsworth," *Wordsworth Circle* 28, no. 1 (winter 1997): 41–48. Jules David Law touches on Ruskin's epigraph from *The Excursion* in examining Ruskin's figures of reflection, understood as confused in a way that reveals impasses in the larger project of modern empiricism from Locke to Ruskin (*The Rhetoric of Empiricism: Language and Perception from Locke to I. A. Richards* [Ithaca, N.Y.: Cornell University Press, 1993], 231–32).

10. Ruskin treatment of the pathetic fallacy arises in *Modern Painters* III (5: 201–20). It is well to recall that he does not condemn such projection entirely, despite the pejorative connotation of the word *fallacy.*

11. Lord Byron, *Childe Harold* 14, verse 17.

12. J. B. Bullen, "Ruskin and the Tradition of Renaissance Historiography," *The Lamp of Memory: Ruskin, Tradition, and Architecture*, ed. Michael Wheeler and Nigel Whiteley (Manchester: Manchester University Press, 1992), 56.

13. By definition, individual agency and providence are problematically compatible, at best, at least as regards the ultimate purview of individual agency: to the extent that our actions are fated, they are not willed in the strongest sense. The opening chapter of

John Beer's *Providence and Love* offers a literary-historical overview of providentialism from the late seventeenth century up to his book's romantic and Victorian focusing points. See also Thomas Vargish, *The Providential Aesthetic in Victorian Fiction* (Charlottesville: University Press of Virginia, 1985). Mary Poovey has argued suggestively that the discourse of providence softened from the 1790s to the 1830s in service to developing needs to navigate between ideas of factuality and theory in economic science. *A History of the Modern Fact: Problems of Knowledge in the Sciences of Wealth and Society* (Chicago: University of Chicago Press, 1998).

14. While Ruskin is not concerned enough with consistency for added citations to be conclusive here, it seems worth noting his language in an 1860 letter to Harriet Beecher Stowe: "So you are coming round to Venice, after all? We shall all have to come to it, depend on it, some way or another. There never has been anything in any other part of the world like Venetian strength well developed" (36:338).

15. For a literary deconstructive account of Ruskin's rhetoric of truth, see Gary Wihl, *Ruskin and the Rhetoric of Infallibility* (New Haven, Conn.: Yale University Press, 1985). Wihl is adept in tracing the convoluted workings of metaphor in Ruskin's thinking, but, as my own exposition implies, I do not share Wihl's sense that Ruskin's works become thereby "unreadable" (xi). It's a tenet of my study overall that even contradiction and undecidability are eminently readable constructs in terms of the interest that they arouse and sustain in modern critical thinking; for a fuller discussion of this point, see the concluding section of Chapter 4 below and the study's conclusion. Jules David Law's 1993 study *The Rhetoric of Empiricism* offers a useful account of Ruskin's projects in epistemological terms (204–44).

16. Ruskin's assumption about the straight line's fundamental nature in this scheme probably reflects the providential thinking from which he draws so much of his rhetoric, especially in his earlier years. Straightness, as a figure of maximal economy in the traversal from point to point, will seem allied to a value of sufficient reason. This principle, in turn, plays a role in ontological proofs of God's existence.

17. See *Modern Painters* II (4:138); also *The Seven Lamps of Architecture* (8:249).

18. John Ruskin, *Ruskin in Italy: Letters to His Parents, 1845*, ed. H. I. Shapiro (Oxford: Clarendon, 1972), 209.

19. Ibid., 139.

20. John Ruskin, *Examples of the Architecture of Venice* (Sunnyside: G. Allen, 1887), iii.

21. Treating Ruskin's relation to Venetian architecture, Kristine Otteson Garrigan touches on his predilection for fragments, but with her concern to explain Ruskin's interest in two-dimensional (or planar) representation—especially suited to Venice, where space and waterways conspire to grant such importance to facades—Garrigan's account leaves us with more to do if we are to think about the fragmentary nature of the casts. (The casts are, for one thing, distinctly three-dimensional.) See Kristine Ottesen Garrigan, "Visions and Verities: Ruskin on Venetian Architecture," in Rhodes and Janik, eds., *Studies in Ruskin*, 156–58. Jules David Law accounts smartly for Ruskin's engagement with images of surface and depth, although Law's emphasis goes to Ruskin's treatment of painting rather than architecture. Law places Ruskin in a British empirical tradition with a rich but problematic relation to ideas of perception and reflection. *Rhetoric of Empiricism*, 204–33.

22. For Ruskin's concern to control aesthetic response in others and to contrast proper with profligate pleasure in art, see Siegel, *Desire and Excess*, (189–92).

23. At several points in *Stones*, Ruskin mentions such response to expediency as a point of nobility in Gothic architecture generally (e.g., 9:212–13; 10:212).

24. *Works* 37:6. Ruskin offers the line in quotation marks. It is a reference, with the pronoun gender switched, to a line in Tennyson's *Maud* (part 1, section 18).

25. *Works* 29:539. For Ruskin's treatment of Scott in *Fors*, see *Letters*, 31–33 (27:562–623).

26. This list of admired figures bears noting. Ruskin's comments on Scott tend to cast him as a simple but vigorous creator, a miracle of well-tuned and uncomplicated responsiveness. Ruskin's interest in Scott recalls the idealization of spontaneity and unreflectiveness that Faust admired in Gretchen. As one could say regarding Turner and Carlyle, Ruskin himself was more Faust than Gretchen, and it seems, in the end, that he rather wished he were like Scott than felt himself to be so.

27. See the 1871 lecture "The Relation Between Michael Angelo and Tintoret" (22:73–110). Some listeners opposed Ruskin's lecture on general art-historical grounds, regarding the higher estimation of Tintoretto as absurd. But a specifically Oxonian investment in the glories of Michelangelo has to be noted as well, for the University Galleries had an extensive collection of the artist's works, to which Ruskin referred, and rather harshly. For this context, see the editors comments in *Works* 22:xxx–xxxiv.

28. Ruskin's principal late writings on Venice are *Guide to the Principal Pictures in Academy of Fine Arts at Venice* (1877) and *St. Marks Rest: The History of Venice* (1884). For Ruskin's later comments on his own relation to Venice, see *Praeterita* and *Fors Clavigera*, letter 76 for April 1877 (29:82–97, esp. 87–91).

29. Tim Hilton, *John Ruskin: The Early Years, 1819–1859* (New Haven, Conn.: Yale University Press, 1985), 95.

30. Giorgio Vasari, *Lives of the Painters, Sculptors and Architects*, trans. Gaston de Vere, 2 vols. (New York: Knopf, 1996), 2:509. Note: readers must consult the second edition of Vasari's *Lives*, as there was no notice of Tintoretto in the first. For a recent account of Tintoretto as an artist peculiarly defined by his role of navigating between older and newer protocols of artistry, see Tom Nichols, *Tintoretto: Tradition and Identity* (London: Reaktion, 1999).

31. For my sense of Tintoretto's historical reception, I am indebted to commentary and source materials in Anna Laura Lepschy, *Tintoretto Observed: A Documentary Survey of the Critical Reactions from the Sixteenth to the Twentieth Century* (Ravenna: Longo, 1983).

32. One constant companion for eighteenth-century Grand Tourists, Addison's Italian travel guide, is typical in this regard. Addison casts Tintoretto as at once overrated and now chiefly a figure favored only in his Venetian hometown. *Remarks on Several Parts of Italy, &c. in the Years 1701, 1702, 1703* (London: J. Tonson, 1705), 86.

33. Goodall's account is excerpted by Cook and Wedderburn in their edition of Ruskin's *Works* (4:xlv n. 4). Samuel Rogers is best known to Ruskin scholars as the author of the poem *Italy*. An 1830 edition, with steel engravings from Turner, was a crucial gift to Ruskin at the age of thirteen. In his adulthood, Ruskin befriended Rogers.

34. Some readers will be interested in a subsequent line of French existentialist interest in Tintoretto. Jules Vuillemin's essay in Sartre's journal *Les Temps modernes* established the image of Tintoretto as a *peintre maudit*. See "La Personalité esthétique du Tintoret," *Les Temps modernes* 9 (1954): 1965–2006. Jean-Paul Sartre developed that account by identifying Tintoretto's with class struggle: "Le Séquestré de Venise," *Situations IV* (Paris: Gallimard, 1964). In each of these accounts, Titian embodies the flaws of establishment fixity, and Tintoretto, even in his imitation of establishment forms, is construed as an agitant, located both within and without the establishment. Sartre also wrote an account of one of Tintoretto's paintings: "Saint-Georges et le dragon," *L'Art* 30 (1966): 33–52.

35. In fact, Ruskin's comments on finish are not easily reconciled to one another. He famously asserts in *Stones*, "Never demand an exact finish for its own sake, but only for some practical or noble end" (10:197), but his mind is set there on the lower order of workers in architectural sculpture, and he goes on to say of painting that "delicate fin-

ish is desirable from the greatest masters, and is always given by them" (10:199). A lengthy footnote in *Modern Painters* V (1860) provides his most concerted attempt to put order into his seemingly contradictory positions on finish (7:356–58). The upshot there: finish is a noble thing but the "imperative demand for finish is ruinous, because it refuses better things than finish" (358). So, with a logic that differs markedly from his above statement in *Stones*, Ruskin would probably justify Tintoretto's lack of finish on grounds of the painter's immersion in sincere and passionate expression.

36. Ruskin's entire letter is printed in Ruskin, *Ruskin in Italy*, 211–13.

37 For references to Tintoretto's *Paradise*, see, for example, *Works* 7:289; 10:438; and 22:102–05. The picture's great size renders impossible any meaningful reproduction here.

38. For a lucid treatment of Ruskin's relation to an alternative conception of the sublime that Ruskin was no doubt more self-conscious about, see Elizabeth Helsinger's treatment of the Burkean and the English-romantic sublimes (*Ruskin and the Art of the Beholder*, 111–39).

39. See the chapter "On the Sublime of Self-Disgust: Or How to Save the Sublime from Narcissistic Sublimation," in Charles Altieri, *Postmodernisms Now: Essays on Contemporaneity in the Arts* (University Park: Pennsylvania State University Press, 1998), 257–82.

40. Nietzsche's comment arises in *On the Genealogy of Morals* (1887), "There is *only* a perspective seeing, *only* a perspective 'knowing'; and the *more* affects we allow to speak about one thing, the *more* eyes, different eyes, we can use to observe one thing, the more complete will our 'concept' of this thing, our 'objectivity,' be." Friedrich Nietzsche, *On the Genealogy of Morals*, trans. Walter Kaufmann and R. J. Hollingdale. [With *Ecce Homo*.] (New York: Vintage, 1989), 119.

41. In 1852, for example, a writer for *The Guardian* deplored the self-contradictory nature of Ruskin's argumentation in his recent work, which included volume 1 of *The Stones of Venice* and also *Examples of Venetian Architecture*, nos.1–3. The reviewer argued that Ruskin had made a mess of the relation between art and religion, and Ruskin wrote to his father, "When I work over a volume for two years, and weigh *every word* in it, and a dim-brained rascal like this of the *Guardian* walks up to me and tells me that 'half of my statements are diametrically opposed to the others,' simply because the poor long-eared brute cannot see that a thistle has two sides, it *does* worry me considerably, and makes me very angry, and yet depresses me at the same time" (qtd. 9:xlii).

42. Ruskin's urging of Turner's exactness—and, indeed, of his unequivocal greatness—became more complicated with time. For an astute account of Ruskin's evolution, see Dinah Birch, ed., *Ruskin on Turner* (Boston: Bulfinch [Little, Brown], 1990), esp. 120–21.

43. Regarding disorderliness in Ruskin's later writing, a widely rehearsed remark in Ruskin scholarship is Cardinal Manning's to Ruskin that *Fors* "is like the beating of one's heart in a nightmare" (qtd. in Ruskin, *Works* 36:lxxxvi), and prominent responses thereafter—for example, Frederic Harrison's of 1902—place Ruskin's idiom there at the furthest limit of rationality (Frederic Harrison, *John Ruskin* [London: Macmillan, 1902], 181). But much of the best recent work on Ruskin focuses on his later career and *Fors* in particular. Tim Hilton's biography declares a mission to establish not just the neglected but indeed the greater character of the later career (*John Ruskin*, x–xi). Judith Stoddart's *Ruskin's Culture Wars* is an excellent study of Ruskin in the 1870s, and a fine new edition of *Fors Clavigera* seems bound to speed this line of thinking along: John Ruskin, *Fors Clavigera*, ed. Dinah Birch (Edinburgh: Edinburgh University Press, 2000). Dinah Birch has an excellent article about *Fors*: "Ruskin's Multiple Writing: *Fors Clavigera*," in Birch, ed., *Ruskin and the Dawn of the Modern*, 175–87. See also Francis O'Gorman, *Late Ruskin: New Contexts* (Burlington, U.K.: Ashgate, 2001).

Chapter 3. The Work of Imposture

1. Of the three legitimate pro-Claimant weeklies, two were launched in the summer of 1872 between the civil and criminal trials: the *Tichborne Gazette* and the *Tichborne News and Anti-Oppression Journal*; *The Englishman*, in turn, began its run in 1874 after the Claimant's criminal conviction. An issue of the "impostor" newspaper, a satire entitled the *Tichborne Times*, is held at the Bodleian Library, Oxford (John Johnson Collection, "Tichborne Case"). That same file also contains examples of an anti-Tichbornite weekly, *The True Briton: The Avowed Enemy and Antidote to Dr. Kenealy's "Englishman"*, with a run from 25 April 1874 to 30 May 1874.

2. This shorthand account of the narrative passes over many details and allows an assumption—that the Claimant was indeed Arthur Orton—which is open to some question. Several modern scholars have treated this history at greater length than I can here. Rohan McWilliam's doctoral dissertation is the definitive social-historical treatment of this case to date: "The Tichborne Claimant and the People: Investigations into Popular Culture, 1867–1886" (D. Phil., University of Sussex, 1990). His redaction of this work has been published: "Radicalism and Popular Culture: The Tichborne Case and the Politics of 'Fair Play,' 1867–1886," in *Currents of Radicalism: Popular Radicalism, Organised Labour, and Party Politics in Britain, 1850–1914*, ed. Eugenio F. Biagini and Alastair J. Reid (Cambridge: Cambridge University Press, 1991), 44–64. See also Douglas Woodruff, *The Tichborne Claimant: A Victorian Mystery* (London: Hollis and Carter, 1957). Woodruff's account remains the most comprehensive factually. For a study centered on popular culture and Edward Vaughan Kenealy, a controversial legal counsel for the Claimant, see Michael Roe, *Kenealy and the Tichborne Cause: A Study in Mid-Victorian Populism* (Melbourne: Melbourne University Press, 1974). For key earlier accounts of the case, see Lord Maugham, *The Tichborne Case* (London: Hodder & Stoughton, 1936); J. B. Atley, *The Tichborne Case* (1899).

3. *Daily Telegraph* (6 March 1872), 4f. Newspapers across the spectrum voice this reminder: "The chief matter at issue is his identity" (*Reynolds's Newspapers*, 10 March 1872, 4); "Indeed, the whole case comes back to the question of identity" (*Times*, 27 April 1872, 12).

4. McWilliam, "Radicalism," 44. McWilliam notes, furthermore, that most historians overlook the Tichborne affair when they suppose that the mass platform expired on the Kennington Common in 1848. Such oversight is brought about by excessively class-based analytical procedures, which throw relatively little light on episodes only partially explainable in terms of traditional class struggle. "Radicalism," 45; 52–53.

5. For divergent perspectives on the Millwall visit, see the *Tichborne News* (13 July 1872); the *Hampshire Chronicle* (13 July 1872), 3. For discussion and further references see McWilliam, "Tichborne," 97–99.

6. See especially Roe, *Kenealy and the Tichborne Cause*; McWilliam, "Radicalism."

7. McWilliam, "Radicalism," 45.

8. *Saturday Review* 33 (30 March 1872), 401.

9. The anti-Catholicism, often styled as anti-Jesuitism, was at times quite rabid. One of the Claimant's two key supporters in Parliament, the Liberal G. H. Whalley, was himself largely responsible for linking the Claimant's case with an alleged Jesuit-Catholic conspiracy, an irony given that the Claimant himself professed to be Catholic. On Whalley, see Michael Roe, *Kenealy and the Tichborne Cause*, 50. The Claimant's counsel in the second trial, Sir Edward Vaughan Hyde Kenealy, was also very exercised by this theme, as his writings in his weekly newspaper the *Englishman* (1874–86) make plain. For general accounts of anti-Catholicism in mid-Victorian Britain, see D. G. Paz, *Popular Anti-Catholicism in Mid-Victorian England* (Stanford, Calif.: Stanford University Press,

1992), and Frank H. Wallis, *Popular Anti-Catholicism in Mid-Victorian Britain* (Lewiston, N.Y.: Edward Mellen, 1993).

10. These weight figures translate the sixteen-stone and the twenty-seven-stone, ten pounds figures referenced in Woodruff, *The Tichborne Claimant*, 81.

11. For a discussion of how populist movements would come to oppose thrift, moderation, the work-ethic, and associated mainstream shibboleths, all understood as part and parcel with corrupt establishment values, see Roe, *Kenealy and the Tichborne Cause*, 43ff.

12. For a prose historical account of the family curse in the context of the Tichborne sensation see, "The Tichborne Dole," *Gentleman's Magazine* 7, new [5th] ser. (1871): 172–75. That article is followed two years later by a poem on the same theme: "The Tichborne Dole," *Gentleman's Magazine* 10, new [5th] ser. (1873), 262–64. For a scholarly gloss, see Woodruff, *Tichborne Claimant*, 5–6.

13. Edward FitzGerald, *The Letters of Edward Fitzgerald*, ed. Alfred McKinley Terhune and Annabelle Burdick Terhune. 3 vols. (Princeton, N.J.: Princeton University Press, 1980), 3:427.

14. See Anthony Trollope, *Is He Popenjoy?* (London: Chapman & Hall, 1878); Charles Reade, *The Wandering Heir* (1872).

15. See Richard Mullen, *Anthony Trollope: A Victorian in His World* (London: Duckworth, 1990), 594.

16. Guildford Onslow, *200 Facts Proving the Claimant to be Roger Tichborne*, 4th ed., De Morgan's Popular Series, no. 2 (London: George Howe, n.d.), 21. This rare title and numerous other pamphlets of the sort are held at the British Library.

17. For a popular account of the non-suit as a legal stratagem in this context, see the *Daily Telegraph* (6 March 1872), 4.

18. *Morning Post* (7 March 1872), 6e.

19. The *Observer* estimated the 26-day address to occupy 140 hours (25 February 1872), 2. As one would expect, letters to the editor of the *Tichborne News and Anti-Oppression Journal* reflect suspicions about the attorney general's motives. See, for example, the letter from "A Clergyman," 29 June 1872, 3; and the letter from John Bailey, 13 July 1872, 2. Similar suspicions also arose in much more mainstream contexts. In the months preceding the criminal trial, the *Solicitor's Journal* openly criticized Coleridge's decision to put the criminal trial before the bar rather than going through a simpler procedural setting: "We cannot help suspecting that his judgment in the matter is not quite as good as it might be if he had not been so long occupied with the case." *Solicitor's Journal & Reporter* (27 April 1872), 478.

20. *Standard* (5 March 1872), 4.

21. *Observer* (10 March 1872), 4.

22. The charge of forgery arose because the Claimant had signed the name of Sir Roger Tichborne during a bond scheme to raise funds for himself. The charge was dropped not for lack of cause, but as a technical expedience, because forgery trials required the total sequestration of the jury. See McWilliam, "Tichborne," 116. The bonds were to be repaid upon the Claimant's possession of the Tichborne estate, so their purchase was both a form of speculation and a sign of widespread faith in his cause. Because the bonds could be traded subsequent to their purchase, their rising and falling values can also be taken as one measure of public sentiment on his prospects.

23. This popular rumor has powerful documentary confirmation. Already during the course of the first trial, in which Cockburn was not involved, Shirley Brooks had written in his diary for 20 June 1871 that "Sir A. Cockburn wishes he were counsel in it—he 'could have doubled the fellow up much quicker.'" See G. S. Laayrd, *A Great*

"Punch" Editor: Being the Life, Letters, and Diaries of Shirley Brooks (London, 1907). Qtd. in Roe, *Kenealy and the Tichborne Cause*, 46–47.

24. Kenealy's doings after the Claimant's conviction at the criminal trial are varied and interesting, including a brief stint as Member of Parliament (understood then much as Jesse Ventura's election as governor of Minnesota has been understood in our time) and several lawsuits against him and his *Englishman* newspaper for libel. I make my case with only passing references to Kenealy, because his story been well documented already in Michael Roe's *Kenealy and the Tichborne Cause.*

25. The rhetoric of these reports is highly charged and could repay closer examination than I offer here. For perhaps the earliest report on the verdict, see the late edition of the *Daily Telegraph* for 28 February 1874. Of the Sunday papers, several went to press with reports dated 1 March 1874: the *Weekly Times, Lloyds,* and the *Observer,* the Sundays by *Reynolds's* and the *Sunday Times* apparently went to press too early to report the final verdict and had to wait until the next week (8 March 1874). The broadest array of reporting appears with the dailies on Monday, 2 March 1874, for which dates see such papers as the *Times,* the *Pall Mall Gazette,* the *Morning Post,* the *Standard,* the *Morning Advertiser,* and also a substantial follow-up report by the *Daily Telegraph.* For a relevant Saturday weekly, the *Hampshire Chronicle,* see 7 March 1874.

26. Joseph Brown, *The Tichborne Case Compared with Previous Impostures of the Same Kind* (London: Butterworths, 1874), 5.

27. The state refused to prosecute in a case involving the banking house Overend and Gurney, in the 1860s, and the popular perception was that class and insider privilege had bought impunity from the law. This instance is mentioned as a concern for the Tichbornite faction in Woodruff, *Tichborne Claimant,* 220.

28. *Weekly Times* (10 March 1872), 4.

29. For a reconstruction of the Claimant's itinerary of meetings, which came to number about sixty, see McWilliam, "Tichborne," 299–300.

30. Ibid., 304, 305.

31. *Tichborne Gazette* (13 May 1874), 3.

32. Regarding the Education Act of 1870—which ensured that state-funded nondenominational elementary schools would be raised up to fill in the gaps left over from the traditional system of religious schools—Nonconformists initially supported a nondenominational or even secular state school system in the months leading up to the Education Act. One could erroneously see the Nonconformists as "bracketing" their religious preferences in service to a liberal-minded tolerance. But it seems that Nonconformists adopted this tack largely because they felt that the Anglican Church would get the better of a state system in which any denominational instruction at all was specified. See Gillian Sutherland, *Elementary Education in the Nineteenth Century* (London: The Historical Association, 1971), 21. In all these concrete political contexts referenced here, we should only suggest broader cultural meanings with an eye as well to the complexities invariably at hand.

33. A regular signature in *Reynolds's Newspaper,* "Gracchus" was G. W. M. Reynolds's brother Edward, but perhaps also Reynolds himself at times. See Rohan McWilliam, "The Mysteries of G. W. M. Reynolds: Radicalism and Melodrama in Victorian Britain," in *Living and Learning: Essays in Honour of J. F. C. Harrison,* ed. Malcolm Chase and Ian Dyck (Aldershot, U.K.: Scolar, 1996), 189.

34. *Reynolds's Newspaper* (22 February 1874), 3.

35. *Lloyds Weekly London Newspaper* (17 March 1872), 5.

36. *Standard* (8 March 1872), 4.

37. *Morning Post* (7 March 1874), 4.

38. *Daily Telegraph* (6 March 1872), 4.

39. *Standard* (8 March 1872), 4.

40. McWilliam, "Tichborne," 69.

41. Despite their common hostility to the Claimant, these newspapers are hardly equivalent in their practical political perspectives. The *Standard*, for example, was a Conservative newspaper, so caution is warranted whenever one tries, as I do here, to apply ideas of "liberal" or "middle-class" culture very broadly. To understand the grounds for being more careful in preserving these distinction in my argument, it would be necessary to mount a more exhaustive examination of mid-Victorian editorializing than I have been able to do. It would be interesting to see, for example, whether the *Standard*'s editorial stance toward the working classes that supported the Claimant tended to change after it became clearer that the working classes had moved in increasing numbers to support the Tory party under Disraeli after 1874.

42. The *Morning Post* (7 March 1872), 4.

43. *Observer* (3 March 1872), 7.

44. Reports in the anti-Claimant *Hampshire Chronicle* often drip with sarcasm: "The [pro-Claimant] meetings seem generally to have been pretty unanimous, and it is pleasing to know that one or two individuals who ventured to express disapprobation regarding the statements made were duly hauled on the platform, hissed, and otherwise punished for the temerity of their conduct." *Hampshire Chronicle* (15 June 1872), 5. Public feeling ran high in Hampshire, where the Tichborne family estate was located. The Hampshire public itself seems to have been of a piece with the rest of England in dividing sharply along class and other social lines.

45. The *Bee Hive* was founded in 1861 with an announced concern to boost for working-class representation in Parliament. See Ian Machin, *The Rise of Democracy in Britain, 1830–1918* (New York: St. Martin's, 2001), 54.

46. Other mainstream press accounts of this demonstration, which became an annual Easter Monday event for a decade, include "The Tichborne-Kenealy Demonstration," *Times* (30 March 1875), 6; "Demonstration in Hyde Park," *Daily Telegraph* (30 March 1875), 6; *Pall Mall Gazette* (30 March 1875), 6; "Kenealy-Tichborne Demonstrations," *Lloyd's Weekly London Newspaper* (4 April 1875), 3; and two articles in *Reynolds's Newspaper* of 4 April 1875, "Monster Demonstration in Favour of the Claimant" (3) and "The Tichborne Demonstration" (4). For a predictably affirmative account, see "The Hyde Park Meeting" in Kenealy's *Englishman* (3 April 1875), 815–16.

47. [Walter Bagehot,] "The Orton Demonstrations," *The Economist* 33 (3 April 1875): 391. The article is on one page, so further quotations to Bagehot in this discussion can take this note as the reference.

48. Louis Althusser, "Ideology and Ideological State Apparatuses (Notes Towards an Investigation)," *Lenin and Philosophy and Other Essays*, trans. Ben Brewster (London: NLB, 1971), 127–86; Michel Foucault, "Governmentality," *The Foucault Effect: Studies in Governmentality, with Two Lectures and an Interview with Michel Foucault*, ed. Graham Burchell, Colin Gordon, and Peter Miller (Chicago: University of Chicago Press, 1991), 87–118; Pierre Bourdieu, *Distinction: A Social Critique of the Judgement of Taste*, trans. Richard Nice (Cambridge, Mass.: Harvard University Press, 1984); Catherine Gallagher and Stephen Greenblatt, *Practicing New Historicism* (Chicago: University of Chicago Press, 2000).

49. Charles Dickens, *David Copperfield* (Harmondsworth, U.K.: Penguin, 1996), 526.

50. It seems that Lowe's original remark was uttered before rather than after the passage of the Reform Bill. The parliamentary record gives his words as follows: "I believe it will be absolutely necessary that you should prevail on our future masters to learn their letters"; *Hansard's Parliamentary Debates*, 15 July 1867, col. 1549. Due to its popular career, Lowe's remark is often miscited, implicitly located after the bill's passage, typi-

cally in keeping with the title of Thomas Wright's reflections on the rifts between working-class and middle-class culture: *Our New Masters* (London: Strahan, 1873).

51. Wright, *Our New Masters*, 157.

52. Roe, *Kenealy and the Tichborne Cause*, 39.

53. Samuel Smiles, *Self-Help*.

54. This Seventh Earl of Shaftesbury was a Tory MP before his accession to the House of Lords in 1851, so his exemplarity as a "liberal" here is loose. It was characteristic of Shaftesbury, however, that his Evangelicism and sense of moral principle predominated over his party or even national interests, as in his opposition to the opium trade. To this extent, he proceeded according to reflections on duty and principle, much in keeping with a general spirit of critical moral liberalism. Geoffrey B. A. M. Finlayson, *The Seventh Earl of Shaftesbury, 1801–1885* (London: Eyre Methuen, 1981); John Charles Pollock, *Shaftesbury, The Poor Man's Earl* (London: Hodder and Stoughton, 1985); Virginia Berridge and Griffith Edwards, *Opium and the People: Opiate Use in Nineteenth-Century England* (London: Allen Lane, 1981).

55. This view of the middle-class progressive relation to the working classes is smartly argued in Lauren M. E. Goodlad, " 'Making the Working Man Like Me': Charity, Pastorship, and Middle-Class Identity in Nineteenth-Century Britain; Thomas Chalmers and Dr. James Phillips Kay," *Victorian Studies* 44, no.4 (summer 2001): 592–617.

56. *Times* (5 August 1872), 6. A short notice of the occasion also appears in one of the pro-Claimant weeklies, apparently by way of an excerpt from the *Times*: *Tichborne News and Anti-Oppression Journal* (10 August 1872), 4.

57. The Artisans, Labourers, and General Dwellings Company was founded in 1867 in response to the broad areas laid waste by railroad building and other urban developments. "On every estate purchased by the company a suitable space will be reserved as a re-creation ground, a co-operative store will be built for the especial benefit of the tenant, and publichouses will be absolutely forbidden." *Times* (5 August 1872), 6.

58. On the relation of masculinity metaphors and Victorian self-fashioning more generally, see James Eli Adams, *Dandies and Desert Saints: Styles of Victorian Masculinity* (Ithaca, N.Y.: Cornell University Press, 1995).

59. Garrett Stewart, *Dear Reader: The Conscripted Audience in Nineteenth-Century British Fiction* (Baltimore: Johns Hopkins University Press, 1996).

60. Michel Foucault, "Governmentality."

61. See especially Roe, *Kenealy and the Tichborne Cause*; McWilliam, "Radicalism."

62. McWilliam, "Tichborne," 97–99.

63. Roe, *Kenealy and the Tichborne Cause*, 27, 117.

64. McWilliam, "Radicalism," 49.

65. See, for example, one of the Claimant's parliamentarian supporters, Guildford Onslow, as he refuses the accusation that he is setting class against class: *Tichborne News* (31 August 1872), 2.

66. *Sunday Times* (10 March 1872), 4. I have corrected a misprint in the original, allowing *evident* for the original's *evidently*.

67. *Tichborne News* (7 September 1872), 2.

68. *Hansard's Parliamentary Debates* (9 August 1872), 852. More generally, see *Hansard's* for 9 August 1872, 846–53; and 10 August 1872, 866–67.

69. The Claimant's "Appeal" was printed in the *Standard* of 25 March 1872, according to Douglas Woodruff, *Tichborne Claimant*, 223. I could not locate it in the issue that I examined, but the letter was soon reprinted in several newspapers, such as the *Times*, from which I quote (27 March 1872, 5).

70. A typical newspaper account in this vein purports to outline a "defect in the En-

glish law of bail." A closer inspection reveals, however, the defect was that the particular legal circumstances of the Claimant's arrest restrained the judge from withholding the option of bail from the Claimant. The argument only makes sense, then, on the assumption that it would be a plain and simple wrong to allow bail to the Claimant. See the *Daily Telegraph* (14 March 1872), 4. For another article making the same point, and in the same spirit, see the *Hampshire Chronicle* (16 March 1872), 3.

71. *Times* (27 March 1872), 5.

72. See, for example, *Tichborne News* (15 June 1872), 1; *Tichborne News* (6 July 1872), 3.

73. Thomas Wright, *Our New Masters* (London: Strahan, 1873), 150.

74. Wright, *Our New Masters*, 155. There is room for a cultural history of kleptomania, it seems: Wright's point is reiterated high and low in the early 1870s: see chap. 23 in *Middlemarch*, 234; also *Reynolds's Newspaper*: "Kleptomania, as well as insanity, is one of those convenient loop-holes and pleas whereby the wealthy and powerful contrive to escape from the judicial fangs which fasten so closely upon the poorer delinquent." (3 March 1872, 2). According to the *Oxford English Dictionary* the term *kleptomania* is Victorian in origin.

75. The weekly papers devoted to the Tichborne case give glancing but continual representation to the debates. Fuller statements are at hand in more general press organs devoted to the working classes. The most important of these was surely *Reynolds's Newspaper*, which took a consistently radical and sometimes ranting approach. The *Morning Advertiser*, which supported the Claimant expressly, was a paper for the Licensed Victuallers Association, and it reported on legislation having to do with drinking hours and tariffs. The Tichborne weeklies often excerpted their stories from these two papers. On the specific features of various working-class and lower-middle-class newspapers in mid-Victorian Britain, with an eye to their concrete differences (e.g., according to their appeal to artisanal and shopkeeping audiences), see Virginia Stewart Berridge, "Popular Journalism and Working-Class Attitudes, 1854–1886: A Study of *Reynolds's Newspaper, Lloyd's Weekly Newspaper* and *The Weekly Times*" (D.Phil. University of London, Birkbeck College, 1976).

76. "The Tichborne Claimant's Appeal," *Saturday Review* 33 (30 March 1872): 402.

77. Roe, *Kenealy and the Tichborne Cause*, 43.

78. Sigmund Freud, "On Narcissism," *The Standard Edition of the Complete Psychological Works of Sigmund Freud*, trans. James Strachey, 24 vols. (London: Hogarth Press, 1953), 14: 88–89. For Freud on the human fascination with roguery in the context of social life, see *Civilization and its Discontents*, vol. 21 in the *Standard Edition* (57–145).

79. *Morning Advertiser* (8 March 1872), 4.

80. *Sunday Times* (8 March 1874), 5.

81. *Observer* (10 March 1872): 4.

82. *Daily Telegraph* (7 March 1872), 4.

83. *Standard* (8 March 1872), 5.

84. *Morning Post* (2 March 1874), 3. Qtd. in McWilliam, "Tichborne," 131.

85. *Tichborne News and Anti-Oppression Journal* 11 (24 August 1872): 3.

86. Uday Singh Mehta, *Liberalism and Empire*, 164.

87. Ibid., 27.

88. Charles Taylor, *Sources of the Self: The Making of the Modern Identity* (Cambridge, Mass.: Harvard University Press, 1989), 521.

89. The relations between legal culture and political-moral thought during the Victorian period are a key theme in Stefan Collini, *Public Moralists: Political Thought and Intellectual Life in Britain, 1850-1930* (Oxford: Oxford University Press, 1991), esp. 251–307.

90. Bentham's writings were directed against Blackstone beginning already with his

A Fragment on Government (1776). See *A Fragment on Government*, ed. J. H. Burns and H. L. A. Hart, Cambridge Texts in the History of Political Thought (Cambridge: Cambridge University Press, 1988); Bentham's *Comment on the Commentaries of Blackstone*, written 1774–76, was not published in his lifetime, nor was other relevant argumentation. See his *A Comment on the Commentaries; and A Fragment on Government*, ed. J. H. Burns and H. L. A. Hart (London: University of London Press, 1977); and his work of the 1780s, *Of Laws in General*, ed. H. L. A. Hart (London: University of London Press, [Athlone], 1970).

91. Blackstone is widely noted for epitomizing the acceptance of natural law in this statement from his *Commentaries on the Laws of England*: "This law of nature, being co-eval with mankind and dictated by God himself, is of course superior in obligation to any other. It is binding all over the globe, in all countries, and at all times: no human laws are of any validity, if contrary to this: and such of them as are valid derive all their force, and all their authority, mediately or immediately, from this original." *Commentaries on the Laws of England*, 4 vols. (Portland: Thomas B. Wait, 1807), 1:40–41. Modern legal historians understand Blackstone's actual commitment to natural law theory as less dogmatic and complacent than Bentham made it out to be. It seems that Bentham's account gained its notoriety and its influence in part because Blackstone disdained to answer the polemic of the young Bentham. For an updated account of differences between Blackstone and Bentham, see Richard A. Cosgrove, *Scholars of the Law: English Jurisprudence from Blackstone to Hart* (New York and London: New York University Press, 1996), esp. 21–87.

92. Legal positivism's key issues ramify quickly into problems too remote from my argument to repay discussion here. But I can paraphrase H. L. A. Hart's usefully compact characterization, whereby the term means one or more of the following: (1) that law equals human commands; (2) that law and morality have no necessary connection; (3) that the practice of legal analysis can and should be distinguished from historical, sociological, and critical appraisals centered on law's purposes and functions; (4) that law is a closed system of meanings and rules, with correct decisions following on adequate realization of the underlying rules; and (5) that values, unlike facts, cannot be established by rational argumentation or proofs. According to Hart, only the first three points were affirmed in the legal positivism associated with the two nineteenth-century figures relevant to my discussion, Jeremy Bentham and John Austin. See H. L. A. Hart, *The Concept of Law* (Oxford: Clarendon, 1961), 253

93. Lecture 5 in John Austin, *The Province of Jurisprudence Determined*, ed. Wilfred E. Rumble (Cambridge: Cambridge University Press, 1995), 157.

94. For a conceptual argument along these lines, see Roberto Mangabeira Unger, *Knowledge and Politics* (New York: Free Press, 1975), esp. 63–103.

95. The 1873 Judicature Act, with amendments in 1875 and thereafter, has been seen by social and political historians as a signal development in the rationalization of law since the argument to that effect in R. C. K. Ensor, *England, 1870–1914* (Oxford: Clarendon, 1936), 17. A textual examination of the 1873 Act itself can begin with chap. 66, "The Supreme Court of Judicature Act, 1873," in *The Public and General Acts of the United Kingdom of Great Britain and Ireland* [36th and 37th Regnal Yrs] (London: George Edward Eyre and William Spottiswoode, 1873), 191–222. A detailed account of the Act and its various amendments is available in what legal historians call "Chitty's Statutes." See "Judicature," *The Statutes of Practical Utility*, 5th ed., ed. J. M. Lely, Vol. 6 (London: Sweet & Maxwell, 1895), 1–21. For more accessible and compact discussion, see Raymond Cocks, *Foundations of the Modern Bar* (London: Sweet & Maxwell, 1983), 135-61. Historians specializing in legal history often emphasize that actual changes in legal practice were slow to come. See Richard A. Cosgrove, "The Judicature Acts of

1873–1875: A Centennial Reassessment," *Durham University Journal* 37, no. 2 (1976): 196–206.

96. Charles Dickens, *Bleak House* (London: Penguin, 1996), 118–19.

97. Equity's precedence over common law might be taken as another sign of the decline of the natural-law approach, which figures powerfully in the common-law tradition. But it bears noting that equity had been deemed to supersede common law since the times of James I. The 1873 Judicature Act followed therefore on an early modern practice. For this point I am indebted to A. W. Brian Simpson.

98. See especially *Punch* 64 (10 May 1873): 193. The image depicts two impish figures, labeled "Law" and "Equity," at the point of being plunged into a cauldron marked "Fusion."

99. Charles Dickens, *Our Mutual Friend* (Oxford: Oxford University Press, 1989), 140.

100. Wilfred E. Rumble, "Nineteenth-Century Perceptions of John Austin: Utilitarianism and the Reviews of *The Province of Jurisprudence Determined*," *Utilitas* 3, no. 2 (November 1991): 199–216.

101. Mill had admiringly reviewed Austin's *Province* when it appeared in 1832, but he also foretold a poor public reception: the present age, said Mill, is too busy in its reading to welcome a book so clearly indebted to meditation. John Stuart Mill, "Austin's Lectures on Jurisprudence," *Collected Works of John Stuart Mill*, 21:53, 51–60. Later, in 1863, Mill reviewed the posthumous publication and republication of Austin's work, at which point Austin became widely and hotly debated: "Austin on Jurisprudence," 165–205.

102. *Swansea & Glamorgan Herald* (3 July 1872), 4.

103. The *Tichborne Gazette* resumed publication in 1874 for exactly this reason. The lead editorial answer a charge that the newspaper might weaken the pro-Claimant movement by dividing public attentions between itself and Kenealy's *Englishman*. "Unfortunately, however, the 'Englishman' week after week put forth matters relating to its gifted author in the fore-front and those of Sir Roger in the rear; and as it was felt by the friends of Sir Roger's cause generally, that his interests should take rank, in a paper professing to uphold the Tichborne cause, before those of his advocate, it was resolved to fall back again upon the original intention of again publishing the TICHBORNE GAZETTE." *Tichborne Gazette* (13 May 1874), 3.

104. A proper discussion of the movement's fragmentation after the Claimant's conviction lies outside my charge here. On the relations between radicalism, libertarianism, the free-born Englishman ideal in terms of the Tichborne cause, see McWilliam, "Tichborne," and his briefer treatment in "Radicalism."

105. Matthew Arnold, *Culture and Anarchy*, in Matthew Arnold, *The Complete Prose Works of Matthew Arnold*, ed. R. H. Super (Ann Arbor: University of Michigan Press, 1965), 5:121.

106. McWilliam, "Radicalism," 45.

107. Ibid., 55–56, 60–62.

108. Blair Worden, "The Victorians and Oliver Cromwell," in *History, Religion, and Culture: British Intellectual History, 1750-1950*, ed. Stefan Collini, Richard Whatmore, and Brian Young (Cambridge: Cambridge University Press, 2000), 132.

109. Ibid., 122.

110. *The Tichborne News and Anti-Oppression Journal* 5 (13 July 1872): 2.

Part II. Aesthetic Agency

1. I discuss Linda Dowling's work in this study's opening chapter. The most relevant Dowling reference here is *The Vulgarization of Art.*

2. Pierre Bourdieu, *The Rules of Art.*

3. Fredric Jameson, *The Political Unconscious: Narrative as a Socially Symbolic Act* (Ithaca, N.Y.: Cornell University Press, 1981). For Jameson's view of utopia, see his *Marxism and Form*, 111.

4. Immanuel Kant, *Critique of Judgment*, esp. 35–38.

5. Jonathan Freedman, *Professions of Taste.* Citations are given parenthetically in the text. See also two works by Regenia Gagnier: *Idylls of the Marketplace: Oscar Wilde and the Victorian Public* (Stanford: Stanford University Press, 1986); *The Insatiability of Human Wants.*

6. Walter Benjamin, "Central Park" [1937–38], *New German Critique* 34 (1985): 37.

7. The key figure arguing for agency as born within or through subjection is Louis Althusser, whom I read in Chapter 5 below. See Louis Althusser, "Ideology and Ideological State Apparatuses (Notes Towards an Investigation)," *Lenin and Philosophy and Other Essays*, 127–186. For current critical purposes, the key figures who posit resistance through working within and from interpellated identities are the later Michel Foucault and Judith Butler. This tradition from Althusser forward is cogently rehearsed in Judith Butler, *The Psychic Life of Power: Theories in Subjection* (Stanford, Calif.: Stanford University Press, 1997).

Chapter 4. Replicating Agency

1. For a list of eighteen showings during Rossetti's lifetime, see Alicia Craig Faxon, *Dante Gabriel Rossetti* (Oxford: Phaidon, 1989), 22, 228 n. 8.

2. "The Royal Academy II," *The Graphic* (13 January 1883), 50.

3. Theodore Watts[-Dunton], "The Truth about Rossetti," *The Nineteenth Century* 13 (1883), 408. My account proceeds from numerous contemporary journalistic reviews of the Rossetti shows. See the anonymous articles "Contemporary Art—Poetic and Positive: Rossetti and Tadema—Linnell and Lawson," *Blackwood's Edinburgh Magazine* 133 (January–June 1883): 392–411; "Memorials of Rossetti," *Atlantic Monthly* 51 (April 1883): 549–55; "Rossetti at Burlington House," *Spectator* (6 January 1883), 14–15; "Rossetti at Burlington House (Second Notice)," *Spectator* (27 January 1883), 115–17; "The Rossetti Exhibition," *Times* (12 December 1882), 3; "The Royal Academy I," *The Graphic* (6 January 1883), 22; "The Royal Academy II," *The Graphic* (13 January 1883), 50; "Royal Academy—Winter Exhibition (First Notice)," *Athenaeum* (6 January 1883), 22–23; "Royal Academy—Winter Exhibition (Second Notice)," *Athenaeum* (13 January 1883), 58–59; "Royal Academy—Winter Exhibition (Third Notice)," *Athenaeum* (20 January 1883), 93–95. See also the by-lined articles of Francis Hueffer, *Italian and Other Studies* (London: Elliot Stock, 1883), 83-105; Cosmo Monkhouse, "Rossetti's Pictures at the Royal Academy," *Academy* 23, no. 557 (6 January 1883): 14–15; Cosmo Monkhouse, "Rossetti at the Burlington Club," *Academy* 23, no. 559 (20 January 1883), 50-51; F. W. H Myers, "Rossetti and the Religion of Beauty," *Cornhill Magazine* 47 (January–June 1883), 213–24; Harry Quilter, "The Art of Rossetti," *Contemporary Review* 43 (January–June 1883): 190–203. During the exhibitions the *Athenaeum* ran a public exchange of letters on the matter of copyright and Rossetti's works, with figures such as H. Virtue Tebbs, George Price Boyce, William Bell Scott, and William Michael Rossetti weighing in (*Athenaeum*: 17 February 1883 [222–23]; 24 February 1883 [254–55]; 3

March 1883 [287]; 10 March 1883 [319]. For notices before and after the public sale of Rossetti's works, see the *Times*: 9 May 1883 (5); 14 May 1883 (6).

4. The details of the Royal Academy show are in the catalogue of the annual Winter exhibition for 1883: *Exhibition of Works by the Old Masters and by Deceased Masters of the British School; Including a Special Selection from the Works of John Linnell and Dante Gabriel Rossetti*, Winter Exhibition [Royal Academy], Fourteenth Year (London: Wm. Clowes and Sons, 1883), 56–76. For the catalogue of the Burlington Fine Arts Club show, see *Pictures, Drawings, Designs and Studies by the Late Dante Gabriel Rossetti. Born 1828; Died 1882*, with a preface by H. Virtue Tebbs (London: Metchim and Son, 1883).

5. Cosmo Monkhouse, "Rossetti at the Burlington Club," 50. Monkhouse lent item 121 to the Burlington Club show—a pen-and-ink sketch of Tennyson reading from "Maud"—and that version was one of two replicas made by Rossetti from the original, itself owned by Robert Browning. This point seems worth noting, insofar as owning a replica might be thought to dispose Monkhouse well toward them generally. On the versions of this drawing, see item 526 in Virginia Surtees, *The Paintings and Drawings of Dante Gabriel Rossetti (1828–1882: A Catalogue Raisonné*, 2 vols. (Oxford: Clarendon, 1971), 198–99. Surtees's work does not number its two volumes, one of which offers plates while the other offers text. In this chapter, all of my references refer to the text volume.

6. The Burlington Club was second in line for Rossetti's works, notwithstanding Rossetti's diffidence in his lifetime toward the Royal Academy and the mainstream London art world that it represented. Frederick Leighton, organizer of the Royal Academy show, wrote to George Price Boyce about space restrictions at the Royal Academy in hopes that some of the items that owners sent to Leighton might be taken by the Fine Arts Club show. See Frederic Leighton, letter to George Price Boyce, 25 December 1882, Lord Leighton's letters 16740, Royal Borough of Kensington and Chelsea Libraries, London. According to William Bell Scott, Boyce shared the organization of the Burlington Club show with H. Virtue Tebbs. See William Bell Scott, letter to James Leathart, 18 January 1883, Special Collections and Archives, University of British Columbia, Vancouver. The general effect of this division was that the Royal Academy offered a more concentrated view of Rossetti, emphasizing his imaginative and poetically oriented works, while the Burlington Club featured replicated versions of major works and also numerous portraits and sketches. So the Burlington Club provided, as one reviewer would note, a more "intimate communication with his [Rossetti's] personality." See Monkhouse, "Rossetti at the Burlington Club" (50).

7. Dianne Sachko Macleod, *Art and the Victorian Middle Class* (Cambridge: Cambridge University Press, 1996), 320. Excepting Macleod, scholarly discussion focused on replication remains minimal. But see also Marjorie B Cohn, Introduction, *Ingres, In Pursuit of Perfection: The Art of J.-A.-D. Ingres*. ed. Patricia Condon, Marjorie B. Cohn, and Agnes Mongan (Louisville, KY.: J. B. Speed Art Museum, 1983), 8–33; Rosalind Krauss, "Originality as Repetition: Introduction." *October* 37 (1986), 35–40.

8. William Bell Scott, letter to James Leathart, 18 January 1883, Special Collections and Archives, University of British Columbia, Vancouver. Part of this quotation is given in Macleod, *Art and the Victorian Middle Class*, 324. Although I quote from original letters here and wherever possible, I want to register my debt to Dianne Sachko Macleod's work for unearthing this reference and several others in the pages that follow.

9. These figures are approximations drawing on several sources. I list them here in chronological order. There is a hastily assembled and spotty appendix in William Sharp, *Dante Gabriel Rossetti: A Record and a Study* (London: Macmillan, 1882), n. p. Sharp's work is chiefly useful as a guide to the ownership of Rossetti's works at the time of his death. There is a similar appendix in William Michael Rossetti, *Dante Gabriel Ros-*

setti as Designer and Writer (London: Cassell, 1889), 263–89; the best period appendix is in H. C. [Henry Currie] Marillier, *Dante Gabriel Rossetti: An Illustrated Memorial of his Art and Life* (London: G. Bell, 1899), 233–62; and modern scholarship is referenced to the invaluable catalogue raisonné by Surtees, on which see note 5 above.

10. Scholarship has so far not treated the end of Rossetti's relation to Dunn, so I will note that some unpublished letters from Dunn to Rossetti place the end of their relationship in the summer of 1881. The letters suggest that financial stresses for Rossetti led him to moodiness in his dealings with Dunn. On 22 July 1881, Dunn writes from Truro, where he has taken extra work to relieve himself of rising debts, apparently occasioned by lack of due payment from Rossetti; on 27 July, Dunn is rather surprised to find himself terminated as Rossetti's assistant, with an understanding that some other person was to replace him. On 1 August, Dunn is removing his things from Cheyne Walk, implying with characteristic caution and solicitude that Rossetti has perhaps been unduly cross with him. In this last letter, Dunn professes regret over Rossetti's "recent disappointment respecting the 'Dante' picture," a large painting that Rossetti had considerable difficulty selling. See Angeli-Dennis papers, box 2, folder 21, University of British Columbia, Vancouver.

11. Henry Treffry Dunn, *Recollections of Dante Gabriel Rossetti and His Circle (Cheyne Walk Life)*, ed. Gale Pedrick (London: Elkin Matthews, 1904), 21. In the 1883 shows, both the Royal Academy and the Burlington Fine Arts Club offered a rendering of *The Loving Cup*, but the catalogue raisonné by Surtees would suggest that still another version had Dunn's hand in it (115). In 1873, Rossetti recalled that he had three watercolor replicas made of the original oil, but he mentioned Walter John Knewstub as the assistant who began one of them with limited success. Dante Gabriel Rossetti, *Letters of Dante Gabriel Rossetti*, ed. Oswald Doughty and John Robert Wahl, 4 vols. (Oxford: Oxford University Press, 1965–67), 3:1135.

12. For a work that makes much of Dunn's role in fashioning replicas, see Gale Pedrick, *Life with Rossetti; or, No Peacocks Allowed* (London: Macdonald, 1964). This Gale Pedrick is not to be confused with his father, also named Gale Pedrick, who edited Dunn's memoir, cited in note 11 above. Both Pedricks, in turn, are related to Dunn himself, who was an uncle to the wife of the elder Pedrick and, therefore, a great-uncle to the younger Pedrick. On these relations, see the younger Pedrick's *Life with Rossetti*, 5–6. Some caution seems warranted concerning the younger Pedrick's precision as a historian of Rossetti's replicas. He says, for example, that Rossetti's *Proserpine* was started seven times before a "final picture was completed to his satisfaction" (131), but the idea of a "final" picture is not a factor in this particular tale, where at least two versions, and perhaps three or more, received full finish. For a detailed account of the history of the *Proserpine* images, see Surtees, *Paintings and Drawings*, 131–34.

13. Qtd. in Elzea Rowland, ed., *The Correspondence Between Samuel Bancroft, Jr., and Charles Fairfax Murray (1892–1916)*, Occasional Paper 2 (Wilmington: Delaware Art Museum, 1980), 211. Surtees quotes a different, draft form of this letter (117 n. 2). On Murray's relation to Rossetti, see Carole Cable, "Charles Fairfax Murray: Assistant to Dante Gabriel Rossetti," *Library Chronicle of the University of Texas at Austin* 10 [n. ser.] (1978), 81–89.

14. Qtd. in Virginia Surtees, *Paintings and Drawings*, 85. See also an 1890 letter from William Michael Rossetti to Murray, which makes clear that both men were watchful in regard to false Rossetti works, which, in this instance, they wished to have removed as lots from an 1890 Sotheby's auction. William Michael Rossetti, *Selected Letters of William Michael Rossetti*, ed. Roger W. Peattie (University Park: Pennsylvania State University Press, 1990), 544.

15. D. G. Rossetti, *Letters*, 3:1263. A large number of Rossetti's letters to Dunn are

held at the National Art Library in the Victoria and Albert Museum. There is some uncertainty about how adequately these letters are reproduced in the Doughty-Wahl edition of Rossetti's letters. See William E. Fredeman's two excellent reviews of the published letters, "Rossetti's Letters," *Malahat Review* 1 (1967), 134–41; and "Rossetti's Letters: Part 2," *Malahat Review* 6 (1968): 115–26. From the papers that remain after Fredeman's death, a newly authoritative edition of D. G. Rossetti's collected letters is appearing. Three volumes have appeared to date. See Dante Gabriel Rossetti, *The Correspondence of Dante Gabriel Rossetti*, ed. William E. Fredeman, 9 vols. (Oxford: Boydell & Brewer, 2002–).

16. Qtd. in Surtees, *Paintings and Drawings*, 16. Surtees suggests that the pupil in question was W. J. Knewstub (16 n. 3). Knewstub is said by William Michael Rossetti to have had a position "something between that of pupil and of artistic assistant." William Michael Rossetti, *Rossetti Papers, 1862 to 1870* (London: Sands, 1903), 15.

17. For the complex details of Rossetti's versions of *Proserpine*, see entry for item 233 in Surtees, *Paintings and Drawings*, (131–34).

18. Surtees dates Graham's version of *The Blessed Damozel* at 1875–78, item 244; the other version, purchased by Leyland, is dated 1875–79, item 244, R.1.

19. Fredric Leighton, letter to William Michael Rossetti, 19 November 1882, Special Collections and Archives, University of British Columbia, Vancouver. Qtd. also in Macleod, *Art and the Victorian Middle Class*, 324.

20. The Royal Academy had originally allotted only one room to Rossetti items, but in an early notice in the *Times*, Francis Hueffer protested the crowding of the images (one of the issues that had always kept Rossetti shy of exhibition). Leighton promptly doubled the space with another gallery. The articles appeared in the *Times* in three notices: 30 December 1882 (6); 13 January 1883 (4); and 15 January 1883 (8). They are reprinted in Hueffer, *Italian and Other Studies*, 83–105.

21. Macleod, *Art and the Victorian Middle Class*, 324.

22. The minutes are held at the archive and library of the Royal Academy, London. I examined the years 1880 to 1885.

23. Hueffer, *Italian and Other Studies*, 85. This notice appeared originally in the *Times* (30 December 1882), 6.

24. William Bell Scott, letter to James Leathart, 18 January 1883, Special Collections and Archives Division, University of British Columbia, Vancouver.

25. These and subsequent points in this paragraph draw on the Royal Academy's 1883 exhibition catalogue, *Exhibition of Works*.

26. Although the comment does not turn on replicas, it seems worth noting William Michael Rossetti's recollection in his diary at this time that Leighton "views with some disfavor the general run of Gabriel's works produced within the last 4 or 5 years." William Michael Rossetti, *Selected Letters*, 436 n. 3).

27. Francis L. Fennell Jr., ed., *The Rossetti-Leyland Letters: The Correspondence of an Artist and his Patron* (Athens: Ohio University Press, 1978), 70. As it happens, Leyland did not purchase *Astarte Syriaca* (referred to as *Venus Astarte* in Rossetti's letter). Rossetti sold the work, at his chosen price, to Clarence Fry (see item 249 in Surtees, *Paintings and Drawings*, 146.)

28. Qtd. in Fennell, *Rossetti-Leyland Letters*, 44.

29. Sigmund Freud, *Beyond the Pleasure Principle, Standard Edition*, 18:20–21.

30. Christina Rossetti, "In an Artist's Studio," *Poems* (New York: Knopf, 1993), 56.

31. *Daily News* (6 July 1882), 5. The next day, Theodore Watts [-Dunton] disputed the suggestion that Rossetti was a sad figure: *Daily News* (7 July 1882), 2.

32. "Contemporary Art—Poetic and Positive: Rossetti and Tadema—Linnell and Lawson," 398–99.

33. J. B. Bullen, *The Pre-Raphaelite Body: Fear and Desire in Painting, Poetry, and Criticism* (Oxford: Oxford University Press, 1998).

34. *Mnemosyne* was, in fact, an early attempt at a conception that went on to be realized in *Astarte Syriaca*. As often happens with Rossetti, some cutting and pasting and recasting brought him to conceive one bit of work in a new context. See Surtees, *Paintings and Drawings*, 156.

35. Bourdieu, *The Rules of Art*, 167.

36. Qtd. in C. L. Cline, "Dante Gabriel Rossetti's 'Last' Letter," *Library Chronicle of the University of Texas at Austin* 9 [n. ser.] (1978): 76.

37. William Graham, letter to Dante Gabriel Rossetti, 7 November 1871, Special Collections and Archives, University of British Columbia, Vancouver.

38. Editor's reply to letter from "Canadian," the *Collector* 5, no. 1 (1 November 1893).

39. For such a claim, see Faxon, *Dante Gabriel Rossetti*, 21–22.

40. Graham's letter is quoted in Dante Gabriel Rossetti, *Letters*, 3: 969 n. 1.

41. On the evolving response among patrons to replicas, see Macleod, *Art and the Victorian Middle Class*, 319–24.

42. For criticisms of the long-standard edition of letters, see the reviews by Fredeman, cited in note 15 above.

43. To judge by the appendix in Sharp's 1882 study of Rossetti, the names listed in this paragraph account for the ownership of approximately 35 percent of Rossetti's total output of paintings and studies (139 of 395 works listed).

44. Bourdieu, *Rules of Art*, 141–73.

45. Macleod, *Art and the Victorian Middle Class*, 2.

46. Fennell, *Rossetti-Leyland Letters*, xxv, xvi.

47. Lady Charles Eastlake, "Memoir of Sir Charles Lock Eastlake," in Charles L. Eastlake, *Contributions to the Literature of the Fine Arts*, 2d ed. (London: John Murray, 1870), 147. Several art historians have noted that Lady Eastlake overstated the indifference of new middle-class collectors to old masters. See C. P. Darcy, *The Encouragement of the Fine Arts in Lancashire, 1760–1860*, Remains of the Chetham Society, 3rd ser., vol. 24. (Manchester: Manchester University Press, 1976), 122–55; also Macleod, *Art and the Victorian Middle Class*, 5. For broadly figured arguments against invoking a monolithic bourgeois or middle-class sensibility in the study of nineteenth-century British art, see John Seed, " 'Commerce and the Liberal Arts': The Political Economy of Art in Manchester, 1775–1860," in *The Culture of Capital: Art, Power, and the Nineteenth-Century Middle Class*, ed. Janet Wolff and John Seed (Manchester: Manchester University Press, 1988), 45–81; Janet Wolff, "The Problem of Ideology in the Sociology of Art: A Case Study of Manchester in the Nineteenth Century," *Media, Culture, and Society* 4 (1982), 63–75.

48. D. G. Rossetti, *Letters*, 3:1003. Surtees quotes this remark and indicates that the Beatrice here refers to a replica of *Beata Beatrix* currently held at the Chicago Institute of Art (95). It is Figure 24 here.

49. Ibid., 1175.

50. On Rossetti's only major quarrel with Leyland, which arose in the months following this remark, see Fennell, *Rossetti-Leyland Letters*, xx–xxiii.

51. The gender inflection implied in the image of the prostitute can be related to other constructions of femininity in aestheticist discourse. On this prospect, see Kathy Alexis Psomiades, "Beauty's Body: Gender Ideology and British Aestheticism," *Victorian Studies* 36, no. 1 (fall 1992): 31–52. For the prostitute in terms of broader issues of cultural agency in the Victorian period, see Amanda Anderson, *Tainted Souls and Painted Faces: The Rhetoric of Fallenness in Victorian Culture* (Ithaca, N.Y.: Cornell University Press, 1993); Catherine Gallagher, "George Eliot and Daniel Deronda: The Prostitute and the

Jewish Question," *Sex, Politics, and Science in the Nineteenth-Century Novel*, selected papers from the English Institute, 1983–84, n. ser. 10, ed. Ruth Bernard Yeazell (Baltimore: Johns Hopkins University Press, 1986), 39–62.

52. Anderson, *Tainted Souls*, 2.

53. For an illustrated presentation of the Jubilee in England, especially London, see John Fabb, *Victoria's Golden Jubilee* (London: Seaby, 1987).

54. This list, taken from an announcement on the front page of the *Manchester Guardian* for 5 May 1887, reflects the popular conception of the exhibition's organization. The actual administrative organization differed slightly from this model, notably in the linkage of Handicrafts and the replica of Old Manchester and Salford; for such details, see *Royal Jubilee Exhibition, Manchester, 1887. Report of the Executive Committee*, ed. Andrew A Gillies, rev. ed. (Manchester: John Heywood, 1890).

55. *Official Guide to the Royal Jubilee Exhibition, Manchester, 1887* (Manchester: John Heywood, 1887), 4.

56. "The Manchester Exhibition," *The Graphic* 35 (7 May 1887), 470.

57. K. Luckhurst, *The Story of Exhibitions* (London: Studio, 1951); Paul Greenhalgh, *Ephemeral Vistas: The Expositions Universelles, Great Exhibitions, and World's Fairs, 1851–1939* (Manchester: Manchester University Press, 1988).

58. *Royal Jubilee Exhibition. 1887. Report of the Executive Committee*, 254.

59. "Old London" was part of the 1884 International Health Exhibition, and it seems to be the first such historical replica in British exhibitions. One press account notes, "No actual street has been taken, but a number of well-known old houses have been grouped together in a street about the width of the thoroughfares as they existed before the great fire of 1666." *The Graphic* 29 (17 May 1884): 483. For illustrations and brief discussions of "Old London," see *Illustrated London News* (10 May 1884), 1; *The Graphic* 29 (17 May 1884): 476, 483; *The Graphic* 29 (14 June 1884), 569–70; A similar mission drove the Edinburgh replica, which was part of the 1886 Edinburgh exhibition and featured "reproductions only of such buildings as are now among the things of the past, as have vanished before the invasion of modern utilitarian improvement." J. M. Gray, "Old Edinburgh," *Magazine of Art* 9 (1886): 437. In 1887, Liverpool also fashioned a city replica for its version of the Golden Jubilee exhibition.

60. *Relics of Old Manchester and Salford, Including Drawings, Portraits, Prints and Curiosities* (Manchester: John Heywood, 1887), 3. Notwithstanding this writer's own words, it seems that there were not in fact any Chartist pikes at Old Manchester and Salford. This point bears noting here, as I will soon be underlining the antimodernity of the city replica.

61. Alan Kidd, "The Industrial City and its Preindustrial Past: The Manchester Royal Jubilee Exhibition of 1887," *Transactions of the Lancashire and Cheshire Antiquarian Society*, vol. 89 for 1993 (Otley: Smith Settle, 1995), 54.

62. "Model Manchester," *Punch* 92 (14 May 1887), 233.

63. Qtd. in *Manchester Guardian* (2 May 1887), 8.

64. "Some Aspects of Our Jubilee Exhibition," *Manchester City News* (30 April 1887), 4.

65. For a standard account of Manchester in its Victorian context, see Asa Briggs, *Victorian Cities*, [1963] (Berkeley: University of California Press, 1993). See also Alan J. Kidd and K. W. Roberts, eds., *City, Class, and Culture: Studies of Social Policy and Cultural Production in Victorian Manchester* (Manchester: Manchester University Press, 1985); Alan Kidd, *Manchester*, Town and City Histories (Keele: Ryburn Publishing, for Keele University Press, 1993).

66. Briggs, *Victorian Cities*, 89.

67. Friedrich Engels, *The Condition of the Working Class in England*, trans. W. O. Hen-

derson and W. H. Chaloner (Oxford: Blackwell, 1958; rpt. Stanford, Calif.: Stanford University Press, 1968), 63.

68. *Works* 29:224.

69. Michael E. Rose, "Culture, Philanthropy, and the Manchester Middle Classes," *City, Class, and Culture: Studies of Social Policy and Cultural Production in Victorian Manchester* (Manchester: Manchester University Press, 1985), 110.

70. Ulrich Finke, "The Art Treasures Exhibition," *Art and Architecture in Victorian Manchester* (Manchester: Manchester University Press, 1985), 102–26.

71. See Macleod, *Art and the Victorian Middle Class*, however, on the tendency of art historians to overestimate this singularity; she notes that the Manchester City Art Gallery's permanent collection of Pre-Raphaelite works is largely a matter of twentieth-century purchasing (139).

72. "Wanderings in the Machinery Annex (By an Outsider)," *Manchester Guardian* (1 June 1887), 8.

73. Bourdieu, *Rules of Art*, 178–84.

74. My characterization of the Mancunian mind-set underplays some interesting class differences, which I want to note here as matter for further research. Very generally, it seems that the historical city replicas were more appealing to middle-class visitors than to working-class visitors, but this characterization is precisely what further research should test, as contradictory points are not far to find. The city replica figured prominently in middle-class reportage but was relatively neglected by working-class organs. *Ben Brierley's Journal*, for example, was a dialect weekly published in Manchester. Aimed at a working-class audience, it followed the exhibition closely with a report each week. The reports conjure fictionalized discussions between visitors to the exhibition's various sections, but one looks in vain here for any explicit discussion of the replica's supposed delights. On the face of it, one could expect a readership interested in historically significant dialect speech might be interested in representations of local history as well. But, according to Martha Vicinus, the dialect writers, far from recovering a former idiom, were principally engaged in "mingling of the old and the new, the urban and the rural." Martha Vicinus, *The Industrial Muse: A Study of Nineteenth-Century British Working-Class Literature* (London: Croom Helm, 1974), 190. Vicinus discusses Brierley (200–07 and passim). Her general argument about dialect writers is that they lost their concretely working-class character after the fall of Chartism and bought into the mind-set, and the larger audience, marked out by self-improving, middle-class ideology. These writers, as she has noted, were themselves distinguished by practicing a kind of nostalgic recuperative fabrication. On the cultural work of dialect writings, see also Patrick Joyce, *Visions of the People: Industrial England and the Question of Class, 1848–1914* (Cambridge: Cambridge University Press, 1991), esp. 256–304. My survey of newspaper and pamphlet accounts suggests that lower- or working-class interests in the exhibition generally were directed toward the technology and industry displays and toward the less fancy and costly elements of domestic design and decoration. The city replica of Old Manchester and Salford, like the fine arts displays and the lavish home furnishings, was seldom treated by working-class papers with the kind of interest or admiration that one sees routinely in middle-class organs.

75. *Royal Jubilee Exhibition. Report of the Executive Committee*, 122.

76. "Manchester Royal Jubilee Exhibition," *Gorton, Openshaw and Bradford Reporter* (30 April 1887), 6.

77. George Milner, Introduction, in Alfred Darbyshire, *A Booke of Olde Manchester and Salford* (Manchester: John Heywood, 1887), 14.

78. Richard Altick, *The Presence of the Present: Topics of the Day in the Victorian Novel* (Columbus: Ohio State University Press, 1991). Treating a larger conception of

modernity, critics as diverse as George Steiner and Theodor Adorno have addressed the increasing privilege of novelty over originality. Theodor Adorno, *Aesthetic Theory* [1970], trans. Robert Hullot-Kentor, ed. Gretel Adorno and Rolf Tiedermann (Minneapolis: University of Minnesota Press, 1997); George Steiner, *Real Presences* (Chicago: University of Chicago Press, 1989). For a lucid examination of Adorno's treatment of the new as an aesthetic category, see Peter Bürger, *Theory of the Avant-Garde*, trans. Michael Shaw, Theory and History of Literature 4 (Minneapolis: University of Minnesota Press, 1984), 59–63.

79. George Milner, Introduction, 14.

80. Alfred Darbyshire, *A Booke of Olde Manchester and Salford*, 22, 20.

81. Ibid., 22.

82. "The Manchester Exhibition," *Times* (5 May 1887), 3.

83. "Round the Exhibition VII: Handicrafts in Old Manchester and Salford," *Manchester City News* (25 June 1887), 5. A modified version of this passage appears in a commemorative book with excellent illustrations of the exhibition: see Walter Tomlinson et al., *The Pictorial Record of the Royal Jubilee Exhibition, Manchester, 1887*, ed. John H. Nodal (Manchester: J. E. Cornish, 1888), 127.

84. Sigmund Freud, *Civilization and its Discontents*, Standard Edition, 21:70.

85. Freud's penchant for archeological images is also at hand in "Fragment of an Analysis" (7:12) and "Constructions in Analysis" (23:259–60) in the *Standard Edition*. On Freud's affection for such metaphors and rhetorical figures, see Donald P. Spence, *The Rhetorical Voice of Psychoanalysis: Displacement of Evidence by Theory* (Cambridge, Mass.: Harvard University Press, 1994). Spence argues that Freud's habits here have spawned a mode in psychoanalytic criticism generally that works against the pursuit of scientific evidence.

86. "The Exhibition: Handicrafts in Old Manchester," *Manchester Guardian* (28 May 1887), 9.

87. This viewpoint on the Manchester replica is passingly offered in Alan Kidd's historical discussion, "Industrial City." On this idea more generally, see Jean Baudrillard, "The Precession of Simulacra," *Art after Modernism: Rethinking Representation*, ed. Brian Wallis (New York: New Museum of Contemporary Art, 1984), 253–81; and Umberto Eco, *Travels in Hyperreality: Essays*, trans. William Weaver (San Diego: Harvest, 1990), esp. the title essay, 3–58.

88. Jerome McGann, *Dante Gabriel Rossetti and the Game that Must Be Lost* (New Haven, Conn.: Yale University Press, 2000), 10.

Chapter 5. Against Originality

1. Letter from C. G. Stuart to Dante Gabriel Rossetti, dated 1 September 1881. Special Archives, University of British Columbia. Angeli-Dennis papers, box 4, folder 11. The limerick is on the otherwise-empty fourth page.

2. Private communications with Vivien Allen and also Jan Marsh have assisted me in my speculations about this limerick. Allen refers to a letter from Caine to his brother, pointing out Rossetti's facility with limericks, and there Caine says that he took every opportunity to write them down whenever a bit of paper was available. Jan Marsh notes that the Fales Library at New York University has a collection of limericks attributed to Rossetti.

3. It seems that Wilde's name has been misspelled as a deliberate pun, for Jonathan Wild was a notable robber in the eighteenth century, but he was no kind of poet. Dick Turpin (1705–39) and Jack Sheppard (1702–24) were thieving heroes celebrated in his-

torical romances by Harrison Ainsworth: *Rookwood* (1834) featured Dick Turpin, and it was followed by *Jack Sheppard* (1839). My thanks to Stephen Holcombe and Patrick Leary for clues to these references.

4. See, for example, Wilde's pilferings from Walter Pater's "The School of Giorgione" in "L'Envoi," his introduction to Rennell Rodd's 1882 collection of poems *Rose Leaf and Apple Leaf.* Oscar Wilde, *The First Collected Edition of the Works of Oscar Wilde,* ed. Robert Ross, vol. 14 (London: Methuen, 1922), 30–41.

5. When Wilde responded once to someone's witty remark, "How I wish I had said that," Whistler added with characteristic drollery, "You will, Oscar. You will." Hesketh Pearson, *Life of Oscar Wilde* (London: Methuen, 1964), 97. On the various possible sources of this widely quoted exchange, see Richard Ellmann, *Oscar Wilde* (New York: Knopf, 1988), 132–34. For a probably subsequent public exchange between Whistler and Wilde, see two letters from Wilde and the editorial apparatus, reproducing Whistler's share, in Oscar Wilde, *The Letters of Oscar Wilde,* ed. Rupert Hart-Davis (New York: Harcourt, Brace & World, 1962, 1963), 253–54.

6. W. B. [Willie] Maxwell, one of the young men who lingered about Wilde and went on to be a novelist, reaped the benefit of Wilde's incessant storytelling by writing down at least one tale and publishing it under his own name. Wilde's response was to assure Maxwell, "Stealing my story was the act of a gentleman, but not telling me you had stolen it was to ignore the claims of friendship." W. B. Maxwell, *Time Gathered* 97, referenced in Ellmann, *Oscar Wilde,* 309.

7. It is a related truth that Wilde also called property rights as such into question, notably in "The Soul of Man under Socialism," *The Artist as Critic: Critical Writings of Oscar Wilde,* ed. Richard Ellmann (New York: Random, 1968, 1969), 255–89.

8. Qtd. in Ellmann, *Oscar Wilde,* 146.

9. I have in mind, for example, Denis Donoghue's preference for Walter Pater, couched in a plea that we resist Ellmann's supposed overstatement of Wilde's claims on our interest: *New Republic* 198 (15 February 1988): 25–6.

10. Ellmann, *Oscar Wilde,* xvii.

11. Intervening playfully in the Shakespeare industry was among Wilde's enticements in writing "Mr. W.H." In the years immediately preceding Wilde's writing of this story, and preceding his own publication in that same journal of his "Critic as Artist" dialogues, a more earnest venture in this vein appeared: see Charles Mackay, "A Tangled Skein Unravelled; or, the Mystery of Shakespeare's *Sonnets,*" *The Nineteenth Century* 16 (August 1884), 238–262.

12. Oscar Wilde, "The Portrait of Mr. W.H.," *Oscar Wilde: Complete Shorter Fiction,* ed. Isobel Murray (Oxford: Oxford University Press, 1979), 139. Murray reprints the shorter 1889 version of this story, the only version published in Wilde's lifetime. It appeared in *Blackwood's Edinburgh Magazine* for July 1889. Like Murray, I find the story's central ideas better served by the initial version, but serious study of the tale requires a view to the longer version, as well. The longer version features more extensive reading in the Shakespeare sonnets, underscoring the homoeroticism of the poems and also adding a more general account of Platonic love—featuring references to Plato, Michelangelo, Montaigne, and others—that Wilde would echo in a famous outburst during his trials only a few years later. For the longer version, see "The Portrait of Mr. W.H.," *The Artist as Critic,* 152–220.

13. Matthew Arnold, "The Function of Criticism at the Present Time," *The Complete Prose Works of Matthew Arnold,* ed. R. H. Super, vol. 3. (Ann Arbor: University of Michigan Press, 1980), 258; Oscar Wilde, "The Critic as Artist I," *The Artist as Critic,* 369.

14. Periodic debates of the 1880s show that Wilde was unique more in the panache he brought to these concerns than in having the concerns in the first place. See J. C.

Robinson—whom I take to be Sir John Charles Robinson (1824–1913), a cataloger and bibliographer of art history—"On Spurious Works of Art," *The Nineteenth Century* 30 (November 1891): 677–98; also Henry G. Hewlett, "Forged Literature," *The Nineteenth Century* 29 (February 1891): 318–38.

15. Walter Benjamin, "The Storyteller: Reflections of the Works of Nikolai Leskov," Illuminations, 83–109.

16. Wilde, *Letters*, 443.

17. Sos Eltis, *Revising Wilde: Society and Subversion in the Plays of Oscar Wilde* (Oxford: Oxford University Press, 1996). On Wilde's Irishness, see Terry Eagleton, *Saint Oscar* (Lawrence Hill: Field Day, 1989); and Vicki Mahaffey, *States of Desire: Wilde, Yeats, Joyce, and the Irish Experience* (Oxford: Oxford University Press, 1998).

18. Jonathan Dollimore, *Sexual Dissidence: Augustine to Wilde, Freud to Foucault* (Oxford: Clarendon, 1991); Ed Cohen, "Writing Gone Wilde: Homoerotic Desire in the Closet of Representation," *PMLA* 102, no. 5 (1987): 806.

19. As ideas of constitutive contradiction underlie both Marxist and Freudian theory, it is plain that such a project of self-critique has a much larger and voluminous history. For ambitious argument that explores the common stake of Marxian and Freudian paradigms in questions of normativity, see Jürgen Habermas, *Knowledge and Human Interests*, trans. Jeremy J. Shapiro (Boston: Beacon Press, 1971). In Habermas's view, both Marxian and Freudian paradigms are implicitly committed to positivistic and empiricist viewpoints that lead practitioners to disavow certain forms of critical reflection and to remain lodged in forms of partial critique. I comment on the resulting issues for cultural historiography in "Replicas and Originality: Picturing Agency in Dante Gabriel Rossetti and Victorian Manchester," *Victorian Studies* 43, no. 1 (Autumn 2000): 67-102, esp. 92–97 and 98 n23.

20. Deidre Lynch discusses character, and revises prior accounts of the term, in treating the crisis of modern agency driving the rise of the novel in the eighteenth century and beyond. See *Economy of Character: Novels, Market Culture, and the Business of Inner Meaning* (Chicago: University of Chicago Press, 1998).

21. Catherine Gallagher shows how novelistic form came to reflect prevalent authorial uncertainties about how to render the relation of plot and character: *The Industrial Reformation of English Fiction* (Chicago: University of Chicago Press, 1985). See also Amanda Anderson, *Tainted Souls*.

22. For an influential account of promising as performative action, understood to indicate language that does rather than simply describes, see J. L. Austin, *How to Do Things with Words*. For a discussion of his theme in a Victorian context, see Randall Craig, *Promising Language: Betrothal in Victorian Law and Fiction* (Albany, N.Y.: SUNY Press, 2000).

23. Oscar Wilde, *The Importance of Being Earnest*, *The Complete Works of Oscar Wilde* (London: Collins, 1966), 363.

24. P. S. Atiyah, *The Rise and Fall of the Freedom of Contract* (Oxford: Clarendon, 1979), 139–76, 330 ff.

25. There are remarkable resonances between Nietzschean and Wildean thought, but it seems that neither writer was aware of the other. It bears noting, however, that both writers admired Ralph Waldo Emerson, and work on Emerson over the last decade has found in his thinking some lines of thought about human agency that resemble what my own argument locates in Wilde and Nietzsche. See, in particular, Stanley Cavell, who attributes to Emerson an idea of subjectivity that does not fall back on idealist assumptions about the transcendental subject and instead conjures an idea of subjectivity as an embodied and situated process of positioned action. In this, Emerson is styled as a forerunner of Wittgenstein, who offers the most concerted and detailed ac-

count of agency as an embodied process rather than as the power borne by some underlying abstract subjectivity. Cavell, *Conditions Handsome and Unhandsome: The Constitution & Emerson Perfectionism* (Chicago: University of Chicago Press, 1990).

26. Freud *Standard Edition*, 21:57–145; Michel Foucault, *Discipline and Punish*; Judith Butler, *The Psychic Life of Power*.

27. John Stuart Mill, *On Liberty, Collected Works of John Stuart Mill*, 19:240.

28. Oscar Wilde, *Salome* (London: Elkins, 1894); rpt. Oscar Wilde, *Oscar Wilde: The Major Works*, ed. Isobel Murray (Oxford: Oxford University Press, 1989, 2000), 321; 299–329.

29. Oscar Wilde, *The Picture of Dorian Gray*, in *Oscar Wilde*, ed. Murray 47–214.

30. In *The Psychic Life of Power*, Judith Butler proposes to unite the Foucauldian inquiry into power with an inquiry into power as a specifically psychoanalytic concern as well, and she takes as her premise something much like the relation that I here propose between Dorian Gray and the portrait: "Subjection consists precisely in this fundamental dependency on a discourse we never choose but that, paradoxically, initiates and sustains our agency" (2).

31. Wilde's revisions underline his concern to put a state of consciousness specifically at issue. In the Clark Library (UCLA) typescript for the 1890 *Lippincott's* text of *Dorian Gray*, Sibyl declares, "Tonight, for the first time, I *saw* that the Romeo was hideous, and old, and painted, that the moonlight in the orchard was false, that the scenery was vulgar, and that the words I had to speak were unreal, were not my words, not what I wanted to say" (leaf 86). I underscore from this passage the word *saw*, which Wilde crossed out and replaced with "became conscious" for the published version. In another correction, the moment fixed in Dorian's portrait was originally his "unconscious boyhood," which Wilde changed to his "then just conscious boyhood" (Clark Typescript 91).

32. Louis Althusser, "Ideology and Ideological State Apparatuses (Notes Towards an Investigation)," *Lenin and Philosophy and Other Essays*, 127–186. For recent accounts of Althusser's essay, see Judith Butler, *Psychic Life*, 106–31; Mladen Dolar, "Beyond Interpellation," *Qui Parle* 6, no. 2 (1993): 73–96.

33. Earlier, Dorian remarked to Basil, "I offer no explanation, and you are not to ask for one." This exemption from explanation can be figured in a simple sense, as Dorian's refusal to explain something that he knows. But the mode of existence that he there appropriates also is suggestively similar to that mode that Kant would attach to the aesthetic: that which does not bear explanation.

34. Exodus 3:1–15.

35. Exodus 4:10–13.

36. In the *Ethics*, Spinoza's central statement on human action, he establishes a determinism perhaps congruent with Marx and an overseeing God, understood along the lines that Althusser invokes, when he observes in connection with religious ideology that "there can only be such a multitude of possible religious subjects on the absolute condition that there is a Unique, Absolute *Other Subject*, i.e., God" (178). See Charles Altieri for a brief but telling location of Spinoza in terms of current agency issues: *Subjective Agency*, 24, 85–87.

37. I take it to be a fact that most critics who bother to touch on the justification of literary-critical study tend to deploy such more or less "political" language. A notable exception is Stanley Fish, who avows a motive in pleasure and disputes that justification itself makes any sense. See *Professional Correctness: Literary Studies and Political Change* (Oxford: Clarendon, 1995).

38. Diana Fuss's *Essentially Speaking* remains the readiest gloss of essentialism and antiessentialism in contemporary criticism.

39. This suggestion that manners trump morals echoes some eighteenth-century currents of thought. For a powerful discussion relating languages of virtues, rights, and manners in the eighteenth century, see J. G. A. Pocock, *Virtue, Commerce, and History: Essays on Political Thought and History, Chiefly in the Eighteenth Century* (Cambridge: Cambridge University Press, 1985).

40. Dollimore, *Sexual Dissidence*, 15

41. Ibid. Dollimore digests the Wilde passage at p. 16; his reference to Gide is at p. 5.

42. Wilde, *Letters*, 352.

43. In the mystical developmental scheme of Yeats's *A Vision*, Wilde is not included with the dandies and decadents of the sensualist phase thirteen, but rather occupies a later phase—nineteenth out of the twenty-eight—wherein the mind has just lost its "Unity of Being" and will consequently be able to dramatize only those fragments of truth available to it. William Butler Yeats, *A Vision* (New York: Macmillan, 1961), 147–51.

44. Eve Sedgwick's work on Willa Cather, for example, isolates in Cather a "refracted" sensibility, and this refraction does not merely indicate a departure from normative constructions of desire—as if to constitute lesbian desire an alternative sexual truth. Instead, this refraction amounts to the very condition of desire itself, where straight and "queer" desires are understood as constituted in their equivocal relations to any order of sexual truth. Eve Sedgwick, "Across Gender, Across Sexuality: Willa Cather and Others," *South Atlantic Quarterly* 88 (Winter 1989), 68-9; see also her *The Epistemology of the Closet* (Berkeley: University of California Press, 1990); and Judith Butler, *Bodies that Matter: On the Discursive Limits of "Sex"* (New York: Routledge, 1993).

45. See Laura Mulvey, "Visual Pleasure and Narrative Cinema," in *Narrative, Apparatus, Ideology: A Film Theory Reader*, ed. Philip Rosen (New York: Columbia University Press, 1986), 198–209. Indeed, Lord Henry's comments here are couched in gendered terms: he comments that "women never know when the curtain has fallen. They always want a sixth act." In other words, women, who go in for reminiscences and memory, play the part of an intractable and uncontainable reality that impinges on the pretty orders that the aesthete might pass the hours contemplating.

46. Ellmann, *Oscar Wilde*, 518.

47. Oscar Wilde, *More Letters of Oscar Wilde*, ed. Rupert Hart-Davis (Oxford: Oxford University Press, 1985), 165.

48. For the classic argument along these lines, see Max Horkheimer and Theodor W. Adorno, *Dialectic of Enlightenment* [1944], trans. John Cumming (New York: Continuum, 1994), esp. the chap. "The Culture Industry: Enlightenment as Mass Deception."

49. Anthony Cascardi, *Consequences of Enlightenment* (Cambridge: Cambridge University Press, 1999).

50. Bourdieu, *Rules of Art*, 215–16. See also p. 21.

51. Ibid., 28.

52. For a very keen reading of Bourdieu along the same lines I take here, see John Guillory, "Bourdieu's Refusal," *MLQ: Modern Language Quarterly* 58, no. 4 (December 1997), 367–98.

53. Bourdieu, *Rules of Art*, 98

54. Ibid., 95–98.

55. Ibid., 100.

Index

Acknowledgments

A great number of people and institutions made this book possible. Current and onetime colleagues at the University of Michigan provided continual and invaluable support, inspiration, and critical readings. In the English Department, Sadia Abbas, Lee Behlman, Richard Cureton, Jonathan Freedman, Andrea Henderson, Kerry Larson, Adela Pinch, John Kucich, Yopie Prins, Marjorie Levinson, Suzanne Raitt, Michael Schoenfeldt, Tobin Siebers, Michael Szalay, Rei Terada, and Martha Vicinus; in History, Geoff Eley and Kali Israel; at the School of Law, Tom Green and A. W. Brian Simpson; and in Philosophy, Ian Proops and James Tappenden. I have benefited from several on-campus reading groups, most notably the Nineteenth Century Forum, with membership primarily in English and History; and the Aesthetics Discussion Group, centered in the Philosophy Department. The University of Michigan itself has suported me generously with a term of leave and with research, travel, and publication assistance.

Scholars at institutions elsewhere shared time, materials, knowledge, and gracious advice; clarified innumerable local questions; and commented on work in progress: Vivien Allen, James Eli Adams, Charles Altieri, Amanda Anderson, Timothy Barringer, Megan Becker-Lekrone, Joseph Bristow, James Deardon, Allen Dunn, Frances Ferguson, Pamela Gilbert, Howard Horwitz, Gerhard Joseph, Alan Kidd, Steven Knapp, George Levine, Dianne Sachko Macleod, Jan Marsh, John McGowan, Rohan McWilliam, Andrew H. Miller, Talia Schaffer, Jonah Siegel, Judith Stoddart, and Stephen Wildman. I also want to thank the collective membership of the VICTORIA electronic discussion group. A dissertation on Oscar Wilde prepared my thinking for the present study, so here I fondly thank my graduate advisors in English at the University of California, Davis: Peter Allan Dale, Michael Hoffman, and Sandra M. Gilbert. Joseph Aimone and Carl Eby have been longtime friends and intellectual supporters. Vincent Pecora is unlikely to know how much I benefited from sitting in on his 1996 Marx seminar at UCLA. And I am grateful to the teachers and students gathered at Dartmouth College for the School of Criticism and Theory in 1995, especially Judith Butler, for her seminar, and Gustavo Guerra, for his friendship and critical engagement.

My arguments have benefited from public responses at conferences and campus visits over the years, including the Victorian Studies Group of the CUNY Graduate Center; the Dickens Project at Santa Cruz; several meetings of the Modern Language Association; the Northeast Victorian Studies Association (NVSA); the Midwest MLA; the Ruskin Centenary Symposium at Lancaster; and Interdisciplinary Nineteenth Century Studies (INCS). The journal *Victorian Studies* published a version of Chapter 4 in its autumn 2000 issue (43, no. 1). Elements of Chapter 5 appeared in "The 'Strange Music' of *Salome*: Oscar Wilde's Rhetoric of Verbal Musicality," *Mosaic: A Journal for the Interdisciplinary Study of Literature* 33, no. 1 (March 2000): 15–38; other material from that chapter appeared in "Decadent Critique: Constructing 'History' in Peter Greenaway's *The Cook, The Thief, His Wife & Her Lover*," in *Perennial Decay: The Aesthetics and Politics of Decadence in the Modern Era*, ed. Liz Constable, Dennis Denisoff, and Matthew Potolsky (Philadelphia: University of Pennsylvania Press, 1999), 101–18.

For access to archival materials, I am indebted to more institutions than I should try to itemize here, but I mention places with especially important material holdings and persons who went out of their way to facilitate my work. I am grateful to Peta Motture and Diane Bilbey of the Sculpture Department at the Victoria and Albert Museum, London; Christopher Marsden at Blythe House, the registry of the Victoria and Albert Museum; Colin Stevenson, Morag Wray, and other staff at the London Library; Alison Morton at the Ruskin Galleries, Sheffield; Stephen Wildman, Ruth Hutchison, and Rebecca Patterson at the Ruskin Library, Lancaster; Andrew Russell at the National Art Library, London; and Peter Newman at the Tate Gallery, London. Among North American collections, the William Andrews Clark Memorial Library of UCLA deserves special acknowledgment: I held a three-month predoctoral fellowship there for work in an incomparable collection of Oscar Wilde papers. The Clark staff at that time—Steve Tabor, Suzanne Tatian, Renee Chin, and Steve Sloan—provided my lucky introduction to the professionalism and humanity of archival staff generally. Other valuable research locations include the Bodleian Library, Oxford (special thanks to Colin Harris and Julie Anne Lambert); the British Library, especially the Newspaper Library at Colindale and the Rare Books and Manuscripts Division at the main branch; the Karpeles Manuscript Library, Santa Barbara (thanks to Miriam Hospadar); the New York Public Library; the Pierpont Morgan Library, New York; the Royal Academy Archive, London; the Royal Borough of Kensington and Chelsea Libraries, London; the Special Archives of the University of British Columbia,

Vancouver (thanks to George Brandak); Vassar College Library; and the Yale Center for British Art.

I dedicate this book to my wife, Barbara, my son, Colin, and my family more generally, all of them in so many ways the *sine qua non* of this effort.